Sweet Life

Sweet Life

ADVENTURES ON THE WAY TO PARADISE

Barry Manilow

McGraw-Hill Book Company

New York   St. Louis   San Francisco   Auckland   Bogotá   Hamburg
London   Madrid   Mexico   Milan   Montreal   New Delhi   Panama
Paris   São Paulo   Singapore   Sydney   Tokyo   Toronto

1 2 3 4 5 6 7 8 9 D O C D O C 8 7

ISBN 0-07-039904-2

LIBRARY OF CONGRESS CATALOGING-IN-PUBLICATION DATA

Manilow, Barry.
  Sweet life.
  1. Manilow, Barry.   2. Rock musicians—United States—Biography. I. Title.
ML420.M23A3   1987   784.5'4'00924 [B]   87-3283
ISBN 0-07-039904-2

BOOK DESIGN BY PATRICE FODERO

Acknowledgments

I feel the need to give my humble thanks to all the people who saw me through the creation of this book. My friends, family, fans and business associates have all been brutally honest and incredibly helpful in this undertaking.

Special thanks go to Garry Kief and Roberta Kent for the hours and hours of input.

Very special thanks go to Gladys Justin Carr, Editorial Director and Chairman of the Editorial Board at McGraw-Hill, for her attention and talent in helping to bring this project together.

But most of all, my very special deepest loving and heartfelt thanks go to Maureen Lasher who, with her husband Eric, has seen me through each and every page of this experience. It's been a strange way of getting to know someone, but I think Maureen and I have formed a bond of friendship that will endure. Her enormous editing talent and her sensitivity and caring have been invaluable and I'll never forget her.

Contents

Contents

Contents

Introduction

There are a load of gold and platinum records on my wall. They hang in the room where I keep my musical instruments and synthesizers. The room is mostly made of glass windows and has a breathtaking view of canyons and mountains in Bel Air, California. They make a very intimidating arrangement for people who come into the room for the first time.

"Are they *real* gold?" some people ask.

"You must be very proud," others say.

I am proud. I am so proud of the work that those records represent I could burst. Ten years of my life, filled with exhilaration and laughter, depression and confusion, wonder and inspiration.

Sometimes I sit and stare at them as the sun is going down. Every time I do, memories come crashing back to me as vividly as if they had happened yesterday. A lot of the memories are wonderful. A lot of them are horrible.

Sometimes I think I should melt them down and wear them on a hat or a uniform like you would in a war. Sometimes I think that these gold and platinum mementos represent more than how many records were sold. Each one is a medal for a battle won. And each one represents an adventure.

I decided to write this book not because I wanted to tell the story of my life. It's not yet time for me to do that. I want to tell you the story of an average guy on the way to the rest of his life, who made a right turn on Broadway and Fifty-seventh Street and wound up in Bel Air with a wall full of gold and platinum medals. I want to tell it to you because there aren't many who are lucky (or unfortunate!) enough to have experienced this phenomenon called fame.

I know you won't believe me when I tell you I never went after it. My old friends tell me I was always ambitious and goal-oriented and always seemed to be reaching for the top. Maybe I was, but I don't remember it like that. I only wanted to do the best job I could. I never even fantasized about the kind of success that has been bestowed upon me or about the arena in which I found myself. My only commitment was to my music.

It's been an unbelievable trip. One I'm still on, but one I feel I can now, for the first time, look back on without freaking out.

Writing this book has been one of the most profound experiences in my life. (And I thought making a record album was complicated! Forget it.) It has given me new respect for writers. I really don't know how Shakespeare or Jackie Collins did it.

Whenever I've recorded an album, I've lived and breathed it for all the time it took to make it. I thought of nothing else and finally, when it was done, I was able to sleep for the first time since I had begun it. Usually my albums have taken two, three months to record.

This book has taken over three *years* to write. Considering the fact that I'd never written anything but a few English reports in school and some letters home from Camp Ma-Ka-Bee, this seemed like *Mission Impossible*. I wrote no less than fifteen versions of the book and drove everyone around me crazy.

To remind me of past incidents, I began to call friends I hadn't spoken to in years. I renewed friendships that I thought had faded away and solidified friendships that had needed a shove. I visited my old neighborhoods, I listened to old audio tapes and watched old video tapes. I reread press clippings and my daily journals I've been keeping for twelve years.

This experience has made me reevaluate my entire life. It reminded me of what I always wanted and what I never really wanted. It made me appreciate my friends and family more and made me feel grateful to all the people who believed in me. It helped me to put the past into perspective and the future into focus.

Even if this book were never published, I have gotten so much out of this experience it has been worth all the effort. I hope you have a good time with my book. I hope you see yourself in it and are able to relate to many of its moments.

Now when I look at my wall of gold and platinum I know that each record really represents a stop, an adventure on the way to Paradise, which was right under my nose (pardon the expression) all along.

Prelude

I sat in the back of the cushy black limousine and looked out the window as it sped over the Williamsburg Bridge toward my old Brooklyn neighborhood. Over there was the Schaefer brewery just as I remembered it. Near it was the huge aircraft carrier; and there was the gold dome of the Williamsburgh Savings Bank. The solid cement pavement of the bridge suddenly turned into the familiar metal grating and the tires howled as they rode over the iron. The subway train roared by on my left and I could see the passengers all bundled up because it was so cold out, staring glumly out the windows of cars covered with graffiti.

How many times, I thought, had I been one of those straphangers? Hundreds? Millions? Everywhere I glanced, dozens and dozens of stories and memories flashed through my mind. I had taken this trip countless times as I grew up.

It was 1984. I was headlining that week at Radio City Music Hall. Performing in New York has always been a potent emotional experience for me. But playing at Radio City was especially meaningful. Earlier that day, as I stood on the stage and rehearsed in the magnificent theater, I kept remembering my childhood and the powerful impact Radio City had had on me. I got so lost in the memories I could barely concentrate on the music. Finally, I

1

let my band and staff carry on the rehearsal without me as I wandered through the empty lobby and stairways.

After the rehearsal I couldn't seem to lose the nostalgic feeling I had, so I decided to go with it. I told my associates and friends I'd see them in a few hours.

"Clinton," I said to my driver. "Take me over the Williamsburg Bridge."

It was late in December and it was freezing. The sleek black limousine crawled slowly through my old neighborhood and I peered out the tinted windows. I could see out, but nobody outside could see in. The neighborhood was a disaster. I mean, it had never been Park Avenue, but now, it looked like Germany after the war. Buildings had literally crumbled along my old familiar streets. Tough-looking kids stared at the car suspiciously as it drove by, while the older men and women looked on sympathetically—the only time a limousine made an appearance in this neighborhood was for a funeral. I was sure they all thought someone had died.

"That's where I was born, Clinton."

"No! *Really*, Mr. Manilow?" he said in shock as we passed 100 Broadway. Garbage was piled along the outside of the building. The stores that once lined the ground floor were boarded up with metal and wood. Foul words and graffiti covered everything. Even though the sun was still shining, people walked by briskly heading for warmth. We rounded another corner.

"That's the second place I lived, Clinton." I pointed to a small brownstone. "And that was my apartment on the ground floor."

Everything looked smaller. My memories were of huge looming apartment buildings and long streets that stretched on and on. But everything seemed so tiny. We passed my high school, the library, candy stores, movie theaters, the barber shop, the grocery stores. I thought it would take hours—I remembered an enormous neighborhood. It took fifteen minutes.

As we rounded a corner, the neighborhood turned quieter and cleaner. Trees lined the street and the brownstones were better kept. This was the neighborhood of the synagogue I had been bar mitzvahed in.

As we stopped for a red light, I noticed a small boy walking toward the corner. He must have been ten or eleven years old, and he was all bundled up, a knit hat and ear muffs on his head, gloves tied with a string to his coat.

He stopped at the corner and looked around, waiting for the light to change. I kept staring at him. He looked so sweet and innocent—polite, shy, and lonely.

"That's me," I thought. "That's exactly what I looked like when I was his age."

I knew where the boy was going. I knew exactly what he was feeling, what kind of life he was living. I had been there. Man, had I been there.

The Early
Adventures

In the Beginning . . .

I stood in the cold waiting for the light to turn green so I could cross the street. I was really feeling low. I had just come back from my monthly visit to the orthodontist and he had put even *more* junk in my mouth. I was eleven years old and very skinny. I had a long nose, big ears, and an Adam's apple that looked as if I had swallowed a baseball. And now I had a mouthful of nuts and bolts. Understand, we're not talking just a few little wires, we're talking the Iron Works—I mean springs, screws, and caps. When I smiled people in Brownsville needed sunglasses. And now, he had put in rubber bands, so that when I least expected it, they would snap and fly out of my mouth, sometimes hitting the person in front of me.

I hated them. I knew that my front teeth protruded and that I probably needed these things, but I hated them. As I walked home from the bus stop, I decided I wouldn't smile anymore.

"Hello, Barry," Mrs. Greenblatt said as she passed me.

"Hello, Mrs. Greenblatt," I mumbled, head down, not smiling.

I rounded the corner and walked quickly toward my apartment building, passing the dozen or so storefronts: Sal's Shoe Repair, Kleiner's Grocery, Dave's Candy Store, the Hebrew Book Store.

We lived on the ground floor of a brownstone on Division
Avenue in Williamsburg, Brooklyn—my mother, my grandmother, my grandfather and me. We'd been living in this building
for three years.

When you walked into the apartment, you walked directly
into the dining room. Off the dining room was the kitchen, my
little bedroom, and the living room, which had been divided into
two rooms, so that Gramma and Grampa would have their own
bedroom. Mom slept on a sofa in the dining room.

I marched briskly into the apartment. I could smell the chicken
and potatoes cooking. It was Friday night and Friday night was
roast chicken night. It smelled great.

"Hello, *tatteleh*," Gramma said.

"Hello, Gramma," I mumbled, head down, walking into my
tiny bedroom. I sat down on my bed, sulking.

She followed me in. "Did he put more braces on your teeth?"
she asked. I nodded glumly. She sat on the bed and put her arms
around me.

"I know you can't believe this, but you'll be happy your mother
put braces on your teeth when you grow up. She went through
a life of buckteeth and she couldn't stand thinking that you'd have
to go through that too," she said, stroking my head.

I loved Gramma's hands. They were old, wrinkled and weath-
ered from years of hard work and dishwater. She made me feel
better.

"Take off your coat, darling. You'll get overheated," she said
as she went back to the kitchen. "Have some milk and cookies
and then you'll practice your accordion."

*   *   *

I was born Barry Alan Pincus, the son of Harold Kelliher, a thin
Irishman who drove a truck for the Schaefer brewery. I don't
know anything else about him because my parents were divorced
when I was a baby. All he gave me was his mother's maiden
name, Pincus.

I was raised by my mother, Edna, and my grandparents, Esther and Joseph Manilow. They wouldn't allow my father to visit and the few times his name was mentioned it was always with loathing. I grew up thinking I'd better stay away from this guy.

But I grew up loving my grandmother, although the rest of the family feared her; adoring my grandfather, although the rest of the family derided him; and worshiping my mother, although the family never understood her.

My grandparents were immigrants from Russia, who, along with hundreds of other immigrants, wound up living in a tenement apartment in Williamsburg, Brooklyn, New York. The apartment was in an enormous building near the elevated BMT subway and a few blocks away from the Williamsburg Bridge and the East River. The apartments they lived in were small and cold. There was hardly any furniture; they could afford barely enough food to sustain them.

They met when their families had both moved into the apartment building. Grampa always kidded that he fell in love with Gramma "at first fight." She was a breathtakingly beautiful woman and even as a teenager, she had carried herself with dignity.

Gramma had been rich for about thirty seconds. For the first eight years of her life she was raised in a wealthy household in Russia. But her father was killed in the war, and before she knew it, she was part of a penniless family on their way to America. But she never forgot that she was once rich and always behaved as if she still were. When she arrived in America, she wouldn't open her mouth to speak to anyone until she learned English; I'll always remember her trying to speak grammatically. Gramma saw what America had to offer and wanted the finer things in life.

Grampa, on the other hand, knew nothing of the finer things in life. He was not terribly bright, not terribly good-looking, and had very little ambition. But he was sweet. He was possibly the sweetest guy you could ever meet.

Gramma married Grampa not out of love, but because her mother demanded it. She eventually wound up loving him (how could she not?) but she was always frustrated at her lot in life.

He got a job in a garment factory and tried to support Gramma and their two children, Rose and Edna, but there was never enough money. Out of desperation, Gramma found a job. And what a job!

It was in a factory for men's hatboxes located in a basement with no windows. Gramma sweated bullets in the summer and froze in the winter, and she stood on her feet all day long. Gramma, who wanted the finer things in life, did this for fifteen years.

The years in the basement of the box factory made Gramma tough, bitter, and hard to live with. She took out her frustrations on Rose, my mother, and Grampa. She was the boss, the *balla-buster* (Yiddish for ballbuster). The rest of the family always steered clear of Gramma.

She hit the roof when she heard my mother wanted to marry Harold Kelliher. Not only was he a lowly truck driver, he wasn't even Jewish! My mother had been desperate to get out of living with Gramma. Her sister Rose had already married and moved to Philadelphia, so Edna convinced my father to change his name legally to his mother's Jewish maiden name, Pincus. Gramma gave in, and at nineteen years old, my mother was a married lady.

They moved into an apartment four blocks away and within two months my father was drafted into the army, so my mother moved back in with Gramma and Grampa. Grampa was happy to have her back; he loved her dearly and it kept Gramma off his back. But Gramma continued to make her life miserable, berating her relentlessly about the bum she had married. When my mother found out she was pregnant, she didn't dare tell anyone. She knew Gramma wouldn't approve and she wanted the baby badly.

When she reached her fifth month of pregnancy, she told Gramma. Predictably, Gramma hit the ceiling.

"How can you afford to have a baby?" Queen Esther screamed. "You stupid girl!" And she hit her and broke her nose.

Nothing could upset my mother. She was so happy—she was going to have a baby! She went around telling everyone it was going to be a boy, the most beautiful boy. Gramma grumbled.

On June 17, at 9:00 A.M. in Beth Moses Hospital in Brooklyn, Mrs. Harold Pincus had a boy after sixteen hours of labor. A tired but happy Edna sighed, "He's the most beautiful boy in the world, just like I said he'd be."

"Edna, *mammeleh*, you should rest," Grampa said.

When my mother and Grampa looked at Gramma, they saw a smile and a gentleness on her face they had never seen before as she stared at me.

"Yes, Edna, you rest. I'll take care of him," Gramma said.

*   *   *

Gramma loved me. I mean *really* loved me. It was as if I made up for all her suffering. She was bitter and frustrated at her lot in life, and when she looked at Grampa or her daughters, she just blamed them. But I was not to blame, so she used me to pour out forty years of bottled-up love. I could do no wrong in Gramma's eyes. Ever. I think that if I had wound up a serial killer instead of a musician, Gramma would still have loved me.

My mother and father divorced soon after he returned from the army and both of us moved back into Gramma's apartment on Broadway and Berry Street for good. Gramma's apartment was on the sixth floor, a major hike for anyone over fifteen years old. There were six apartments on each floor, three on one side of the floor and three on the other. Our apartment was between Nettie Allisburg, the manicurist's, and the Blumenthals', who didn't speak much English.

It was a three-room apartment. You walked down a long foyer into the kitchen. There was a bedroom on either side of the kitchen. Gramma and Grampa slept in one bedroom, and my mother and I in the other. Since there was no living room, everything happened around the kitchen table: eating, reading, arguing, planning. The kitchen window looked out on Broadway, and on many hot nights my mother would sit on the fire escape, singing to me and holding me until I fell asleep.

The neighborhood's a slum now, but then, although poor people lived there, it wasn't. No one was afraid to walk through the streets or sit on the stoops in the evening. Everyone left the doors unlocked and everyone knew everyone else. On summer evenings, groups of parents would sit outside Eppy's candy store way into the night because it was too hot to stay inside. The kids would play and make noise running through the streets in front of them. The sounds of talking, laughing or hollering constantly filled the apartment building. Kids clomped down the stairs at breakneck speed while their mothers yelled, "If you fall down those steps and break both your legs, don't come running to me!"

Smells of stuffed cabbage and gefilte fish hung in the air for weeks. Maybe years. Maybe you can still smell it if you visit there today. I'll bet you can.

My mother was so young when I was born, Gramma really raised the two of us. We were very poor, but I never knew it. I was given a secure upbringing and I always felt loved and wanted. Gramma and Grampa taught me Jewish traditions and raised me to be polite, caring, and sensitive, a gentleman. I loved them both with all my heart.

But I was crazy about the black-haired beauty who was my mother. She wasn't really beautiful—she was skinny and gawky and had buckteeth and a long nose. But she was beautiful to me. She was young, full of life, and outrageous. The mothers of my friends in the neighborhood were from the "old country" and all reminded me of my grandmother. I proudly realized that I was the only kid on the block with Auntie Mame for a mother.

Into our apartment she'd stride after her day's work, wearing spiky high heels and a tight-fitting dress, smoking, smiling, laughing, shouting "Hiya, babe!" to me. The radio, which had been silent while I did my homework in the afternoon, would go on and she'd sing along with the popular songs of the day. Sometimes we'd pretend she was a great singer and we'd make Gramma and Grampa sit and watch. "Ladies and Gentlemen, Miss Edna Manilow!" I'd yell and we'd all applaud as she stood and sang into the broom handle.

As soon as I could, I began to sing along with the radio. And as soon as Grampa heard me, he took me to Times Square, found a "Record-Your-Own-Voice" booth, plopped his quarter into it, and said, "Sing, Barry." Of course, I wouldn't.

"Sing Heppy Boidday to your cousin Dennis, Barry," he coaxed me in his Yiddish accent.

I stood there looking at the microphone, saying nothing.

Grampa started to panic, seeing his quarter going down the drain. "Don' you vanna sing anyting?" he pleaded.

"No," I squeaked.

So Grampa sang "Heppy Boidday to You" to my cousin Dennis by himself with his thick Yiddish accent. At the end of the record he once again tried to coax me into singing, but I started to cry and wouldn't stop until we got back home.

Determined to encourage my musical talents, my mother decided I should begin lessons on the dreaded accordion. I really didn't enjoy practicing, but I was pretty good at playing the thing.

I was raised an only child among adults. My mother and grandfather worked Mondays to Saturdays, all day long, which left me with Gramma. She was very protective. Too protective. I had no friends for the first ten years of my life, and I was very shy and introverted. My cousins and relatives were warm and loving, but Gramma kept me pretty much to herself during those years.

With my mother and grandfather at work all day, it was Gramma and me, me and Gramma. I'd sit and squeeze out melodies on the accordion and Gramma would actually stop her cleaning or cooking and sit and listen to me. Sometimes she'd smile and hum along and I felt loved and happy that I could make her smile.

*　　　*　　　*

Other than my immediate family, the three most important people in my young life were Larry, Fred, and Willie.

Larry Rosenfeld was my first friend. He was five-eight—I'll never forget it because he always felt he was too short. He had jet black hair and a perfect nose (everyone had a perfect nose compared to me). He was outgoing, with a great sense of humor which got better as he got older. He was bright and had his academic future mapped out long before I even thought about mine. Larry was warm and funny and generous. He introduced me to his group of friends and encouraged me to join in with them. Because of Larry, I slowly began to emerge from the isolated life that I had with Gramma.

Larry introduced me to Fred Katz, my second real friend. He lived across the street with his father, younger sister, and brother. His mother had died of cancer the year before—he could have gone in a million directions. He could have dropped out and become a street kid or worse, but he became my friend. We adopted Fred. He became my grandmother's third grandson, my mother's second son—my brother.

The three of us had that kind of wonderful inseparable friendship you can only have when you're growing up. My apartment became our base of operations. After school, the three of us would burst into Gramma's kitchen, gulp down the milk and cookies she'd have waiting for us, and tear out into the street. We'd race down Division Avenue, past the police station, past Kitzel Park, where all the old Jews sat, until we got to the school yard, where we'd meet the rest of the gang and roller skate on the newly paved street in front of the school.

Larry, Fred, and I teamed up with the usual cast of school characters. We began going to after school parties where the girls taught the boys to dance as *American Bandstand* played on television. We'd all rush home from school to watch the show at three o'clock and got very involved in the lives of Bob, Justine, and the other regulars on the show. We learned how to Stroll and Lindy and Philly.

We began to date at our parties and paired off to discover the opposite sex. I had the hots for Michelle Goldberg because she was a poet, but she was already going with Richie Klein, who was fat. Madeline Kantor had the hots for me, but she had underarm odor.

Carole Tubb gave me my first soul kiss when she dragged me behind the couch at Rita Stein's Halloween party. Carole came dressed as a harem girl. I found out later she had soul-kissed every boy in the room. Made me feel *real* special.

I found a steady girl. Her name was Maxine Horn. She was a sweet girl. Tall and skinny like me, with a great sense of humor. Her family was bright; her brothers and sisters were all college graduates, something very rare in Williamsburg. Once when I got home from dropping Maxine off after a school dance, I called

Fred and excitedly told him that when I kissed her good night, her leg went up in the back, just like in the movies.

The three of us guys were real city kids. As soon as we were allowed to, we took the subway into Manhattan by ourselves. Our hangouts became Rockefeller Plaza's ice-skating rink, the Museum of Natural History, Times Square, and Thirty-fourth Street. We got to know the short cuts to take on the subways and great places to have hamburgers, french fries, and Coke.

I think my friendship with these two funny, intelligent, gentle souls was the reason I was able to get through an uncomfortable adolescence.

*   *   *

One afternoon, while I was on my way home from Larry's apartment, a Schaefer beer delivery truck pulled up alongside me. A tall skinny guy jumped out of the driver's side and walked over to me.

"Hi, Barry," he said.

"Hi," I said. He looked familiar.

"I'm your father," he said. And I instantly knew he was.

Whenever anyone had ever mentioned Harold's name, Gramma would grumble disgustedly and Mom would get angry. There was only one picture of him in all our photo albums. Gramma had quietly taken the scissors and cut him out of any photos he was in with Edna or me. But I recognized him from that one stray photo.

"How've you been, son?" he asked.

"Okay," I said, looking at the ground, feeling awkward.

"Listen, I know your Grandma hates me and I'm afraid if she sees me she'll call the cops, so I'm not gonna stay long, but tomorrow's your birthday and I brought you a present."

He reached into the cab of the truck and lifted out a reel-to-reel tape recorder.

"Here," he said, handing it to me. "It's not brand-new, but I thought you'd get a kick out of playing with it."

"Thanks!" I said. "This is great!"

"You got a kiss for your old man?" he asked.

I hugged him tentatively and kissed him on the cheek. We let go and he looked at me for a long minute.

"Okay. I've gotta go. You take care of yourself. Hey, how's your mother?"

"She's fine," I said.

"Listen, don't tell anyone I was here, huh? Tell 'em you found the tape recorder or something, okay?" He walked briskly to the driver's side of the truck.

"Be a good kid," he said and waved and drove off in the giant beer truck.

I stood there with my new tape recorder, bursting with excitement, but feeling funny too. For as long as I could remember, I had thought of Harold as this monster person who had been mean to Mom and was uncaring and ugly. Now, here was this nice-looking, gentle guy, treating me affectionately, remembering my birthday and giving me a great gift. That was my father? He wasn't so bad after all.

I brought the tape recorder into the apartment.

"Where'd you get that?" Gramma immediately asked.

"Where'd I get what?" I said, stalling.

"Where'd you get that machine?" she said.

"What machine?" I said, still stalling, trying to think of where I could possibly have gotten it.

"*This* machine, in your hands, where did you get it?" she said, losing her patience.

"Oh, *this* machine," I said, finally acknowledging the tape recorder.

"Yes, darling, that one. Where did you get it?"

I'm a terrible liar. Always have been. I just couldn't lie to her. "Well," I said, taking a deep breath, "the funniest thing happened just now, Gramma. Harold drove by in his truck and gave it to me for my birthday," I stuttered out. "Are you gonna hit me?"

"*Harold?*" she yelled. "That *monster!* Where is he?" She ran out into the street.

I ran after her. "Gramma! Gramma! He's gone. Come back!"

She ran up the street looking for Harold, the monster, while

I got some milk and cookies. When she came back, she was muttering to herself and I was in my room, glowing over my new tape recorder.

"If I didn't see you loving this thing so much," she said, "I'd throw it out in the garbage."

I was very quiet. I was hoping she'd just forget it.

When Mom came home and heard about my visitor, she was upset too. It was a topic of discussion for a few days and then the subject was dropped. Soon we all began to enjoy the new tape recorder because Mom sang a song into it and suddenly the machine wasn't so bad after all.

I never felt the need to go searching for my father, and so I never did. I got so much love and I felt so secure with my family and my friends that finding my real father never became an issue. Besides, the family would have gotten really upset and I was never one to make waves. But the image of that gentle man, Harold the Monster, who hugged me and gave me my first tape recorder for my eleventh birthday, stayed with me.

*　　*　　*

When I was twelve years old, I began going to Hebrew school in preparation for my bar mitzvah at thirteen. I took it all very seriously. I would get up with the sun each morning to say the Hebrew prayers. I'd stand by the window in the dining room wearing a yarmulke on my head and a prayer shawl around my shoulders. I'd moan and hit my chest with my fist the way they showed me to as I babbled in my newly learned Hebrew language.

My mother, trying to sleep on the sofa in the dining room and nursing her hangovers, tolerated her born-again son. Gramma and Grampa nodded their heads in approval. Of course, it was easy for them to approve since they slept in a separate room and couldn't hear me.

Being bar mitzvahed means that a boy becomes a man. It is a very big step for any Jewish boy. My name, Barry Alan Pincus, had always bothered my mother. There was no Pincus in our family. She had gone back to being called Manilow when she divorced my father. Even my father changed his name back to Kelliher. Here I was, about to enter manhood with a name that didn't mean anything to anyone.

The thing that clinched it was Grampa. He was the last Manilow male and if he were to die, so would the name. So, with my approval, a few weeks before my bar mitzvah, Edna had my name legally changed to Barry Manilow.

My bar mitzvah gifts included cashiers' checks, fountain pens, and a stepfather. While I was learning about the suffering of the Jews, my mother was getting serious about William E. Murphy.

Willie had known my mother when they were kids. He lived in the Irish neighborhood near the river and was friends with Harold, my father. They both worked at the Schaefer brewery as truck drivers.

He remembered Edna as a skinny, bucktoothed little girl from the Jewish neighborhood. When they met on the subway years later he was amazed to find that she had turned into an attractive woman.

Willie was a great-looking Irishman with sandy blond hair and steel-blue eyes. His body was strong and solid from years of lugging cases of beer. He had two kids and had just recently gotten divorced. His large Irish family was as close and loving as our Jewish family was.

Willie loved to drink and fight. His nose had been broken a few times from street brawls. He also happened to be brilliant. He had little formal education, but he read voraciously. His taste in music, art, and clothes was stylish and sophisticated. He was a true Gemini—a street punk on one hand, an uptown gentleman on the other.

By this time, my mother was managing a toy firm's showroom on Fifth Avenue. She introduced Willie to her well-bred executive friends, and he talked with them about everything from politics to painting. He was also able to drink them all under the table. He was accepted into her professional life immediately.

After much protesting from Gramma, they married. But eventually Willie's charms worked on Gramma. Although he wasn't

Jewish, he was obviously a good man and was good for my mother and me.

They moved into an apartment on Keap Street ten blocks away from Division Avenue. Before they moved in, they let me decide where I'd like to live—with Gramma or with them. I chose to live with them. They were young and fun and musical and attractive—and Gramma was only ten blocks away. I moved in two weeks after they were married. Three Geminis in a three-room apartment. Crazy.

The apartment on Keap Street was in an old four-story brownstone owned by Evelyn Steinberg and her family, who inhabited the first three floors. We lived on the fourth floor above Rose Berger and her blind dog Pola. In order to get to our apartment, we'd have to pass the other families, who could see us walk by. We had no secrets on Keap Street.

The apartment was made up of a living room, a small kitchen, and a bedroom with its own closet. I moved into the closet. There was a second door in the closet that led out to the hallway, so I had my own entrance. The room was tiny, but we managed to squeeze in a daybed, a desk, and a chest of drawers.

I was nuts about Willie. He brought home books I had never heard of and read magazines I had only glanced at. His taste in everything was way above what I'd been exposed to. But most of all it was his music that changed my life.

Willie had a phonograph and lots of record albums. His phonograph was a small boxlike thing that sat on the floor, with speakers on all four sides. Under the lid was a turntable. It wasn't anything spectacular, but to me it sounded magnificent.

It was the first time I began to take music seriously. Up until then, I had played the accordion for the family's sake, and paid no attention to the popular music on radio. I really did not like Elvis Presley or "Rock Around the Clock." At the parties I went to I enjoyed dancing to "Chances Are" or "Teenager in Love," but I never listened to music for my own pleasure. My mother had tried to introduce me to the music she loved, but aside from being walloped by one stunning performance by Judy Garland at the Palace, I wasn't really a serious music lover.

Willie's record collection was like a treasure chest to me. I'd sit on the floor as close to the speakers as I could get, trying to crawl into the phonograph. I'd spend hours listening to all of Willie's albums. I fell in love with the jazz singers Chris Connor and June Christy. I discovered Sinatra. I memorized the Count Basie arrangements. I couldn't get enough of the bands led by Shorty Rogers, Woody Herman, and Duke Ellington. Among his jazz albums were some of the finest Broadway cast albums. I'd sit, mesmerized, listening to *Carousel, Kismet, The King and I.*

Willie saw how I was reacting to music. So one weekend, he bought two tickets for us to see Gerry Mulligan at Town Hall. Like the time I had seen Judy Garland, it was a thunderbolt in my life. I heard music I'd never even imagined existed—such rhythms, harmonies, chords. When it was over, I couldn't stop talking about it.

For my birthday that year, Willie bought me a tiny transistor radio. If I held it really close to my ear, I could hear the bass! I'd sleep with it turned on under my pillow.

I went to sleep one night, the radio murmuring softly under my pillow. Sometime after midnight, I woke up hearing great music. I had discovered Symphony Sid!

Symphony Sid hosted a three-hour jazz show on WEVD radio every night at midnight. He played the latest along with the classic jazz cuts. Listening to his show each night was a revelation to me. Within weeks I had dark circles under my eyes when I went to school. As I listened to his show, I discovered the Modern Jazz Quartet, Cal Tjader, Lambert, Hendricks and Ross, and Bill Evans. I learned about the difference between cool West Coast jazz and energetic East Coast jazz. I found Miles Davis, John Coltrane, Cannonball Adderley; I wallowed in Sarah Vaughan, Carmen Macrae, Nina Simone, Joe Williams, Mel Torme. I couldn't get enough. I tried playing some of this new music on my accordion, but it sounded silly.

*   *   *

One flight down, Rose had a grand piano in her apartment. On my way upstairs one day, she invited me to play it. I sat down

at the instrument and hesitantly began to play "Don't Blame Me."
Because of my knowledge of the accordion keyboard, playing the
piano was easy.

From then on, I'd sit at Rose's piano and play all the songs I'd
been hearing on Willie's albums and on Symphony Sid. Finally,
my mother and Willie decided to buy me a piano.

I was home alone when it arrived. It was an $800 Wurlitzer
spinet and it took my mother five years to pay for it. Have you
ever seen piano movers deliver a piano? It's inhuman.

I had been waiting for hours for them to arrive. When the
delivery man rang the bell from the street, I ran to answer it.

"Up here!" I yelled from the fourth floor.

I ran to the window and saw them rolling the piano out of
the van. They wrapped it in a heavy cloth and rolled it into the
building. Then they began bouncing it up the stairs as if it were
an old shoe. You could hear the strings ringing at every bounce.

"Take it easy!" I yelled and I ran downstairs to them.

"Out of the way, kid. It ain't hurtin' the piano," one of the
big delivery men told me. "We do this all day long."

I couldn't watch. I went back upstairs and into my room as
they bounced my new piano up the stairs. When they got up to
our apartment, I pointed them toward the living room. They
were right. They hadn't hurt it. After they left, I sat down at the
piano and began playing. That's how Willie and my mother found
me when they got home from work.

I've played on hundreds of pianos, from uprights to nine-foot
grands. My Wurlitzer spinet is still one of the best pianos I've
ever played. It stayed with me for fifteen years. The piano lives
at my mother's apartment now, and she still has it tuned each
month. It's got old cigarette burns on it and it's scratched up, but
it still plays great.

Playing the piano that September afternoon was the moment
my life began. It was my mother who gave me life, but it was
that piano that gave my life direction. It was also the key to the
door out of Brooklyn.

My mother and Willie continued to introduce me to the music
they loved. When they saw my passion for the piano, they began

bringing home albums by pianists. They introduced me to Ahmad Jamal, Marian McPartland, Dave Brubeck, and George Shearing. I spent a whole month trying to perfect Marian McPartland's version of "Lush Life" on the spinet. I drove everyone in the building crazy, but I mastered it. While all of the gang was doing the Stroll, I was practicing Shearing's version of "Lullabye of Birdland."

When I got Willie Murphy for a stepfather, so did Larry and Fred. When I discovered music, so did Larry and Fred. Soon it was the three of us harmonizing to Lambert, Hendricks, and Ross songs on the subway.

*   *   *

I think that by the time you enter high school, you arc who you're going to be. You're just a younger version of who you're going to be for the rest of your life. When I entered high school, I was me. My weaknesses, my strengths, my likes, my dislikes were all formed and they've never really changed. Even my response to people was already formed. The problems I would have in dealing with people in the future were already laid out for me.

I was an average kid. I never got into trouble, did my homework, got average grades, and had no idea what I wanted to do with my life.

Larry, Fred, and I began attending Eastern District High School across the street from my house. With my mother and Willie away at work, our apartment was where we lived.

Larry had proven to be extremely bright; I envied his aptitude in math and science. He'd whiz through homework assignments that took me hours. His sense of humor turned razor sharp and he was hysterical to be around. But it was Fred who I wanted to be. He was so cool and good looking. All the girls had crushes on him. He was bright too, but he got through school more on his charm than on his brains. He was strong and yet vulnerable, qualities I envied and admired.

By the time I was fourteen years old, I was a musical snob. I crossed pop music off my list of things to be taken seriously. I didn't care for the popular television programs or the music on the commercial radio stations. Who could compare that kind of music with the artistry of jazz great Chet Baker?

As I became more and more proficient at the piano, I began discovering music arrangers. I was fascinated with why the orchestra did what it did. Why did the sound of a plaintive oboe make me sad, or the power of the trombones excite me? I wondered. Who told them to do it? Was it the conductor? Why did "Don't Blame Me" sound different on one album from the way it did on another? Who conceived the difference? How come no one else was affected by these things? I'd struggle to listen to the instruments accompanying Sinatra, then I'd run to the piano and try to copy the arrangement.

I discovered a whole new world of people when I looked at the "arranged and conducted by" credit on albums. I found Billy May, David Rose, Don Costa. I began to realize that as moving to me as Sinatra was on "Only the Lonely," Nelson Riddle's arrangements were doing as much.

I began creating my own arrangements to my newly discovered music repertory. I recruited everyone I knew to be singer to my arrangements. I'd make Edna stop preparing dinner to come in and sing while I played. I even got Larry and Fred to sing. I never sang myself. It just never dawned on me to sing. I was the piano player and the arranger, not the singer.

High school was boring. I was only interested in running home after school and making music. During my sophomore year, I put together a band: Larry and Fred on clarinet and background vocals, Rosario Rizzo on trumpet, and Harry Lewis on drums. I played piano and arranged. We rehearsed in the school auditorium or my apartment. We'd drag Harry's drum set all the way up four flights, move all the furniture up against the walls of the tiny place and blast away. It was a dreadful band and I don't blame *Ted Mack's Amateur Hour* for turning us down. But it didn't matter to me. Music had become my obsession.

Even though I was only fourteen, once a month Willie would sneak me into Eddie Condon's jazz club or Birdland. I'd sit in awe as Stan Getz or Thelonious Monk tore up the small club. I'd feel very grown up, sneaking a smoke from Willie or sipping from his cocktail.

Throughout these years, my mother and Willie gave me support and encouragement. They did the same for Larry and Fred. When any of us got good grades in school, we'd run to show Edna and Willie. If any of us had problems, we'd discuss it with them and they'd give us advice. In our tiny Brooklyn apartment on the fourth floor, we would discuss the merits of West Coast jazz over East Coast jazz. It was as if all three of us belonged to them. And we did.

*   *   *

Willie had always been a drinker. Now, meeting my mother at the office bars after work, they'd both start drinking at five o'clock. By the time they arrived home, they were always loaded. And they had begun to argue.

In the beginning their arguments were harmless and would be over within hours. Soon, the arguments were about money and the pressures that not having enough of it brought. Their arguments became louder and more serious. Willie would storm down the stairs and sometimes not come home until the next morning, which drove my mother nuts.

Hearing them stumbling up the stairs each evening became the norm. I'd wait until I saw how bad they were before I'd give Larry and Fred the signal to split. My mother would always try to make some kind of dinner, but most of the time I'd received a slurred phone call, telling me to "pop in a frozen."

I lived on Swanson's frozen dinners during my high school days. I didn't mind. My mother and Willie were lovable drunks. They were never abusive, except sometimes to each other.

*   *   *

During the summer I turned sixteen, Willie got me a temporary job at the brewery. Working at Schaefer's convinced me that I was cut out for better things.

I worked midnight to eight, the morning shift, and I was terrible. They tried me out in five different jobs. I screwed up all five. Finally, they made me a "helper" delivering beer on the trucks.

Each morning, the truck drivers would be assigned their helpers for the day. I was a terrible "helper." I was skinny and clumsy. I'd drop whole cases of cold beer. Instead of lugging five cases at once to save time, I'd take one. The daily route should have taken two men four hours to complete. It would take us eight. By the second week, drivers were dreading getting me as their helper.

"Oh, no, I got Manilow!" they'd moan.

The End came one sunny day in Jersey. One of my responsibilities was making sure that all the huge rolltop doors around the truck were pulled down tight after each delivery.

After making a delivery to the basement of a bar in Passaic—and encountering a vicious German shepherd—I shut the rolltop doors and hopped into the cab of the truck. We sped off and made a turn at the corner. Suddenly we heard a loud, long crash.

"Christ! What was that?" I asked the driver.

He didn't even flinch. He calmly pulled over to the side of the empty street.

"Barry," he asked, lighting a cigarette. "Did you close the doors?"

"Absolutely, John. No question about it. I closed 'em. Yes I did," I said, certain that I had.

"Look behind us," he said, staring ahead.

I looked out my window and behind the truck the street was totally filled with bottles and crates all engulfed in foaming beer suds.

That was the end of my career at the brewery. I never liked beer anyway.

*　　　*　　　*

As I entered my last year in high school, two important things happened. My teeth got released from jail and I met my future wife, Susan. I was pretty happy, even though I didn't know or care where I was heading. I was obsessed by music, but thought of it as a hobby, not a future. Fred and Larry and I weren't the most popular guys at Eastern District High, but we had enough dates, parties, and girlfriends to keep us busy.

I met Susan at the beginning of my senior year and couldn't believe it when she seemed to fall for me as hard as I fell for her. She was a year behind me in school and was adorable, small, with great legs and a voluptuous figure. She had jet black hair, dark brown eyes, and a smile that lit up the room. She was warm, funny, sensitive, and bright. During all my years with Susan, I never once met anyone who wasn't crazy about her.

President of every school club, she had boundless energy and was always tearing through the hallways laden down with books or posters. I could never catch up with her. There were always crowds around her. She had loads of friends, and teachers and students alike adored her.

Susan lived way out in Brooklyn with her mother, father, and brother. They had recently moved there, but had decided to let Susan stay at Eastern District rather than make her leave all of her friends. We were great for each other. She was very musical and played piano too.

During the last year of high school, Susan and music were infinitely more important to me than my studies. I joined a jazz group formed by a talented guitar player, Jackie Wilkins, who became a well-respected guitarist. He lived out in the suburban section of Brooklyn and I traveled out there three times a week to play with the group. They made me arranger and I spent hours at my piano writing out charts for the band and composing themes for us to play.

I dug more and more into the concept of arrangers and conductors: Henry Mancini for Andy Williams; Don Costa for Mathis; Nelson Riddle for Sinatra. That magic credit on the albums was where I imagined my name. *Arranged and conducted by Barry Manilow*, I fantasized.

*   *   *

Graduating from high school was not a particularly emotional experience for me. Even though I had made friends in high school, there were really only three friends that mattered: Fred, Larry, and Susan. And I wasn't leaving them.

I look at my high school yearbook picture and I don't recognize that guy. I really don't remember looking like that. Oh, there's a picture of a guy named Barry Manilow, but he sure isn't me. We all looked alike in those pictures, too. It's amazing how that photographer managed to get the same moronic look on all of our faces!

I was glad school was over, but I had no idea what I was going to do. I had made plans to go to City College at night while I worked during the day, but I didn't know what I was going to major in once I got there. If you'd asked me what I thought my future was going to be like, I probably would have told you that I imagined it was going to be pretty conventional. Although I knew that music was the one thing I loved, it never crossed my mind to try to make a career of it. I figured that eventually I would find something in college that turned me on. Then I'd marry Susan, get a house in Long Island with a white picket fence, and have kids, just like everyone else. But it didn't quite work out like that.

Major Decision No. 1

The evening I registered at City College, I still hadn't decided what I wanted to major in. The choices were listed alphabetically, and advertising was first under A. I chose advertising.

I was bored and didn't do well at all, but I stuck it out. I got a job clipping ads in an advertising agency during the days. When the agency went bankrupt, I can't say I was sorry.

Willie had a friend who worked at CBS television and set up an interview for me with the personnel department. "Don't tell them you're interested in music," he warned. "They don't want aspiring actors, actresses, and musicians working in their corporate offices."

"Right," I promised. I began working in the CBS mailroom the next week.

When I got to the mailroom, *all* I found were budding actors, actresses, and musicians! They had also been warned not to tell the truth on their application.

Important things happened for me while I worked at CBS. It was an exciting place to go every morning: it was stimulating, it was filled with music. And I met Marty Panzer. If Fred and I were brothers during high school, then Marty and I went through the college of life together.

Oddly enough, Marty and I were raised in the same Brooklyn neighborhood. We'd gone to the same schools, attended the same movies, stores, and synagogues, but we had never met. We both started working in the CBS mailroom in the same week and recognized each other from passing in the hallway at school.

Marty was unique, his own creation. I'd never met anyone like him. He was hysterically funny, irreverent, sensitive, eccentric, and as bright as you can get. He had dark hair and intense eyes. His brows were always furrowed and he looked as if he had the problems of the world on his shoulders. He chain-smoked and trembled all the time.

Marty was a very emotional guy. His whole life was one big drama. His reactions were bigger than life—when he liked something, he wouldn't stop until he exhausted everyone around him discussing it. He threw himself totally into every project. He was filled with opinions, energy, and passion.

Like me, Marty was enamored of music and show business, but unlike me, he was not moved by cool jazz or interesting melodies. He reacted only to performers and music that had emotion and passion. For every spectacular jazz artist I showed Marty, he returned the favor by introducing me to a great showman. When I showed him Mulligan, he showed me Jackie Wilson. When I showed him Count Basie tunes, he showed me Harold Arlen tunes. And when I showed him Chris Connor, he reminded me about Judy Garland.

He was right. When you combine passion and hot emotion with music, the result is explosive. It was a lesson I would never forget.

* * *

So there I was at nineteen, doing exactly what I thought I should be doing. I took the subway from Brooklyn into Manhattan each morning, wearing my suit and tie. I had a job with a future at a major corporation. Soon I would be promoted to a well-paying position. I was engaged to my high school sweetheart. We would marry, settle down, have a few kids, and grow old together.

And the music? Well, it would stay within me. I loved music, but sensible people couldn't really consider it a career. Sensible people made sure that they got that Friday afternoon paycheck. I mean, look what happened to Willie and Edna. They were always up to their ears in debt, but it was that paycheck each week that bailed them out.

I worked in the corporate headquarters at 485 Madison Avenue, but across the street at 49 West Fifty-second Street were the CBS recording studios. I had to deliver mail there occasionally and I discovered that there were three or four recording studios on each floor.

One of the mailboys called in sick one Monday and I got his route in addition to my own. Even though it was only across the street, I'd never been there. It was a cold New York winter day. I grabbed my armful of mail and took the elevator down to the lobby. The 485 Madison Avenue building was bustling and noisy. The elevator men knew me and greeted me as I walked out the door into the freezing air.

I ran across the street and into the 49 building. The atmosphere was very different. The lobby was empty except for one lone security guard sitting near the elevators. I showed him my identification pass and went into the steel-and-blue elevator. It was very quiet.

I went up to the top floor and found normal offices. After I delivered the mail, I decided to check out the rest of the building. I pressed the 2 button on the elevator. When I got out I found a dark and very quiet floor. There were three huge doors, and above them was a glass sign. Painted in red were the words RECORDING—DO NOT ENTER. None of the signs was lit, so I chose one door and quietly opened it. I found another door with a round glass portal. I stood between the two doors and looked into the room through the glass.

The room was dark, empty, and huge. I opened the second door and stood in awe. My first recording studio. The floors were wooden and the walls were carpeted. Against the walls were microphone stands, music stands, chairs folded up. One wall was made of glass and I could see into an enormous room that had knobs and turntables and recording equipment—the engineer booth. Sitting at the side of the room was the most enormous black grand piano I'd ever seen.

I walked over to the piano, checking behind me to make sure no one had come in, and touched it. It was shiny and spotless. I sat down, opened the lid, and played a few notes. I'd never experienced anything like it. I had been used to the best little piano in all of the world, you remember. But this wasn't even a piano. It was a whole different animal.

Playing my first Steinway was like floating on a silvery white cloud. The sound sparkled. The feel was soft and luscious. *Anything* I played sounded great.

From then on, my mail runs included visits to the studios. Playing the piano in the studios became my first love and I'd reluctantly stop playing to deliver my mail.

Soon, Marty and some of the other mailboys were dropping in. Eventually, the secretaries would come by on their lunch break and listen. I started doing arrangements for budding vocalists and Marty and I began writing songs together.

As much fun as it had been to arrange other people's songs, there was absolutely nothing to compare to creating them. Most of the melodies came easily to me, and because I was so smitten with arranging, I incorporated the tricks I had learned—key changes and grand endings—into the bodies of the songs themselves.

Marty was tentative when he began writing lyrics to my melodies but it was easy to see that he had a knack for it. We spent hours together at the piano and when we'd completed a song, it was satisfying and we were proud. The fun of collaboration is a process I still love to this day.

*　　*　　*

It was time to register at City College for my third semester. As the week went by, I kept stalling. The prospect of another advertising course discussing textiles and factories seemed deadly.

One of the guys in the mailroom was studying classical music at a school called the New York College of Music. The idea of going to any kind of music college had never occurred to me. No one had ever brought up the subject at home. I mean, how could anybody really make music a career? You had to go to work from nine to five, Monday to Friday, and wait for the Friday paycheck. Music school didn't fit into that plan.

I went into the phone booth of the coffee shop located in the CBS building. I called City College and found out that that night was the last time I could register for the next semester. I just stood there, not able to dial.

Then, on a whim, I looked up the number for the New York College of Music. I decided to call and ask about their classes. I found out that this night was the last time *they* were testing applicants for next semester's classes!

I stood in the phone booth wearing my bomber jacket, white shirt and tie. I watched the activity going on outside on Madison Avenue and at everyone running around in the coffee shop. I knew that the decision I was making would affect the rest of my life.

A career in music? What kind of career *is* that? What do you do in it? Can you make money? Can you support your wife and your kids in Long Island in a house with a picket fence? I mean, I loved music, but it just wasn't *sensible.*

Was it?

Someone banged on the door of the booth. I grabbed my stack of mail and left. I walked through the streets and thought about this decision. I thought of all the people I could call for advice, but finally, I knew I'd have to make the decision on my own.

I went back to the 49 building and found an empty studio. I walked into the large, dark, wooden studio and looked at all the music stands and microphones. The control booth on the other side of a large glass window was dark, but I could see shadows of tape recorders and machines.

I loved it here in the studio. I loved the woody smell and the feeling of a soundproofed room. I put my mail down on the piano, sat on the piano stool and played a little. As I played, I thought:

Well, making music feels better than anything I do.

Sitting in City College and trying to be interested in business courses feels worse than anything I do.

Even if I could manage to survive an advertising education, the prospect of a life behind a desk at an advertising agency is depressing.

The prospect of making music for the rest of my life fills me with such joy and excitement that I can't see straight.

But how can I choose something that I *love* to do as opposed to choosing something that I know I *should* do. It isn't sensible. It's irresponsible. Flaky people make decisions based on love. Intelligent, responsible people make decisions based on reality.

I closed the lid of the piano and left the studio. I decided to go to City College and register for the third semester of advertising. I left the building and went back to the mailroom.

A few hours later, as the time drew nearer to leave for the college, I made one more trip across the street. As I crossed the street, I could see the phone booth in the coffee shop. I stood looking at it while people bumped into me.

A little voice inside my head whispered, "Go ahead, Manilow. *Do it!*"

I walked briskly across the street and into the phone booth. I dialed the New York College of Music and made an appointment to take the entrance exam that night.

I didn't talk to anyone about it. I took the subway uptown. I walked blindly forward, not looking right or left, not giving my "sensible" self a chance to question what I was doing. I was afraid that if I thought about what I was doing, I would chicken out.

I took the exam, passed it, and registered for my first semester at music school. When I looked at the subject choices, I smiled. On the list of choices was the magic phrase "Orchestra Arranging." There was actually a class in which I could learn how to do the thing I loved so dearly! I knew I had made the right choice.

Susan

Everyone I told about my decision was happy for me. Edna and Willie were delighted. Larry, Fred, and Marty were excited. Susan was thrilled.

But I was still unsure about committing my life to music. My future at CBS was still extremely important to me. I intended to stay and try to make a career there and wait and see about the music.

Marty and I both left the CBS mailroom a little under two years after we started. He chose to go into On Air Operations. He was responsible for everything that happened on the air. I chose a job as log clerk, which also had to do with the on-air happenings of television. I'd sit in a room, for eight hours a day, and watch four television screens at once. Each monitor showed what was being aired in the four time zones of the country. My job was to keep track of everything that happened. I'd make sure that the programs got on the air all right, that the commercials aired at the right time.

I worked each day from eight until four. Then I ran uptown to school.

Going to music college was a dream. I looked forward to each day at four when classes would begin. I'd finish about eight or nine and meet Susan before going home to Brooklyn.

A year after high school graduation, Susan had gotten a job as a secretary in a toy firm. We'd been going together for a few years by the time we decided to get married. We were in love; there was no question that we were destined to spend our lives together. I loved Susan completely—I loved what she represented as well as who she was. She was independent, she was good through and through, she was smart, pretty, musical, perfect. We'd sit on the subway, holding hands, oblivious to the people around us.

We spent long evenings together playing duets on the piano. I accompanied her while she sang and sometimes we'd sing romantic duets while her family looked on dreamily.

Susan loved her job and, as usual, was always busy. She had continued to cultivate a million friends and was always meeting someone somewhere. She always had time for us, though.

We decided to get married in June, right after my twenty-first birthday. As the time drew near, the two families decided it was time to get to know one another and to discuss the wedding.

Edna and Willie met with Susan's parents—twice. During the first dinner, there was nothing but laughter and smiling. Each couple bragged about their child and they parted after hugging and kissing.

At the end of the second dinner, Edna and Willie left their home in a huff, and that was the end of that relationship.

The argument was about money and the wedding. Nettie and Al wanted a big one, with everyone they'd ever known invited. Edna and Willie said, "Great, but you'll have to foot the bill, because we can't afford to help." And they couldn't. They were still struggling to support Gramma, Grampa, and themselves. The talk became more and more curt and the evening ended in disaster.

Edna was not in favor of my getting married. She really liked Susan, but she believed I was too young for the responsibility of a marriage. She saw my new passion for a career in music and my unsure career at CBS and tried to encourage me to work on one thing at a time. Willie agreed with her.

Even my friends felt that I was rushing into marriage. But I didn't agree. I was on the road to the fantasy life with Susan that I had created years ago: the house in Long Island with the white picket fence and the kids playing in the yard. And I loved Susan. It felt very right to me. When we were together, the world didn't exist. Every time we'd hold each other, it made us both stronger and more determined to marry and begin our life together.

But the bickering between the families was very hard on both of us and we wound up arguing too.

"Your mother called my mother cheap!" I'd yell at her.

"Oh, yeah, well, Edna hung up on my father!" she'd yell back.

The two sets of parents kept fighting about the wedding and finally, Susan and I decided to take matters into our own hands.

After finding a small apartment on Sullivan Street near the Village, we eloped.

One Monday afternoon in May, during our lunch hour, we met at City Hall. Marty, my best man, and Joan DeSantis, Susan's maid of honor, and the two of us.

We were married in a judge's chambers. Before beginning the ceremony, the judge gave us a stern ten-minute speech telling us that this was a very important decision in our lives. He asked us to rethink what we were about to do and left the office for fifteen minutes so we could rethink.

When he returned, we were still determined and he married us in five minutes. We all went back to work after the ceremony. Susan and I met after work and took the subway back to her house. We told her parents that night. They were very upset. So upset they refused to allow us to move into our new apartment together until we were married by a rabbi.

So on our wedding night, I went home to Keap Street and Susan stayed with her parents.

That weekend, we stood under the chupeh in a rabbi's office in Long Island City. Marty, Joan, and the two sets of parents surrounded us. I broke the glass with my foot and kissed the bride. We were finally legally and religiously married. When it was over, my parents went one way and hers the other. We'd been married twice.

The next weekend Nettie and Al threw a wedding reception for us. They refused to invite any of my family, except for Edna and Willie, who wouldn't go. So I refused to go. Tearfully, Edna convinced me to show up. During the reception, Nettie and Al brought in a rabbi and Susan and I were married again, this time in front of her whole family. That made three times.

On the following weekend, Edna and Willie threw a wedding reception for us and didn't invite any of Susan's family. Edna wanted our family to watch me get married, so Susan and I were married once again by a rabbi in front of my family. That made four.

We lay in bed that night, counting the checks our relatives had given us.

"Well, I'd say we are definitely married," I said.

"Yep. I would say that if two people were ever married for keeps, it's us," she said.

"For keeps," I said.

"Forever," she said, and we kissed and turned out the lamp.

*   *   *

We lived in a small one bedroom apartment. The living room doubled as the dining room and had a little indentation in the wall that was laughingly called a kitchenette.

The place was so tiny there was literally no room for furniture, so Susan and I bought platforms, which we placed up against the walls. It was where we sat and relaxed and it left the middle of the room for the dining table and my spinet piano. We positioned the piano facing out so that I could face the room instead of looking at a wall.

The bedroom was small, too, but who cared? We only needed the bed anyway. There were two tiny closets in the place and we crammed everything we had gotten from the wedding(s) into them, along with our clothes and other necessities.

Susan and I loved living in Manhattan. It was exciting and alive. Plus it was only minutes from each of our offices.

The people I made friends with at CBS were friendly and

outgoing. And everyone had a little show business going on the side. Bro Herrod, a director at CBS, owned a little off-off-Broadway theater on Thirteenth Street. We'd meet in the hallway now and then and I told him that I played piano.

He came into my office one day and told me he was reviving the old melodrama, *The Drunkard*. He said that he needed singers because the cast would have to sing during the scene changes. Would I be interested in playing piano?

"Sure!" I said eagerly. Maybe too eagerly. "How much does it pay?" I asked.

"Nothing," he said.

"I'll take it," I agreed. I always drove a hard bargain.

The people I met at rehearsal every evening at the Thirteenth Street Theatre fascinated me. They were "show people." They seemed witty and worldly. They told stories about shows they'd been in and places they'd seen. They spoke of famous performers as if they knew them personally.

"And the next day Ginger and I came in with such hangovers!" David Moyer, our stage manager, related. Ginger Rogers? I was impressed.

"Carol is such a ninny, she forgot her own address!" Chris Cable, our "villain," related. Carol Channing? Hot shit!

They would sing obscure songs from flop shows and I'd play for them with joy. Listening to them talk about their experiences was better than movies or books or television. They seemed as if they were very successful, even though they weren't, and I devoured every story hungrily. But most of all, they seemed to love me! They raved over my piano playing and each of them wanted an original song from me. They fawned over me and flattered me and hired me to play for their auditions. After rehearsals we'd all go out and drink and laugh and sing into the wee hours. The camaraderie was enormously intoxicating. It was a new world for me.

When I'd go backstage to discuss the evening's music, I discovered the freedom that comes with dressing rooms. The Thirteenth Street Theatre was so small everyone dressed in one long room. There were no secrets in that dressing room.

The men would walk around in skimpy bikini underwear and less. The women would sit in panties and bras and laugh with each other and never thought twice about it. The girls with curlers in their hair and just a towel around their bodies would sit next to guys wearing eye makeup and rouge. I had never been exposed to anything like all this and found it daring and exciting.

One night, we all went out to a bar after the show. I felt guilty not having Susan there with me but I promised myself I wouldn't stay long. Carrie, one of the cast members, sat next to me in the booth we were all squeezed into.

We were all chatting away about the show when I felt her hand on my leg. We kept talking to each other as if nothing were happening. I tried to be interested in the conversation going on around me, but she had unzipped my fly and had her hand inside my jeans.

I was still trying to pretend to be part of the conversation and Carrie continued to smile and chat with the others. I couldn't let her continue. It was getting too close. I reached under the table to stop her. When I did, she put my hand under her dress. She wasn't wearing any underwear.

Carrie wasn't the only one trying to seduce me, and after that experience I ran straight home from the theater so as not to be tempted again. But I couldn't deny that I found myself very attracted to the women at the theater. And most amazing of all, they seemed to be coming on to me. No one in school had ever made a pass at me. I couldn't even get dates! When I found myself the center of sexual attention, it was exciting. My luck. I couldn't do anything about it because I was a newly married man with a loving wife waiting patiently for me at home.

It was the beginning of my concern for my marriage. Had I gotten married too soon? Susan tried desperately to be a part of my new show-business life and I really tried to include her. I even got her a role in the first show I conducted.

*   *   *

The Pajama Game was being mounted by the All Souls Players, a community church theatrical group that rehearsed and performed after working hours. I was recommended as conductor by one of the kids in the cast of *The Drunkard*. (Probably Carrie!) I had never conducted or directed a musical in my life, but playing piano for *The Drunkard* had been great fun and I wanted to give it a try.

During the interview, the producer asked, "Have you ever conducted and music directed any shows?" "Of course," said I, and proceeded to recite a list of shows I had directed. In my mind, I was just going through all my favorite Broadway show albums.

When they asked me where these shows were done, I rattled off names of theaters where I had played for auditions. I think they knew I was bullshitting, but I got the job. I remember leaving the meeting with the score of the show under my arm and going directly to the library to find books that might help me. I got home that night laden down with music instruction books and began studying.

I loved doing *The Pajama Game* even more than *The Drunkard*. The cast had three times as many people in it, and I had a small budget that would allow me to hire seventeen musicians. I was going to be able to conduct an orchestra! I dug into the score and began to rearrange the original orchestrations.

Even though I was doing my best to include Susan in my music life, it wasn't really working. She didn't feel comfortable tagging along, and I felt confined. "Love is blind," as the old saying goes. I added, "and marriage is the eye opener."

I was spending more time with the cast than I was at home with my wife. Everyone noticed it and tried to help me. Edna kept telling me, "See, I told you so," as only a Jewish mother can.

I wanted our marriage to work more than anything. But now married life felt confining. And to make it more complicated, this new world of music and show business was spread out in front of me, ready for the taking.

I tried playing the role of loving husband and would visit the in-laws frequently, do the dishes and the shopping when I could, and be with Susan as much as possible. But what sounded ideal to me a year before now paled in comparison to what I saw I could have. Now I wanted more than a house with a picket fence in Long Island. More than a wife and kids tying me down. I wanted to explore the opportunities that were being offered to me. Music, theater, show business, traveling, meeting new people, experiencing everything.

I realized that our dreams and plans were not really the same anymore. The only thing we had in common was our past—not our future.

Once again I found myself faced with the same decision: a life of music versus a conventional life. I would have to choose between the future I had been blindly heading toward, and this wondrous musical adventure that I saw within my reach.

I loved Susan. She was a perfect wife. It was so hard to admit that I wasn't ready to commit my whole life to her. I was too young for marriage. I had to learn more about myself before I could begin to give myself to someone else. I was miserable being married and finally had to tell her. She reacted badly, of course. But leaving Susan, especially before we had any children, was the kindest thing I could do for both of us.

On the night I left, we had both come home from work, and I sat at our dining table wanting to be making music with my new friends. I walked to the window and looked out at the crisp September evening. Susan had begun to wash the dishes, still wearing the dress and high heels she had worn to work. Making dinner for me was so important to her she hadn't even bothered to change into something comfortable.

I lit a cigarette, lowered the lights, and sat down at the spinet piano and began playing a moody piece. Soon she was sitting on the floor in front of me with a cigarette and staring at me. I stared back.

How could I do this to this girl? She deserved someone who would love her with the kind of love I saw in her eyes as she looked at me.

I couldn't bear it. "Susan," I said, "I gotta go."

She started to cry and asked me to think it over a little longer, but I couldn't. It was too hard.

I got up from the piano and went into the bedroom. I stood

there looking at our possessions wondering what I should take with me. I couldn't find anything I wanted.

In the bathroom, as I packed my toothbrush and razor, I could smell the fresh scent of Jean Naté that Susan wore. It reminded me of the good times with her and my knees buckled and I held on to the sink. I had to move quickly or I would never be able to leave.

I packed a suitcase full of clothes and grabbed my brand new Sony tape recorder and my pillow.

Susan sat on the bed and cried as I put on my coat.

"I'll call you before I come for the rest of my stuff," I said. "I'm so sorry. I love you."

I waited for the elevator feeling like shit. As the elevator reached the lobby level, the world became blurry, and through the tears in my eyes I saw colors and heard music from outside in the street.

I walked out of the apartment building and into the pandemonium and chaos of the San Gennaro Festival. The colorful ferris wheel, the loud music, the screaming and laughter of the children, the smells of dozens of street vendors selling fried zeppole, and me standing there in Little Italy with my tape recorder in one hand, my suitcase in the other, and my pillow under my arm, not knowing where I was going.

One Flight Up

I went home to Brooklyn. I went back to security, support, familiar surroundings, Mom, friends, my old room. I went home. But it wasn't the same. I guess it never is.

I had been gone only for a year, but it might as well have been ten. Everything was different. I felt uncomfortable and out of place. My old room was too small; the apartment wasn't as I remembered. Edna and Willie were drinking and fighting. I didn't want to be there.

The truth is, everything was exactly the same. *I* had changed.

The next day, I returned to my apartment in the Village with my friend Steve Mackler and his truck to collect the rest of my things. When I put my key in the door, it wouldn't open. Susan had changed the lock. Which meant she'd probably spoken to her mother.

I called her at her office from a phone booth. And what I heard on the other end was a very distant and hurt woman. She told me I could have my clothes, but nothing else. Not even my piano.

Yep, she had *definitely* spoken to her mother.

I was very upset, but my guilt overpowered me and I let it go. A new start is what I wanted and that's what I was getting.

I looked night and day for an apartment in Manhattan—I wanted that dream apartment to appear. You know, the one you always hear about a friend of a friend finding—one large bedroom, full kitchen, millions of closets, sunken living room, skylight and a small garden right in the middle of Manhattan—for $100 a month? Yeah, fat chance. One week of seeing what was really out there convinced me that it only happened to friends of a friend.

I couldn't wait any longer and rented an apartment deep in the heart of Brooklyn in a nice apartment building in Flatbush. The rent was right for my clerk's salary but the ride to CBS took an hour each way by subway. It was on the third floor and it had a bedroom, living room, kitchen, and bathroom. All the windows except the one in the kitchen overlooked the alley where they stacked the garbage. The kitchen window looked at a brick wall. You couldn't see the sky or the sunshine, but at least it was mine.

Little by little I pulled my new life together. Susan had reconsidered and let me have my piano (but nothing else) and I began furnishing my place modestly(!): bricks and a door for a table, wooden orange crates for end tables, bricks and flat boards for bookshelves. A mattress on the floor was a bed and posters I had bought for two dollars became artwork.

I placed the piano facing out again, so that I wouldn't be staring at a wall when I played. I covered the back of the piano with my favorite album covers. I thought it looked pretty cool.

After a few months I began to feel better. Although I regretted causing Susan pain I knew I had done the right thing for both of us.

Larry and Fred and I tried to stay close but it was very difficult. Fred was deep into his marriage and had a child, and Larry was going to school and was engaged. Our lives were going in different directions and soon the phone calls dwindled.

Marty and I got closer and my new friends at the Thirteenth Street Theatre became my family. *The Drunkard* had become quite an experience for me. What had begun as a piano player job turned into much more. Although I made no money there, the experience I was getting was priceless. I wound up spending most of my free time with Bro Herrod, his lady Diane, and their dog Nellie, who lived above the theater. It was all very glamorous to me.

Bro was a huge man. He was balding and had the most malleable face I'd ever seen. His face was like rubber. When he'd change expressions, his whole face would change—his lips, eyes, and big bushy eyebrows would all just move around his face as if they weren't attached. He was an actor turned director and a real "theater" person. They're a different breed, let me tell you. When he'd get angry, the walls would shake from his strength! When he'd laugh, he'd laugh with his whole body, and he cried very easily. He was mean and brusque to most people because he didn't trust anyone. But when he liked you, watch out—he'd kill for you. He was extremely bright and opinionated. Talent to him was held in religious awe. When he spotted someone with talent, he worshiped him or her. Bro was the first professional person to notice talent in me. He'd sit and stare and smile when I played or worked with the actors. He'd applaud suggestions I made, and he'd teach me everything he could.

I knew nothing about theater or musical comedy. Bro took me by the hand and taught me the ABCs of theater. I worked with him daily, weekly, monthly, on and off for eight years. He became a mentor and big brother.

When Bro mounted *The Drunkard*, he decided to include more music in it than he had originally intended. At first, all he planned to do was to find 1890s-type songs and add them to the script in the appropriate places while the scenes were changed. But soon I began timidly to bring in songs that I had written myself. They were enthusiastically received, and after rehearsing them with the cast we put them into the show. Within a year, I had written an entire score, and *The Drunkard* was an original musical.

I filled every waking moment with work. I couldn't think of getting serious with anyone after Susan, and I kept relationships of any romantic nature at arm's length. While playing for *The Drunkard*, I took a job playing piano in a lounge with a jazz trio from eight until midnight on weekend evenings.

Soon I started my own coaching business on the side. Singers I played piano for recommended me to other singers. Before long I was playing for dozens of performers.

*   *   *

One sunny Saturday afternoon in October while I was working at the piano, the doorbell rang. I opened the door and my mother stood there smiling.

"Ma! What are you doing here?" I asked.

"Hi, honey. I have a surprise for you."

There was a new tenant moving in, because as we spoke moving men were hauling furniture up the stairs behind her.

"Willie and I are moving out of our old apartment in Williamsburg."

"You are? How come you haven't said anything about it to me?" I asked, watching the movers drag some very familiar-looking furniture up the stairs.

"Well, I wanted you to be surprised."

"I am," I said, getting the idea.

"Yes. I've found this great apartment."

"Where?" I asked, not wanting to hear the answer.

"Here! In your building! Directly above you!" she beamed.

I stood with my mouth open. "You're kidding," I said, knowing she wasn't kidding.

"You don't look happy. Aren't you happy?"

"Oh, yeah, it's great, Ma," I said.

"Good. I'm glad it's okay with you. I was a little afraid you wouldn't like the idea. Come on, invite me in and I'll make you a cup of coffee until the moving men are done."

At that point, I was the kind of guy who kept things in. When my mother moved into the apartment above me without even consulting me, I felt outraged and violated, but I didn't know what to say. I had never corrected my mother. She was the parent, I was the son. How could I tell her that I felt she was doing something wrong? Now I wanted to scream at her and slam the door in her face, but I didn't. I invited her in for coffee and kept it all inside.

That night, after she had gone upstairs to her new apartment, I thought seriously of moving into a new place. I went to the newsstand and bought the *New York Times* and began to look for available apartments. As I looked up and down the columns of the real estate section I realized what a pain in the ass it would be to move. To begin looking for another apartment in the middle of my insane schedule was a crazy thought. Besides, I *liked* where I lived. But really, who wants his mother living above him?

After a few weeks, I realized they weren't going to be a problem for me. They must have sensed my negative reaction to their move and made an extra effort to keep their distance. They were at their own jobs during the day, and in the evenings they were having serious problems that didn't involve me. When I realized that I represented the few positive moments in their tumultuous lives, I was happy I could offer something to them.

But as time went by, their relationship disintegrated. They fought a lot and drank more than ever. I could hear them stomping back and forth yelling at each other almost every night. The fights would usually end up with Willie storming out of the house.

One night, just as I was falling asleep, I was awakened by stomping and yelling from upstairs.

"Here they go again," I sighed. They carried on loud and long, cursing and hollering, and finally I heard the inevitable slamming of the door. I knew that Willie had gone.

It was quiet for about half an hour and I tried to fall asleep, but I felt there was something different this time. I couldn't get to sleep. I just lay there in the dark, staring at the ceiling, feeling funny.

Suddenly the phone rang. I picked it up and my mother spoke in a slurred voice. "Honey?"

"Yeah, Ma. What's the matter?"

"He left again. That bastard," she mumbled. And then there was silence.

"Ma?" I asked. "Are you okay?"

"Honey, I love you. I love you the most. You're the best."

"I know, Ma. Are you sure you're okay?"

"I think I've done something stupid again." She started crying.

"Oh shit, Ma. I'll be right up."

*   *   *

The first time my mother had tried to kill herself was a few weeks after I had gotten married. Susan had tracked me down at the Thirteenth Street Theatre while I was writing some music. She told me she was going to pick me up in a cab and that I should meet her outside the theater.

"What's the matter?" I had asked.

"Just be outside. I'll tell you in the cab." She hung up.

As we raced over the Brooklyn Bridge to the hospital, she told me my mother had attempted suicide. Her stomach was being pumped, but she was still in bad shape. We held hands silently and I stared out the window, watching the East River fly by.

"Don't die, Ma. Don't die, Ma," I kept saying over and over as if she could hear. "I have so much music to make for you," I said—as if that would give her a reason to hold on.

She pulled through, but the police physician had told us that if she tried it again and we called them, they'd have to put her into a sanitarium.

The next time my mother tried it was soon after she and Willie moved into the apartment above me. I caught her early enough that time because Aunt Rose called me suspecting something was wrong. My mother had sounded strange to her and she asked me to go and check on her. Sure enough, she had taken a bottle of sleeping pills. I got her off the bed, walked her around and made her drink loads of coffee. I didn't have to call the police.

This was the third time, and she sounded really bad on the phone. I jumped out of bed and threw on my jeans. I ran up the stairs two at a time. I fumbled with the extra set of keys I had to her apartment, and I finally opened the door.

My mother was lying on her bed, an empty bottle of pills on the night table. I slapped her face once, twice. She opened her eyes and closed them again. That was a bad sign.

I couldn't wake her up. My hands were shaking. I blindly ran to the phone and dialed the police emergency number. I kept slapping her face and calling to her, but nothing helped.

I was starting to panic when I heard the heavy footsteps of the police running up the stairs. Outside, lights from the ambulance and police cars flashed. The policemen rushed into the bedroom and told me to wait in the hall. Tenants from other apartments were peeking out of their doors wondering what was happening.

Our landlady, Mrs. Liss, puffed up the stairs. She'd been there the last time, and she looked up at me sympathetically.

"She'll be all right, Barry. Let them do their job."

We hugged each other.

They took my mother out of the house on a stretcher while the neighbors watched. I sat next to her in the ambulance. I was terrified. But for the first time, I was also deeply angry.

I waited in the emergency room alone, smoking, while they pumped her stomach. Then Gramma and Grampa came rushing into the emergency room, and I told them they were working on her. While I was on the phone to Aunt Rose in Long Island, the doctor came into the room.

"We got her in time, folks," he said. We fell apart.

He asked me into his office and listened while I told him her history. As I related the facts, my anger was obvious.

"Look at my family out there!" I shouted to him. "She doesn't care about them. Or me!"

"Sit down, son," the doctor said. "Your mother is a very sad and troubled woman. She needs help and now we'll get it for her."

"What if it doesn't help?" I asked him.

"Look," he said, "the truth is, if your mother wants to kill herself, there's nothing anyone can do to stop her."

My only hope was that she would get some help at the sanitarium they were sending her to.

A month later, I received a letter from her.

Brunswick General Hospital

Hello my darling—

It is now the fourth week that I'm here at Louden Hall and for the first time, I seem to be feeling better. I now know where I am. This is a very nice place—we are two girls in a room—an airy room with a dresser. We get up at 8:30 and

dress and wash and go into breakfast. The breakfast room—
or should I say the dining room is also very nice—table for
four and they serve very nice meals, after which we all go for
sessions with the doctor—which I'm fed up with—he talks
to us as though we are crazy and I know I'm not. The only
reason I'm here is because I was very very depressed, disgusted
and felt like I had nothing to live for. Isn't that stupid? I have
you to live for. But at the time I tried suicide I guess I was
being selfish and I wasn't thinking of you.

I can't tell you how sorry I am for hurting you and feel
like I owe you an explanation.

Willie hadn't come home for ten days—I didn't sleep at
all, but I never missed work. When he did come home he
was drunk and raving. You were downstairs and I didn't want
to bother you with my troubles. Your music career is just
beginning and I'm so proud of you.

Between paying all the bills, and helping Gramma and
Grampa—I didn't tell them either—it was just too much for
me to carry on my shoulders and so I decided to get out of
this world. I know now that it was wrong—who knows why
we do what we do—is it because one is strong or one is selfish
when we try suicide? I tried it twice before for the same
reasons—but now I've decided that it wasn't my time to go.
So I promise I will never try it again.

I don't know how long I have to stay here—I don't
think it will be much longer. Will I go back to Willie—I
don't know.

I wasn't allowed visitors for the first two weeks I was
here. But now I'm allowed visitors on Wednesday and Sunday. Poor Gramma and Grampa—when they came to see me,
the doors were locked and when I wanted to show them the
grounds, a nurse had to go along with us.

And you, my love. Thank you for coming to see me in
the evening on a non-visitors day. About 1/2 hour before you
came the dopey nurse gave me my medication. It made me
shake and made me talk so fast—I know it was terrible for
you to see me like that. I can imagine what you were thinking
when you left. Please forgive me.

My firm paid the expenses, isn't that nice? We have Bingo twice a week, arts and crafts every day, movies once a week and even a beauty parlor on the premises.

When I'm done with this nightmare, let's put it behind us. You're the only thing that's keeping me going. I don't believe in much anymore, but I believe in you. In fact, you're all I believe in.

love,
Mom

Visiting Edna in the sanitarium was uncomfortable. I didn't know what to talk about. I didn't want to upset her so I kept far away from the subject of suicide. She didn't want to upset me, so she pretended to be cheerful.

Even though it was a sanitarium out in the country, it was still a hospital. There were nurses in uniforms everywhere. The patients were sedated and walked slowly and looked terribly sad. Doors were always locked. There were hefty-looking men in white sprinkled around and you *knew* what they were there for. I visited Edna whenever I could and I could see she was defeated.

I didn't know how to cope with the conflicting emotions I felt. All at the same time I was angry, scared, guilty, and confused. I was twenty-two and I had never known anyone who had done anything so violent and potentially dangerous. I had no one to talk to. No sister or brother. My small family was leaning on me for support and *I* had no one to lean on. My friends were there for me, but this was beyond their experience, and they didn't know what to say or how to help.

I felt scared. I had nearly lost her. What if I hadn't been one floor away? My mother would have died, and that was an unbearable thought. I didn't want my mother to die. I loved her and I needed her. We had our problems, but her love, approval, and advice were so important to me. I'd often tried to deny that I cared about what she thought of me, but I was lying to myself. When she said something was okay, it was okay. When she said she loved me and that I made her proud, I could laugh at all the critics in the world.

I felt so bad for her. She must have felt desperate to do this again. I was upset, but this time I was pissed, too. Pissed at Willie and Edna.

I was angry at Willie because he kept walking away from responsibility. They would have their awful fights and he'd leave her in despair. He knew her past history, and yet he'd storm out and leave her alone. Of course she was going to do something terrible. I was angry at him for always deserting her and for leaving me with the responsibility.

When she was recovering, she vowed never to take him back. She called him names and changed the locks on the door. One time she even took a pair of scissors and cut up all his clothes. But she always took him back. I'd get angry at Willie for causing her so much pain and trauma. But then I'd see them together and I'd be glad that things were back to normal. This time, though, I was angry at Willie—but I was pissed at Edna too.

The bond between us was very strong and I'd stand behind anything she wanted. But she kept going back to the same situation again and again. When her life fell apart, she reacted by trying to take it. I had so many questions: Was she counting on my finding her? Did she do it to make me feel guilty? To make us feel sorry for her? Did she do it out of intolerable hopelessness or was it a dramatic way to get attention?

Although my heart was breaking because of her sadness and desperation, I also felt it was a selfish and cowardly thing for her to do. Worst of all, I felt terribly guilty. I didn't know what I had done or why I should feel guilty, but I did. I spent hours, days, thinking about my role in all of it. Why do people have children? Happily married couples have children, among other reasons, so that they can have a child who represents their love for each other, a little piece of each of them to send into the world. Edna and my father weren't one of those happily married couples. I always felt that Edna had conceived me to give her own life meaning, that I gave her a reason to live and put up with all the pressures of life. When I was a child, she felt she was important and necessary because I needed her to be alive. She could bear Gramma's negativity or her struggle to pay the bills because she knew I would be there, needing and loving her. She worked and struggled for me and that was fine with her.

When I left home to get married, she found she was still necessary to support Gramma, Grampa, and Willie. But it must have just seemed as if all she had left were problems. For twenty years she had built a life based on me, not on herself. She had taught me to be independent and strong, so when I left to build my own life as she had taught me, Edna found herself alone with nothing but pressure for company.

So she had run after me to try to keep a piece of me, to try to stay in my life. Living in my apartment building meant she could be close to me again. She had already tried to take her life once and deep in my heart I felt it was because I had left home and she felt deserted. I felt incredibly guilty and confused, because I didn't know what I had done except to live my life. Her letter had said she didn't want to hurt me by dying, so now she would suffer and live. Now I felt guilty for her suffering and living too. I hoped that the therapy at the sanitarium would encourage her to take her life into her own hands and live or die for herself.

Today I look back and realize I don't really know why she did what she did. How can I know? How can anyone know such things?

Edna recovered and never tried to take her life again. Her suicide attempts made me realize how important she was to me—I loved her no matter what. I shed some tears, kicked some walls, and moved on with my life, which was filled with music, joy, independence, compassion, and resilience.

All of which I learned from my mother.

Bye Bye Brooklyn

Living way out in Flatbush finally began to become impractical. I began to spend so much money on cabs to Manhattan and back, I decided to take the plunge and look for an apartment in the city.

I found one on Twenty-seventh Street off Third Avenue, a nice but expensive neighborhood. The apartment was great: a studio with a kitchen and a little garden. I decided to take it, even though it was $200 more than I was paying for the apartment in Flatbush. When I signed the lease, I was so terrified I wouldn't be able to pay the rent that I took most of my savings and paid the first year in full!

I had been in Flatbush for four years and had collected a lot of stuff. When the moving men came to collect my things it took them hours to do it. I waited near the moving van for the men to finish. When they slammed the door of the van I told them I'd meet them in Manhattan at the new apartment and I started for the subway. Then I got an idea. "Hey!" I yelled to the driver. "Can I hitch a ride with you?"

"Sure. Hop in."

I jumped up into the truck, looked at the apartment building and knew that a chapter of my life was closing.

My marriage to Susan had happened too soon. I hadn't grown

up yet when I moved from Williamsburg into our apartment in Manhattan. I had needed more time and I had needed to stay in Brooklyn, which represented childhood, security, education. Manhattan represented adulthood and professionalism.

When that moving van pulled away that day in September, I knew I had finally become an adult. Brooklyn had been as far away from Manhattan as Kansas City. Even though Manhattan was only an hour away by subway, it took me over twenty years to really get there. When I came to Manhattan this time, it was because I was ready.

As we drove away, I said to myself: "Good-bye, Brooklyn. Thanks for everything. I'm never coming back."

And I never did.

The Adventures of
Harry and Ethel

Major Decision No. 2

I first met Jeanne Lucas when she landed the role of Crazy Agnes in *The Drunkard* while I was still married to Susan. She was small, with a curvy figure and flaming red hair. Like Bro, she had an expressive face and was larger than life. She sang great, too. She was a belter and when she hit the big notes, the walls shook.

Jeanne hired me to play piano and do arrangements for her, and we became very close after my break with Susan. She was sympathetic, funny, and bright, and she made me feel better about myself because she agreed with the choice I had made in dissolving my marriage. When I was with her I didn't feel like such a heel.

Jeanne came to New York after graduating Phi Beta Kappa from the University of Michigan. Although she had a degree in English, show business called and she left home to conquer the Big Apple.

We spent a lot of time together selecting songs for her to sing. My arrangements fit her big, brash style perfectly and we quickly became the favorites of the cast. We'd entertain at cast parties and the local watering holes after the show. We worked together for hours at a time. She taught me all the things about theater that Bro hadn't gotten to. Her friends became my friends and mine became hers. She and Marty became very close, and my co-workers at CBS got to know her because she was there all the time waiting for me to have an extra hour to play for her. We'd be with each other every night until the bars closed.

Soon we were working at small clubs around town: the Duplex, the Living Room, and Charlie Bates. We did two shows a night. I was still shy, naïve, and conservative. My uniform was a suit and tie and I carried an attaché case filled with music and appointment books. Although I loved playing piano, I was uncomfortable when the spotlight occasionally landed on me.

At a gig at the Charlie Bates Saloon, Jeanne began to have vocal trouble and asked me to sing so she could rest. We had been doing five sets a night—forty minutes on, twenty minutes off. Having never sung in public before, and having no desire to, I refused time and again, but Jeanne was suffering and finally I agreed to do one or two songs. I was really nervous and rehearsed all day Saturday.

When Saturday night came and Jeanne introduced me, I sang "It Amazes Me," a beautiful song written by Cy Coleman and Carolyn Leigh. I sang it very softly. It went:

> My height, just average
> My weight, just average
> And my I.Q. is what you'd estimate
> Just average
> But evidently she does not agree
> Consequently, if I seem at sea
> It amazes me
> It simply amazes me
> What she sees in me, dazzles me, dazes me
> I'm the one who's worldly wise and nothing much phases me
> But to see me in her eyes
> It just amazes me

Funny that this was the first song I ever sang in public, since it could very well be my view of my singing career.

When I had finished singing, I heaved a sigh of relief. I was glad *that* was over. It was too nerve-racking! But the audience gave me a nice round of applause. They seemed to like it, which really did amaze me!

Whenever I came up with a new arrangement for Jeanne, we'd unveil it for a crowd of appreciative people at the Thirteenth Street Theatre or in the rehearsal hall at CBS. We even learned two songs on which I would harmonize, "Georgy Girl" and "Something Stupid." I would just *ooohh* and *aaaahh* a little, and although they weren't showstoppers, everyone always liked it when I tried to sing.

Jeanne auditioned daily for jobs. She'd go to Broadway calls, off-Broadway calls, summer stock auditions, and out of town tryouts. I accompanied her whenever she needed me. I loved creating arrangements for her. I'd try to make my piano sound like an entire orchestra, but I was just drooling to try orchestrating the arrangements for other instruments as I was learning to do in school. My goal was to become Nelson Riddle or Henry Mancini and conduct a huge orchestra playing my arrangements for some sensational singer. Jeanne fit the bill! She was a little Ethel Merman with more emotion. I really believed in her.

The act we created for Jeanne was very sophisticated. It consisted mostly of songs no one had ever heard of. We included songs that had been dropped from shows before they reached Broadway or songs that had never made it to the hit parade. If there were familiar songs, once I got done arranging them no one recognized them anyway. I arranged fast songs slowly, and slow songs up-tempo. I even wrote some original material for her. It was a musical and clever act, perfect for a New York showcase bar.

Jeanne landed lots of jobs that summer. Summer jobs were easier to get because a pretty girl singer who had her own piano player could always work in the Catskills, the mountainous area in upstate New York where the New York Jewish population goes for the summer. The hotels range from gigantic places like the Concord, Grossinger's, and Kutschers to little bungalow colonies like Lefkowitz's and Blech's Bungalows. Since Jeanne wasn't known, we worked the bungalow colonies.

We gave each other nicknames. I'd call her Ethel, and she'd call me Harry.

"Yes, Ethel. Where to this weekend? The Concord? Grossinger's?" I'd ask her.

"Blech's Bungalows again," she'd sigh.

"Blech!" I'd answer.

We worked in the dining room after dinner and the show would usually consist of a comic, a belly dancer, and us. The bands were always a joke. Most of the time they were made up of an accordion, a drum, and a violin. They were older men who were getting room and board for free and who couldn't read music. The drummer would try to follow me, but it was always hopeless. One night, I felt so sorry for the belly dancer, whose name was Rose Hashonah (I swear), I rushed to the piano to accompany her dance that the band was butchering.

The audiences were polite to us because we were two young hopefuls, but our material was all wrong for that kind of setting. It was frustrating, but I looked on it as a learning experience, and besides, it was good to get out of the hot city and my subway-riding existence. When the summer was over, we went back to playing showcase rooms in the city.

One day at the Thirteenth Street Theatre, Jeanne rushed in and told me breathlessly that an agent had called her. He had an offer out of town and wanted to see her on Monday. I told her I'd go with her.

We both waited in the outer office of the sleaziest office I'd ever seen. Old crinkled photos stared down at us. A very old secretary gave us nasty looks. Finally we were sent in.

The inner office was more cluttered than the outer one. Everything smelled of age. No wonder—the agent was hundreds of years old. He said that he'd seen Jeanne's act and liked it. We were very excited and kept squeezing each others' hands, but acted cool.

He had an opening in a lounge.

I thought to myself, "Lounge. Well, that sounds good. He probably saw how hip the act was and decided to put us in a supper club. Wonder where it could be. The Pierre Hotel has a lounge. Or maybe it's the Waldorf."

I said, "Great! Jeanne's act is a perfect lounge act. At which hotel? The Waldorf?"

"Not exactly," he said. "It's at the Holiday Inn."

Hmm. The Holiday Inn. "Oh! You mean the one on Fifty-seventh Street?"

"No," he said. "I mean the one in Richmond, Indiana."

"Where's that?" I said.

"In Richmond, Indiana," old fart agent said. "And they need a duo. They need a singing duo."

"But it's Jeanne's act, I just play piano for her."

"You sang two songs with her. Can't you learn some more?" he asked.

"But I'm not a singer—"

Jeanne stopped me. "We'll think about it," she said, pushing me out the door. "We'll talk about it and call you in an hour, okay?"

The booking would start in a month. I couldn't go. I just couldn't. How could I leave New York? How could I leave the secure CBS job? School, my friends, my family? Richmond, Indiana? A singing duo? I don't sing. I play piano. It was a ridiculous idea.

We sat in the Howard Johnson's coffee shop on Broadway and Forty-eighth with our fourth cup of coffee. I jumped up.

"Shit! I'd better call the office, it must be past my lunch hour."

"It's four o'clock, Harry. You'd better tell 'em you were hit by a truck."

I looked at my watch. I'd been on my lunch hour for four hours. I sat back down. I was going to lose my job if I didn't cut out the music. Anna, my boss at CBS, couldn't turn her back on my shenanigans forever.

"Think about it," Jeanne said.

"Ethel, it's absurd. What happens after Richmond, Indiana? And what happens to my budding career at CBS?"

"Harry, in your heart you know how good you are. You'll always be able to make a living in music, you know that, too. But you won't if you stay at CBS. You've got to get into the music world and commit to it. I know how scary it sounds. I've been there. It was terrifying leaving home to come to New York. My mother wanted me to stay and get married, but I wanted more. You want more too. You've left Susan and you've got no commitments. What are you waiting for at CBS? For someone to come and discover you and take you by the hand? It's just not going to happen like that. Believe in yourself, Harry. I do."

She had a point. Music *had* become an obsession with me. Although I still held down a steady nine-to-five job, it was meaningless. The true passion in my life was music. I lived for it.

My plans to be married forever hadn't worked out. There was no house in Long Island, no picket fence, no kids. And the plans to climb the corporate ladder to some imagined executive position were bullshit. I couldn't care less about it. If I stayed at CBS, I'd never be able to devote my life to a career in music; it would always be an avocation. But to leave a steady job for a gamble in music went against everything I had learned while growing up. Security was what you aimed for in life. Without that almighty Friday paycheck you were a bum.

The booking agent wanted an answer by the next week. I asked everyone I knew for advice. Everyone said take the job playing piano.

I couldn't.

I was so desperate, I actually wrote a letter to the "Playboy Adviser" in *Playboy* magazine, which they published months later. They sent me a personal reply within a week and they too advised me to take the music job.

Finally, I decided to ask the head of my division, Richard Rector, director of broadcasting at WCBS-TV, for advice. I'd never been in his office, never done more than nod to him in the hallway.

"So you're the piano playing film clerk!"

I was surprised he knew me.

I told him the truth. Told him how much I loved working at CBS, but how the music was an obsession. I told him about my love affair with *The Drunkard* and about music college. And I told him I didn't want to give up the security that CBS offered me, but that the music was coming out of my ears. When I finished, I looked at him.

He said, "Barry, from what I hear about you, everyone thinks you're very gifted. I think you should take the job. If it doesn't work out, I promise you you'll always have a job with me here at CBS."

I'll always be grateful to Dick Rector. He was the last kick in the ass I needed. And I felt somewhat secure knowing I could always come back.

Either I was real brave or real stupid, but I called Jeanne. "Ethel. Start packing. We're going to Indiana!"

Jeanne and Barry: Songs, Dances, and Funny Sayings!

Although we were playing at the Holiday Inn, they put us up at the Motel 400 down the road. We arrived on a Sunday and decided to see the last show of the duo that was then appearing at the Holiday Inn.

Jeanne wore a simple black dress and I wore my usual dark suit and tie. I parted my hair on the side and slicked it back with Brillcream. We set out to walk what we thought was a short distance down the road to the Holiday Inn. Forty-five minutes later we were still walking and covered with dust and dirt. There were no sidewalks, only a dirt road, and the air smelled of sour milk. We found out later that the town was one big dairy farm. This was my first experience out of New York. So far, I wasn't thrilled.

When we got to the lounge, it was filled to capacity with very loud, rowdy people. Most of them were feeling no pain and were singing along with the current duo. The waitress seated us and Jeanne and I got our first look at the competition.

It was a sight I will never forget. They were an older couple. He played (more like pummeled) the piano very badly and sang, and she played a conga drum with brushes and sang. And she had no teeth. And the audience *loved* them.

They sang "When the Saints Go Marchin' In" and the audience

sang along with them loud and clear (they sang that song many more times during the evening). They sang "Hello Dolly" and "Up a Lazy River" and many country songs I'd never heard of. One that everyone seemed to know was "My Bucket's Got a Hole in It." They were terrible, but amazingly, they had the crowd in their pockets.

Jeanne and I just looked at each other—speechless. We saw our lives flashing before our eyes. We just drank.

During their last set, everyone sang a good-bye song to them, and when it was done, the crowd began to disperse. Jeanne and I stayed at the bar for a last nightcap and spotted our own publicity photo staring at us. We had jokingly dubbed the photo "Look, Martha, land!" because in it, we posed smiling brightly, looking into a successful future. Quite a different pose from the one we had sitting at the bar. We tried hiding our faces, but the bartender recognized us and introduced us to the rest of the patrons at the bar.

"Well," said one man, "you sure have a tough act to follow!"

"Good luck, kids!" the bartender said.

Jeanne and I didn't sleep well that night.

We opened the next night. We began the set with our duet of "Georgy Girl." Then Jeanne sang her whole act, and we closed with our duet of "Something Stupid." There were twenty people in the place when we started. We emptied the room in fifteen minutes. The manager fired us two days later.

"Now what?" we asked each other.

We couldn't go back home. It would be humiliating. Besides, we couldn't even afford the plane fare back to New York. We walked to the bus station in silence, the dust making our shoes filthy. Jeanne had been through this kind of thing before, but I hadn't. I had given up a career and a steady job and taken this chance. Now, in less than a week, I was out of a job. I wondered as we walked if I had made a mistake.

*   *   *

We took a bus to Jeanne's mother's house in Dearborn, Michigan. Jeanne and her mother weren't on good terms and it was very tense staying there, but we had no alternative.

Both of us wrote letters back to our friends in New York telling them how great things were going. We just made up things about Richmond, Indiana. Finally we told them that we had landed a job in Detroit and were staying at Jeanne's mother's house because it was cheaper than a hotel.

We spent the days haunting agents' offices in Detroit and working up new material on the upright piano at Jeanne's house. We included many new songs on which I would harmonize. We had learned quite a lesson in Richmond, Indiana. The act needed songs people knew. So we dived in and learned songs that we were sure would be recognizable. But no matter how cleverly I tried to arrange "The Shadow of Your Smile," both of us were bored by conventional popular songs. So we decided to give them our own touch.

Since "When the Saints Go Marchin' In" had seemed to go over so well for the duo in Indiana, we learned it, but we sang it backward.

"Saints the when oh! In marchin' go!" we harmonized loudly.

We learned "The Shadow of Your Smile," but we sang it to the tune of "Hello Dolly." We did "Up a Lazy River," but we did each phrase a bar late. Both of us wrote a parody on the "soul-searching" songs that had become so popular, such as "Where Am I Going" and "I've Gotta Be Me." We called it "Gotta Run Away." In the song we tried to "find ourselves," while Jeanne raced around the stage and I pounded my chest whenever I could. Who knew how they would go over, but people were sure to recognize them and we sure laughed a lot. The comedy material felt great and was a perfect balance for the more serious songs Jeanne sang.

The act became a showcase for both of us. Jeanne was getting arrangements tailor-made for her personality and voice. She was able to stand on a stage and sing, confident that she had a solid backing. I was getting the opportunity to try out arranging songs any way I wanted. She was versatile enough to be able to handle anything from broad show tunes to comedy, even some cool jazz. With her big impressive voice and my arrangements and accompaniments, we knew that if we could land a job, we'd knock 'em dead. But the situation was discouraging.

Jeanne and I would find some dark cocktail lounge and sit and look at each other.

"So," I'd say. "This is show biz, huh?"

"Harry, I've been through it before," Jeanne would say. "The act is coming along great. Let's stay here a little while longer."

We finally landed a job at Paul's Steak House in downtown Detroit. It was a pretty elegant supper club with a grand piano on a small stage. The patrons loved Jeanne and when we would throw in our duets, they really reacted positively. But Jeanne began to have vocal problems again, and she asked me to sing solo so she could rest. I learned a few more songs. Again, I was nervous and didn't enjoy it, but again, the audiences seemed to.

We stayed in Michigan at Paul's Steak House for a few weeks. We were doing pretty well and could have stayed for months, but Jeanne's vocal problems turned into severe tonsillitis and we had to quit so that she could have her tonsils removed. I went back to New York while Jeanne recuperated in Detroit.

I should have been pretty nervous going back to New York with no job but I wasn't. I had broken that damned umbilical cord that binds most people to the nine-to-five life, and a little setback like this wasn't going to scare me. I never once thought about returning to CBS. Even though I wasn't finding fame and fortune in the world, I was happier than I'd ever been. I was able to devote all of my energy to making music and each day was more rewarding than CBS had ever been.

To me, being successful has never meant being number one. Modest triumphs have always felt as fulfilling as the major ones, sometimes even more so. I wasn't making much money and nobody knew my name, but I was surviving and making music and I felt very successful.

I readied myself for the hard times that I knew lay ahead. I put money away; I lived very frugally. I survived. I ate spaghetti and took subways and borrowed from friends, but I survived. Somehow, you just do.

I put ads in the show-business trade papers offering myself as an accompanist. I phoned people I knew to tell them I was back and available. Before too long, I was working as pianist for lots of singers and able to pay the rent. I found that being able to read music and having a technical background was invaluable. Singers could put a sheet of music in front of me and, because I could sight-read, I'd play it. If I came up with an idea for an arrangement, I'd write it out for them; they'd be able to go off to different clubs and be sure that other pianists would play the arrangement the same way.

Lots of accompanists don't have technical abilities and can play piano only by ear. My training at school wound up being the thing that enabled me to survive and make a living from music.

Although Jeanne and I were still quite serious about the act, she too needed to make a living. When she returned to New York, she auditioned for everything she could. She landed a featured part in the road company of *Sweet Charity* that kept her away from our act for four months. She had to take it. She was broke.

We decided to meet near the end of the show's run in Chicago. The show was going to be there for a few months and if I could find a job playing piano somewhere in Chicago in the evening, we could continue to build the act and rehearse during the day. When the show closed, we'd be ready to conquer New York with our act showcasing her as a performer and me as an arranger. But how was I supposed to land a job in Chicago?

A booking agent friend of mine recommended me to a booking agent in Chicago named Hal Munroe. I called him and told him I was a pianist and that I needed work in Chicago within four months. Could he help? He told me he couldn't promise anything, but that he'd look around.

A week later he called back and said he had an opening in a small lounge near Chicago. He said that if I did well there, he was pretty sure he could find me a place to work in Chicago. I told him I'd take it and packed my bags for Kankakee, Illinois.

*   *   *

The Little Corporal Lounge is in a shopping mall. The clientele is local and they usually get roaring drunk. This was my first time playing solo in a piano bar. They had put me in a dismal hotel across the street from the lounge. I was scared. I was alone and I had never ever done anything like this in my life. I put on my new tuxedo in the dreary hotel room, slicked back my hair, and walked to the bar with my attaché case filled with music.

The piano was on a riser behind the bar. I could look down at all the people drinking and they could talk to me and request tunes. When I walked into the club that first night, I felt numb. It was like being dead with none of the benefits. I climbed up to the piano as if in a dream, and when I sat down on the piano bench, I found that the bench was too low and I couldn't see anybody, so I asked for a bar stool. I still sit on a bar stool when I play piano.

As far as the customers were concerned, I was invisible. I remember starting off with "Meditation," the Antonio Carlos Jobim bossa nova—very timidly. Nobody reacted. Nobody looked up. It was as if I weren't there at all. Somehow I got through the first one-hour set.

When I returned after my break, there were a few people around the piano and they were complimentary. I was surprised. But then the strangest thing started to happen to me. Every time I went back to the piano, I felt a little stronger, but when I left the piano I became invisible again. By the end of the evening, I was joking with the patrons and playing as they sang. I even sang a few songs! But every time I left the piano, I became invisible. When I climbed up to the piano stool at the end of the evening, I felt attractive for the first time in my life.

At the end of my first week there, I would walk into the place feeling dull and plain. But I'd climb up to the piano, click on the spotlight with my foot, and I would become attractive, worldly, witty. Women started coming on to me and bought me drinks. I realized that the piano player is always the most attractive person in the place—he's the only one with the spotlight on him!

By the end of my two-week stand at the lounge, the transformation would begin in my little motel room. I'd stand in front of the mirror, comb my hair, put on my tux, and change from invisible Barry to BARRY MANILOW AT THE KEYBOARD, like it said on the sign outside the club.

The next week I landed a gig in Chicago, discovered a blow dryer, and never looked back.

The Last Duet

The job in Chicago was at a restaurant-bar called Henrici's located in the Merchandise Mart, an enormous office building in the Chicago Loop. I played from four to eight and I loved it. I didn't expect to because I really hadn't loved the job in Kankakee the week before; I had only taken the job so I could be close to Jeanne and work on the act. But I loved this. And the customers seemed to like me, too!

I loved playing and singing and cracking jokes and making friends and feeling as if I looked good. It was a big ego trip and I couldn't get enough of it. I was making good money and practically doubling my salary with all the tips I made. Within a few weeks, Henrici's became a popular place to go and it was jammed with people requesting songs and cruising for dates. The bartenders were happy, the waitresses were happy, the manager was happy, and I was feelin' great.

I was still a little uncomfortable being in the spotlight and singing, but I loved making music. Jeanne would stop in before she went to work in *Sweet Charity*. She used to tell me that when she'd watch me sing and play the girls around the piano swooned. She'd tell me what they were saying in the ladies' room and, although it made me feel good, I never took it very seriously. But I *was* getting lucky very often!

73

I enrolled at De Paul University in downtown Chicago to continue studying orchestration. When I was done with class, Jeanne and I would rehearse. Then I'd go to Henrici's and she'd go to *Sweet Charity*. After her show finished each night, we'd try out our new material at various clubs in town and we had a great time. When *Sweet Charity* closed, I gave my notice to the owner at Henrici's. But it was hard to leave.

I felt very secure working there. I could have stayed forever. I was making good money and had developed a following. I had learned a lot and felt much more confident than I ever had. I was even getting that Friday paycheck that was so important to me. There was no job waiting for me or Jeanne in New York. The easy way out would have been to stay, but the easy way out felt wrong. Playing piano in a bar in Chicago could lead nowhere.

I had come this far gambling on myself and on Jeanne. Who knew what awaited me out there? It was scary, all right, but I found myself excited about my future even though I didn't know what it was.

The regulars at Henrici's gave me a good-bye party and the owner told me I would always have a job waiting there. Jeanne and I partied with our Chicago friends way into the night and we left the next day for New York.

When we returned to New York, Jeanne and I landed a job at the famous Downstairs at the Upstairs nightclub, a major coup for us. It was a sophisticated nightclub located in mid-Manhattan. There were two floors. Upstairs at the Downstairs seated a few hundred people at tables, and satirical revues played there. The famous Julius Monk's revues began there, a training ground for many of today's famous stars—Lily Tomlin, Ruth Buzzi, and Jo Anne Worley among others. Downstairs at the Upstairs was smaller and usually the singers and stand-up comedians played there. Landing a job at the Upstairs/Downstairs was a big deal.

We opened for Jackie Vernon for a week. The next weekend starred Joan Rivers. Jeanne and I opened for her for two seasons. Joan was phenomenal even then. She was a smash. I'd never seen anyone work a crowd with more energy and love. We'd do two shows a night from Tuesday to Thursday and three shows on Friday and Saturday. After our set, I'd stand in the back of the house and watch Joan, and even though I got to know her act line for line, I'd still split my sides laughing. Sometimes after our third set I'd stay and watch Joan's third set because I thought she was so great.

We had polished our act and it went over pretty well each night. The act was filled with original songs we'd found or written, and everything had complicated arrangements. We were very proud of it. It was a perfect club for our act and the climax of our career as a singing duo.

We still showcased Jeanne's vocals, but some of the strongest material was the duets. A lot of the material was funny patter between us, and I was singing more solos and doing less *oooohs* and *aaaahhs* in the background. We even hired a choreographer to teach me to stand up and dance! We never did that routine, thank God.

The act had shifted its focus and was now a bona fide duo act, not Jeanne Lucas and her pianist/arranger. Jeanne was beginning to feel more and more frustrated that she wasn't being showcased enough and we were bickering more and more. She'd fallen in love with an actor named Howard Honig and was engaged to be married, so we saw less and less of each other during the days. I began to play for lots of singers and had trouble squeezing in time for the act.

The truth was, I really didn't want to be a singer, certainly not in a singing duo like Steve and Eydie. Jeanne still had her eye on her dream Broadway marquee with her name in lights. We knew our days as a singing duo were numbered.

When Jeanne and I split up, the world didn't mourn; flags weren't lowered to half mast. Nor did very many people care. But for me, it was the end of a valuable learning experience. I learned about resilience and fortitude from Jeanne Lucas. I watched as she was rejected at Broadway auditions, and I watched her wipe away the tears and continue on. I saw first hand a genuine, determined, talented performer who was in show business for no other reason than because she *had* to be. Watching that kind of determination inspired me. I admired her for it, and found myself supporting her ventures, even at my own expense.

Working with her for those years, I was given the opportunity to test my arranging skills. I could have done that without leaving New York, but I stayed with Jeanne because I admired her. She was bright and funny, and I was gaining strength from her determination. I wanted to help her. I wanted to support a woman who wouldn't take no for an answer. As her accompanist, I had gone from the background to the foreground within a year. I don't think I would have ever discovered my own spotlight had I not begun with Jeanne. I think I learned more about show business during my time with Jeanne than at any other time.

After our last night at the Upstairs, we sat across the street having a farewell drink and planning our future as a duo. But both of us knew it was really over.

"The Playboy Club in Chicago made us an offer for next month," she reminded me. But I knew she was really thinking about that Broadway show she was up for.

"Well, let's think about it and talk next week," I told her. I was really thinking about an offer I had gotten at CBS to be music director of a weekly variety show.

We toasted to our past and to an even brighter future.

"To us—the dynamic duo!" Jeanne said.

"To us—watch out, Steve and Eydie!" I said.

But we were really saying good-bye.

The Manhattan Adventures

Adrienne, Amy, and Magic

When Jeanne and I split, I began coaching singers in earnest. I filled up every hour playing piano for struggling entertainers.

I began playing piano for Adrienne Anderson. She was different from any of the other singers and I knew it the moment I heard her sing. She didn't sound like anyone else. She was jazzy and had a lot of music in her—I mean a lot. More than anyone I'd ever worked with or met before.

She was striking, with raven hair and serious hazel eyes that always seemed to be challenging you. Her mother had died when she was a baby and it had devastated her father. He felt he couldn't possibly handle raising his daughter alone, so Adrienne was raised by her aunt and uncle, who were very wealthy and lived in a huge apartment on Park Avenue. Adrienne was my first experience with wealth.

Her attitudes, tastes, and references were all of a world I didn't know. She'd graduated from Columbia University and had attended Carnegie Tech for acting. She'd read F. Scott Fitzgerald and had acted Tennessee Williams. She summered in Martha's Vineyard and had been to Europe twice. Her tastes in clothes, movies, restaurants, and music were all of the highest quality. She was opinionated, intelligent, strong, and beautiful. Just being

79

with her made my head spin. But it was the music that really brought us together. Although we came from separate worlds, when I'd play for her, we came together. Our tastes in music were identical. What began as a professional singer/accompanist relationship turned into something quite deep.

Ever since I had left Susan, my musical experiences had been limited to the Broadway style. The songs Marty and I had been writing were more like standards, and the music Jeanne and I made was cocktail-lounge clever. Adrienne began to introduce me to popular music. Not the bubble-gum, commercial junk they were playing on the radio. I mean the quality rock 'n' roll music of the sixties. Janis, the Stones, the greats from Motown, Jim Morrison and the Doors, and the Beatles.

After the third time we worked together, she invited me to her apartment to show me some records. I walked into Adrienne's apartment with short hair and a button-down suit. Within a year, my hair was shoulder-length and my bottoms were belled.

Our romance was magical and musical. I moved an electric piano into her studio apartment on East Seventeenth and our relationship had a soundtrack going at all times. If I wasn't playing the piano, we were listening to records. We'd leave her apartment occasionally to buy the latest releases, but we were inside together for as much of the time as possible.

She had hired me to help her create an act for herself. She wanted to take a shot at cabaret singing. But putting her act together became secondary to our friendship. I'd cancel appointments to be with her. She'd pay me my fee and I'd spend it on dinner and a movie for the two of us. Our relationship turned out to be one of the deepest I'd ever had. We learned from each other—but to this day I think the scale was lopsided. She taught me so much that she actually changed the direction of my life.

Her standards were higher than those of anyone I'd ever met. I couldn't get enough of her. I wanted to learn everything she knew. When she brought me home to meet the family on Park Avenue, it was the first time I'd ever seen a maid in a uniform and I offered to help her wash the dishes after dinner.

Adrienne was just as unfamiliar with my background. When

I took her to Brighton Beach one summer afternoon, she was appalled at the filth on the beach that I had never noticed. But she adored my close family and friends and was always genuinely interested in meeting them and hearing stories about them.

Marty, Jeanne, and my friends at the Thirteenth Street Theatre all but disappeared during my time with Adrienne. We consumed each other totally and when we were together had little room for anything but each other. We were knocked out by each other's music. Sometimes, in the evening, I'd sit playing the piano and composing a melody and she'd holler from the little kitchen, "That's great! Go back to the first chord—it's delicious!" Soon she was putting lyrics to my melodies and I was encouraging her to.

The arrangements I created for her act were some of the most inventive work I've ever done. Of course, because they were so complicated and daring, the first agent we auditioned her act for didn't even *recognize* "Feelin' Groovy (The Fifty-ninth Street Bridge Song)."

We'd walk through Central Park on sunny afternoons and dream about our musical futures. I was going to be Burt Bacharach and she would be Gracie Slick. After we discovered Laura Nyro, Adrienne was going to be Laura and I was going to be Charlie Callello, Laura's arranger. We began writing songs together and, between my sessions with singing clients, we'd make appointments to try to get our songs published.

Adrienne's career as a nightclub singer never panned out, but I believe it was just an excuse for us to be brought together by whoever arranges those things in heaven or wherever. Never in my life had I felt the joining together of my soul to another as I felt with Adrienne.

When Adrienne and I were done with our love affair, the remaining emotions were strong enough to sustain our friendship for the rest of our lives. We were soulmates.

After Adrienne and I stopped seeing each other romantically, she became very serious about Neil Anderson, the president of the

April Blackwood publishing company. One day, Adrienne showed me a song she had written on the electric piano I had left at her apartment. It was called "Amy" and it was adorable. Neil thought it was commercial and decided to have a record done with it. I was thrilled for Ade.

Neil hired Tony Orlando to produce it. Tony was having a huge success with his record "Candida," and was also an executive at April Blackwood. He sang "Candida" under the fictitious group name "Dawn" because he didn't want to give up his secure job. I could relate to that.

The night of the recording session for "Amy," I showed up to cheer Adrienne on. The background tracks had come out sounding great, but Tony hadn't yet decided on a lead singer. He was planning to hire a studio singer and put the record out under a fictitious group name. But that night, everybody was dying to hear how it would sound with the lead being sung. Tony was hoarse and didn't want to wreck his voice, so I was elected to go into the little vocal booth and sing the lead.

It was a very strange feeling standing in that little booth, staring at the microphone. When they played the track into my headphones, I didn't know exactly what to do, so I just sang the song. When I was done, everyone was applauding.

I came back in and got lots of slaps on my back, but didn't know what they were so happy about. The engineer had forgotten to put my own voice in the headphones so I could hear myself singing, and I didn't know enough to ask him.

They played it back, and I really hated it. My voice was nasal, with a Brooklyn accent, and it was a little out of tune. (Sounds like what the critics say when *they* hear me.) I went back and tried again. This time I was able to hear what I was doing, and adjusted to the track. With all the echo on my voice, it was sort of fun, and with that great track to sing to, I was beginning to like it.

Tony kept talking to me in my headphones, giving me instructions on how to phrase, and little microphone and headphone tricks to use. Within the hour, the vocal didn't sound half bad, even to me, and we all left, happy with the experience.

The next week I got a call from Tony telling me everyone loved the song. I was really happy for Adrienne.

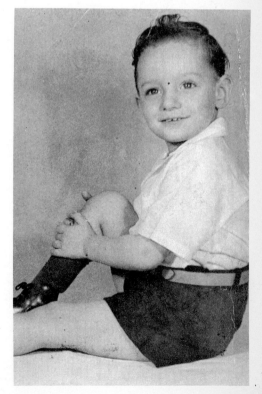

Isn't he cute!

Grampa and a teary-eyed Barry
after he had tried to coax me to
sing for a quarter.

At six

With cousin Dennis and cousin Olivia

Feedin' da boids

The dreaded accordion

With Mom

The serious bar-mitzvah boy

With Fred and Larry

Being cool

With Willie and Grampa

Graduation. What a geek!
(There's hope for everyone!)

With Grampa,
Gramma, Edna
and Willie

Being promoted at CBS

Are you ready? "Barry Manilow at the Keyboard"

Jeanne and Barry. "Look Martha, land!"

CURRENTLY APPEARING
at CHARLIE BATES'

Bob Emma & Company

Jeanne Lucas & Company

Finest act in Detroit?!!!

With Linda Allen

Bagel's first day at home

With Bette Midler

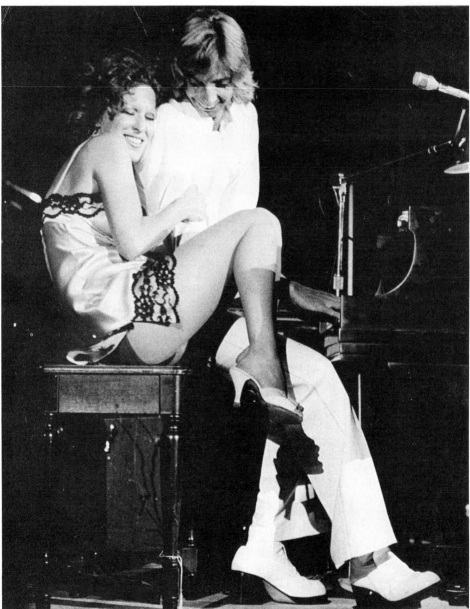

"You gotta have friends"

Conducting for Bette

Xmas on 27th Street

howard stein
presents
friday, june 23   at 8pm

bette
midler
at carnegie hall

barry manilow
music director

TICKETS: $4.50, $5.50 & $6.50 AT CARNEGIE HALL, 154 W. 57th ST., N.Y.C. AND ALL TICKETRON OUTLETS. MAIL ORDERS: SEND STAMPED, SELF-ADDRESSED ENVELOPE AND CERTIFIED CHECK OR MONEY ORDER PAYABLE TO CARNEGIE HALL. BOX OFFICE: 247-7459/ TICKETRON: 644-4400.

"And, Barry, everyone loves your voice."

"What are you talking about?" I asked.

"They all say that there's a vulnerability and warmth to your voice that fits this song perfectly. I'd like to show it to Bell Records."

Bell was the company he was signed with for the Dawn records.

"Tony, you're nuts," I said.

"Maybe, but if it's okay with you, I'll show it to Bell and get back to you."

Well, it sure sounded crazy to me, but why not? Ade and I laughed over the whole prospect, but waited for their decision.

Bell Records loved the song *and* my voice and gave Tony the go-ahead to release the record. I couldn't believe it. It was too funny. I even had to find an attorney to negotiate my record deal! Tony recommended his man, Miles Lourie. We all came up with dozens of names for the ghost group and decided on "Featherbed." So I was Featherbed.

During the month before the record was released, Ade and Neil got married and decided to move to San Francisco. The night before they were to leave, we met in the hotel room they were staying in while their furniture was on its way to the coast and listened to the debut of Featherbed singing "Amy" on WINS, the number-one pop station in New York.

It was a difficult, surreal night for Ade and me. We sat on the floor looking at each other and not knowing what to feel. We both still loved each other, and she was leaving to live three thousand miles away with her new husband. I was the one who was going to be the famous writer/arranger of hip jazz and smart songs, and she was the one who was going to be the famous supper-club or rock singer, and here we were listening to *me* sing a song *she* had written on a *pop* radio station. We lit a joint and opened a bottle of champagne and toasted to a new life. And it sure turned out to be a new life.

"Amy" came out of the box with a bang. Decent reviews in the trades, a few radio stations playing it, and enthusiasm from Bell

Records. As my attorney, Miles took the opportunity to make a small record deal for Featherbed, but he insisted that on the next record they include the credit "featuring Barry Manilow" as they were about to do with "Dawn featuring Tony Orlando."

I found the entire experience amusing. Even when Miles called to tell me Bell would agree to do two more records with Tony and me and that they would put my name on the records, it didn't excite me very much. But the opportunity to write and possibly arrange the next few songs did. With Tony's encouragement, I went to work writing songs with Adrienne—long-distance.

We completed one called "Rosalie Rosie" and waited for inspiration to hit for another song. It hit early one evening the following week. The apartment on Twenty-seventh Street had a small garden that I shared with a young couple named Pam and Bob Danz. Pam was an aspiring singer and Bob was going to school to be a dentist but played the sax as a hobby. Many evenings, we'd get together at my spinet piano and jam. We'd leave the door to the garden open and the neighbors would lean out their windows and applaud.

One balmy summer evening, I got out some of my old classical music books and began playing Chopin, my favorite classical composer. It gave me such pleasure and relaxed me so much to play his gorgeous music after dinner.

After about an hour of playing, Pam and Bob stopped by and we sat and had a glass of wine outside in the garden. When I went back inside, a melody kept going through my head, so I went to the piano, turned on my cassette machine, and recorded it. I played it over and over, putting words to it as I went along. When I was done, I called Pam and Bob in to listen to it and they loved it. I called it "Could It Be Magic."

The next day, when I played the cassette back, I realized that the song I had written was based on the chord structure of the Prelude in C minor by Chopin that I had been playing before I wrote the tune. But the melody and lyrics were mine and I liked it. I sent a tape of the song to Adrienne in San Francisco with a note that read: "Ade, I think I'm on to something. What do you think?"

She called as soon as she got it and raved about it. She said she thought the lyric needed work, but that she was crazy for the song.

Tony reacted positively too, and said that he'd like to try recording both "Rosie" and "Magic," and we agreed to meet about the arrangement in a week.

When Tony and I met to discuss the arrangement of the two songs, I had a few general ideas for "Rosie," but a very definite idea for "Magic."

"Tony," I said, "I hear this song like 'Hey Jude.' It should build and build until you think you can't take it any more. It should be a musical orgasm."

He agreed and I was sure he understood, but on the day of the recording, when I came in to sing, the track to "Could It Be Magic" sounded more like "Knock Three Times" than "Hey Jude." It had a dance beat, cowbells, and girl singers, and sounded like a bubble-gum song. I tried protesting, but I was in no position to make waves, so I reluctantly sang it the way it was. I felt so disappointed that when my friend Lee Gurst drove me home, I hardly said a word.

"Could It Be Magic" was released to the disk jockeys only but didn't get enough reaction to merit releasing it to the public, thank God, and thus ended the short-lived career of "Featherbed featuring Barry Manilow."

Even though the experience of recording those two songs was very frustrating, once again, I learned a lot. Tony was and is a good pop record producer, and watching him work with a band, an orchestra, and his engineer was educational for me, to say nothing of all the tricks I kept learning from him as a singer.

I put Featherbed to rest and wrote it off as another learning experience. I had loved composing the two songs and had really enjoyed working in the recording studio, where the sounds were unreal, better than any stereo system I'd ever heard. I had a feeling that I'd be seeing recording studios again, but certainly not as a singer. Who wanted to sing? Not me.

Linda and Bagel

I met Linda Allen while I was music director for a local weekly WCBS-TV show called *Callback!*, a showcase for up-and-coming young talent. The *Callback!* offices were exactly one flight above the offices I had worked in as a film clerk. Linda worked as production assistant on *Callback!*, and we started dating. Before too long, we were spending every free hour together and began a full-blown love affair.

I was crazy about Linda. She was an attractive redhead, with an angular face and a thin, great figure. She'd come to New York from San Francisco a year earlier. I felt close to Linda very quickly even though we came from different worlds: her childhood had been spent moving from town to town because of her father's job. She had roots all over the country.

Linda was a country girl. She knew about all those things that had eluded me. She cooked, she gardened. She knew about animals and nature. Her personality was completely different from those of the city women I'd been around all my life. She was independent, but she was gentle. She was funny but never vulgar. She was strong, but she was a lady.

Although Linda and I spent much of our time together, I was still living alone in my wonderful studio apartment on Twenty-seventh Street. The small kitchenette barely had room for one person, but it was cheery because I asked my friends and clients to sign their names on the wall in different-colored felt pens. Linda tried to teach me how to cook. I'm the worst cook, but I would have really starved if she hadn't given me some basic training.

We spent hours and hours together. I showed her everything I ever knew or loved about music and she showed me about flowers and cooking. We had a wonderful, warm, deep relationship that has lasted on and on into the years. Our backgrounds were so different that we never seemed to run out of things to talk about.

One night, we began to talk about pets. She had had everything from pet goats to pet rabbits as she grew up. I had never had a pet, and never felt the need to.

So nobody was more surprised than I was when I found myself madly in love with a beagle puppy. I don't know why I called her Bagel, but I just knew, on that chilly day in March 1970, that that little beagle had to be named Bagel.

Linda had called to tell me about her day in Coney Island. She was shooting some promotional Easter spots for WCBS at a store called The Animal Nursery. They had little baby everythings: baby pigs, baby monkeys, baby birds, and baby dogs. She set one shot up in which a baby beagle would be seen chasing a baby chick around a pen and she just fell in love with the beagle.

"So," she told me, "the owner was so thrilled that we were going to show the name of his store in the spot, he offered to give me the puppy for free!"

"Great," I said, "but do you have time to raise a dog?"

"No, so I was thinking maybe you'd want her."

"*Me?!*" I said. "No way."

"Aw, just come to The Animal Nursery with me tomorrow and look at her. Even if you don't take her, it'll be a fun day."

Have you ever been to a pet shop? Have you ever seen those adorable, innocent, helpless little creatures all begging to be adopted? Haven't you just wanted to take them all home with you?

I didn't.

All during the subway ride to Coney Island, I kept telling Linda that I really wasn't interested in getting a dog. I wasn't an animal lover, had never had a pet, except for a parakeet named Skipper which Gramma adopted as her third grandson and taught fluent Yiddish (it was always a little startling to hear *"Squaaawwk, shayneh poooopehleh, squaaawwk!"* coming out of that bird's beak), and I didn't have the patience or the time to change now. I don't even think I'd been in very many pet stores in my life.

So walking into The Animal Nursery was a shock. It stank. It was noisy. It was dirty. I know I must have looked as if I'd just stepped in slime, my face all wrinkled up.

"Hi, Linda!" the owner boomed. "Who's the sourpuss with you?"

Well he didn't actually say that, but I know he was thinking it.

"Decided to take the puppy, eh?"

"Well, John," said Linda, "I'm thinking about it and I wanted my friend Barry to see her."

We went over to the little playpen they kept the beagles in. She was the smallest of all of them because she was the runt of the litter and yet she was the most active. Jumping over all the others, nipping at them playfully, rolling around by herself, never stopping for a second.

John reached in, lifted her out, and handed her to me. She fit into the palm of my hand. And as soon as I held her to my chest, she fell asleep. Just like that. I looked down at this little thing in my hand and then I looked at Linda.

Linda said to John, "I think we'll take her."

It was a nippy spring day, so I put Bagel inside my coat and she slept against my chest all the way back on the subway.

I was hooked.

Training Bagel was really easy, since she was the smartest dog in the world. Really, she was. After a couple of days and nights of barking and having "accidents," she was trained.

I always hate it when people treat their pets as if they were their children. It turns me off. *Cootchy-koo*ing to them, talking to them as if they were human. A cat is a cat, a bird is a bird, and a dog is just a dog.

Except for Bagel, of course. She was a person.

I was running a pretty active coaching profession, and my clients would come to my one-room studio apartment all day long, hour after hour. And they would fall in love with little Bagel. Spoiled her rotten, we did.

She understood my moods, my commands, and the entire English language, I'm sure of it. How many dogs do you know who, when told "Go get your mouse," actually pick out the mouse toy from a box of toys? Or her hamburger toy? Come on now, how many?

I'd take her to Central Park on sunny days and let her off her leash, and she'd run and run. But never away.

I'd come home from a rough day and Bagel would be waiting. Happy to be fed and petted, not caring if the arrangements didn't sound good or if the client hated the melody I'd written.

Bagel was my companion for years. I'd never really taken having a pet seriously, but once I got a dog, my opinion about pets turned totally around. She became as much a part of my life as a friend or a child would be. People would inquire about her health; my schedules had to include her. She was a big responsibility, but worth all the effort, because she was always there and never judgmental. She was a real pal and I loved her.

Musical Therapy

When I was working as an accompanist/vocal coach in New York, my clients were varied. Some were good, some were fair, some were awful. Perhaps two were great. I won't say who they were because I want to keep my friends.

My job was to help them get the part they were auditioning for. I did this by studying their strong points and their weak points and suggesting material for them that would accent their strengths and camouflage their weaknesses.

Before each coaching session there would be a therapy session. I'm not kidding. The first fifteen minutes of each session would start off with the singer pouring out his or her heart to me. About very personal things, too. When I first started coaching, I was very uncomfortable in this role, but as time went on I got used to it. I worked with some real characters.

There was the actress who sang. Of course, she thought she sang great, but she didn't. She acted. And she wanted to sing rock music because she was auditioning for a rock musical. This was a challenge, but with the right selections and the right accompaniment I was pretty sure we could fool the producers into thinking that she could sing rock.

Besides, the show she was auditioning for was about as rock

as *Oklahoma!* From the moment *Hair* had burst upon the Broadway scene, everybody was jumping on the "rock musical" bandwagon, but no one knew what they were doing.

I suggested she sing two songs off the *Dusty in Memphis* album by Dusty Springfield, one of the all-time great pop albums. The songs were "There's No Easy Way Down" by Gerry Goffin and Carole King and "I Don't Want to Hear It Anymore," by Randy Newman. Both had dramatic lyrics and easy melodies and rhythmic structures, which didn't demand too much from her.

We worked on the two songs twice a week for two months, painstakingly tailoring the arrangements to suit her style. When we were ready, you would swear that this girl could handle any contemporary song. She auditioned for the rock musical *Salvation* and got the role on the spot.

Then there was the comedienne who sang. Well, sort of. She was able to carry a tune and was strangely moving, because people who do comedy usually are. The sound of her voice, though, was nasal and annoying. She was always nervous. Manic, almost. Crazy is the word.

She'd start off each meeting by telling unbelievable stories. Her boyfriend had beaten her up last night, or she had just been thrown out of her apartment, or she was fired (or hired) for this show or that show and the director hated her (or loved her) and she couldn't stand him (or loved him).

One time she got very loud and agitated. She paced back and forth in my apartment, talking faster, faster, faster, and then, suddenly, she just grabbed the bottom of her T-shirt and pulled it up and covered her face with it. I found myself staring at a pair of breasts and a face hidden by her T-shirt. I didn't say anything. What was there to say?

As she recovered, she slowly lowered her T-shirt and said, "I'm ready to sing now." This girl is very talented and you know who she is. Some of us here in show biz are just a little more uninhibited than others. I'll say!

After constant work on two specially arranged songs, she got the role she was after. I hope she kept her T-shirt on.

Then there was the Six Million Dollar Man. That's what I

wound up calling him privately. When he called to make an appointment with me, his voice sounded like a road company Alistair Cooke. He had a real phony-sounding name too. Trent Ashley. That's not his real name, but it felt just like that.

When he walked into my apartment, I just stood there, gaping. He looked ridiculous. He looked as if he were pieced together (later I found out he was!). He was over six feet tall, and he had Elvis Presley greasy hair, form-fitting clothes worn too tight, expensive white boots, and a leather jacket with fringes. His face was perfect. Too perfect.

We shook hands and he told me what kind of music he wanted to concentrate on. The more I looked at him, the more I realized that something was screwy. I didn't know what it was, exactly. I knew his speaking voice was phony, and when he sang, he tried to sound like Mario Lanza or something. Now, it's fine to sound like Mario Lanza if that's the way you really sound, but this guy was just imitating a "legit" singer. I knew I was going to have trouble with this one.

During the few months that I worked with Trent, I asked around about him and found out that my first impression had been right. He was a phony. Literally. He was bald as a bowling ball, but had a hair transplant and wore a toupee. He had had everything done to his face that money could buy. His nose, his eyes, his chin, his ears. He had even gone further. His ass, his thighs. He worked out every day to make sure that he wouldn't turn back into his original self.

The more I got to know him, the more I felt sorry for him. We'd talk before each session, and little by little the more comfortable he became with me, the higher his voice became. I found out his real name was something like Arnie Shmendrick and he had spent most of his life trying to become Trent Ashley. He was miserable.

Musically, I didn't know what to do with him. I tried everything, but everything he sang sounded as phony as his teeth. This was one battle I lost. I felt really bad when he stopped calling, too, because I had begun to like Trent (I mean Arnie), and I was fascinated to watch him live this freakish life that wasn't his.

But in acting or in singing it's the truth that ultimately moves people. Even those singers without great voices or great style can succeed if they are truthful. Trent didn't stand a chance. Even with all the tricks I could think of as an accompanist/coach/arranger/therapist, I couldn't really help him. We'd get to an audition, he'd sing the first few notes, and we'd hear the inevitable, dreaded, "Thank you. Next."

A friend of mine told me a story about a girlfriend of his who went to bed with Trent. They were in the heat of passion. But Trent was so cautious he wouldn't let her touch him anywhere. When she finally gently ran her fingers through his hair, it came off in her hands. Trent went crazy. Lost it completely, and the lady wound up running out of the apartment as fast as she could.

I sometimes wonder what those clients of mine think of me now. *They* were the ones who were supposed to become the famous singers. They must be asking "How the hell did *he* get the gig?" How the hell *did* I get the gig?

Welcome to the Seventies

People going in and out of my apartment, staying up till all hours of the night writing arrangements for them, running to auditions at rehearsal halls and theaters, grabbing lunches and dinners wherever I could—this was the way I spent my life. I loved it, but it was beginning to get too frantic. Linda and I would see each other when we could, but the music career left no time for a personal life.

It was 1970, and I was feeling very proud that I had been able to make a living without having a nine-to-five job. Not only was I able to make a living, I was having a ball. I had more business than I could handle.

But I decided my life was just too crazy. I really wanted to concentrate on writing songs, and the coaching business was getting out of hand. I was getting offers to be music director for television shows, and had begun making money doing commercials, so I decided to start turning down singers and to recommend other pianists to my steady clients.

One of my clients, Sheilah Rae, called one afternoon to ask me to play an audition for her.

"Sheilah," I said, "I'm giving up the coaching business and I've got the number of another guy for you to check out."

"Barry, just do this one more for me," she said. "My agent thinks it's important. Please?"

"Okay," I said. "Where do I meet you?"

"Meet me on the corner of Seventy-fourth Street and Broadway. I'm auditioning to sing at a place called the Continental Baths."

It was a freezing cold December afternoon in New York, the kind of cold out-of-towners complain about but New Yorkers don't even notice. This was going to be one of the last times I would play piano for an auditioning singer. I couldn't refuse Sheilah, because we had become very close friends and had worked up some complicated arrangements, and this audition had sounded as if it was important to her.

She was waiting for me, all bundled up in her winter coat and scarf, on the corner of Seventy-fourth and Broadway as planned. I jumped out of the taxi and we started down Seventy-fourth Street.

"I could have sworn you said 'the Continental Baths,' " I said.

"I did."

I could see our breaths in the cold.

"What kind of place is it?" I asked.

"It's a Turkish bath for men only."

I stopped. "It's a *what*?"

"Come on, I'm freezing," she said and walked ahead. "It's very 'in.' They have shows there on the weekends and it's becoming *the* place to be seen singing. My agent says it would be good for me to sing there."

I could see a canopy hanging over a door a few feet away. It said CONTINENTAL BATHS in small letters.

Sheilah was your garden-variety Jewish-American Princess. A very talented singer and a very classy, uptown girl. She belonged on Broadway or in a supper club. This felt weird.

"Sheilah, are you sure? Maybe we ought to call someone and ask about it."

"Oh, come on. It'll be a giggle."

I opened the door and a blast of hot air hit us. I had a heavy winter coat on over my suit and tie and I carried my ever-present attaché case filled with music. We were in a little anteroom. The walls were filled with bulletins, want ads, announcements for shows, and rules and regulations. Sheilah told the ticket taker behind a glass booth that we were here to audition. He pressed a buzzer to let us in another door.

A blast of even warmer air hit us and we both began taking off our coats and scarves. It was darker on the other side of this door, and a stairway led both up and downstairs.

"Go downstairs and see Billy," the ticket taker said. "And good luck!" The door slammed shut behind us.

Dance music wafted up from downstairs and suddenly a naked man passed us going downstairs.

" 'Scuse me hon," he said to Sheilah.

I stood there speechless as he skitted down the stairs. "Okay, let's get out of here," I said, and I pulled Sheilah upstairs.

"Oh don't be such a chicken," she said and kept going down.

The stairway widened, the music got louder, and I saw colored lights, lots of mirrors, and flocked wallpaper. I could see the entire place. There was an enormous swimming pool with fountains spraying in odd directions, an area with tables and chairs near a hamburger and soda stand, and a dance floor in the center. There were lots of men swimming or eating or walking and talking and most of them were stark naked.

"Sheilah, stop drooling," I said.

"I'm not drooling, I'm observing," she said, drooling.

Both of us stood at the bottom of the steps, Sheilah with her mouth open. Finally, Billy Cunningham, a big black man who played piano, came to the rescue. Billy and I knew each other from having met at auditions.

"Barry! Welcome to the tubs! You must be Sheilah. Come on, honey, let's hear you sing."

At one end of the dance floor, there was a small stage with a set of drums and an upright piano on it. While Sheilah got the music out, I saw a tall thin man take a seat at the back of the dance floor.

"That's Steven Ostrow," Billy said. "He's the boss."

Sheilah sang a few of her songs while I played the awful piano. Now and again a door would open directly in front of me and we'd get hit with a huge blast of steam from the sauna. No wonder the piano was out of tune.

When we were done, Steven came over, introduced himself, and told Sheilah how much he enjoyed her songs and said he'd call her agent. While they were talking, Billy and I went to get a Coke.

"Billy, what is this place?" I asked.

"Haven't you ever heard of the baths?" he said.

I hadn't.

"Well, welcome to the seventies!" he smiled and winked at me. "This main floor we're on is the respectable area of the baths," he said.

"Respectable?"

"Yeah, you know, swimming pool, refreshments, barber shop, sauna, massage parlor. So that when the cops check it out everything looks nice and cool."

"Cops? Nice and cool?" I echoed.

"Barry, would you get hip?" He was getting impatient. He leaned closer and spoke softer. "There are two more floors to this place and upstairs there are rows and rows of lockers where you undress and little rooms that you can rent while you're here. And what goes on in those little rooms! Honnn-*eeey!*"

"Welcome to the seventies," I said softly, understanding.

The Continental Baths was the first of its kind, an openly gay Turkish bath where everything was okay. It was an enormous shock to hear what Billy was describing. A few years later there were gay bathhouses in every major city. But in New York in 1970, it was unique. Even the hippest of my show-business friends were stunned when I told them about the place later.

Billy took in my attire and realized I was conservative, uptight, and not very cool. Now that I understood what really went on in this crazy place, I began to feel uncomfortable.

"Listen, they really get some good talent here on the weekends. I've been playing here for a few months, but this weekend is my last. You want the job?"

"I don't think so, Billy."

"The pay's not bad, Barry. One hundred twenty-five dollars to play one show on Saturday night at midnight."

I looked around this very strange place as Sheilah came toward me, Steven helping her on with her coat.

"I enjoyed your playing," Steven said to me in a deep voice.

"Thanks," I said.

He said, "You know, Billy here is leaving. Are you interested in the job?"

"Well, I don't know—" I said.

"The pay isn't bad, you know," Steven said. "One hundred twenty-five dollars to play one show on Saturday night."

Well, I thought, I *am* giving up my coaching business and this would be easy money.

"Yeah, gimme a day to think about it," I said.

"And an extra fifty for a rehearsal on Thursdays," he added.

"I'll take it," I said, driving my usual hard bargain.

Working at the baths was a trip. I inherited a maniac named Joey Mitchell as my drummer, a little black tornado who was so funny and uninhibited that my Jewish middle-class uptightness began to loosen up. Still, I don't think I ever really got used to looking up and seeing naked people roaming around doing clothed-people-type things. Shows you how good I'd be in a nudist colony.

Thursdays rehearsals lasted for an hour or so and they were relatively quiet, but Saturday nights were insane. I found myself in the middle of the wildest situation I could ever imagine. Everything about it had the mark of individuality, rule-breaking, and recklessness. It was decadent, sexual, and shocking—all the things I wasn't. For a few hours a week, though, I was a part of it. It was quite an experience.

The people I met were funny and irreverent, wise-cracking and seemingly without a care in the world. I guess they didn't have a care when they were at the baths. The few people I talked with during breaks would confide to me that they were businessmen or salesmen, sneaking away from their conventional daily lives for a few hours of outrageousness. And boy, was it ever outrageous!

The first show I played at the baths starred two comics and an older black lady blues singer whose name I can't remember. The audience was as enthusiastic as any I'd ever played for—and since there was a lady on the stage, they wore towels.

The following Saturday featured Liz Torres, a wonderfully funny comedienne and singer who was just becoming popular. We rehearsed on Thursday afternoon, and the one serious ballad she was going to do was constantly interrupted by the public-address system which blasted through the place as constantly as the steam from the sauna blasted my piano.

Liz (singing):   The night is bitter, the stars have lost their glitter

PA system: *Free VD tests on Monday in Room 312!*

Liz: And all because of the man that got away
No more his eager call, the writing's on the wall
The dreams you've dreamed have all gone astray

PA system: *The orgy room is off limits for the next hour while it's being cleaned, thank God.*

Liz: The road gets rougher, it's lonelier and tougher
With hope you burn up, tomorrow he may turn up

PA system: *A very strange implement has been left in Room 210. Would the kinky person please claim the thing.*

You get the idea.

The third Saturday night I played at the baths fell on New Year's Eve. New Year's Eve had never really meant that much to me. I had planned to spend it at *The Drunkard* (where I was still playing Saturdays) with the cast after the performance. The show at the baths that night was to feature Liz Torres and two comedians. I had to run uptown for the show at the baths.

The audience at the Thirteenth Street Theatre were feeling no pain by the end of the show, thanks to the free beer. They made the cast take curtain call after curtain call. When the audience had left the theater, the cast gathered in front of the bar in the lobby and we toasted to the new year. After I said good-bye to everyone, I walked down to Sixth Avenue to hail a taxi. Not so easy on

New Year's Eve. I waited in the cold for nearly an hour and finally decided I'd better take the subway.

Taking the subway on New Year's Eve in Manhattan is a little like strolling through the DMZ. I hit the Forty-second Street-Times Square subway stop at precisely eleven thirty P.M. There I was, with my nice neat black suit and my attaché case full of music, trying to ignore the utter pandemonium going on around me in the train. The noise, the humanity being crushed into one another, the total abandon, were unbelievable. These people were crazy! I couldn't wait to get to the baths and some sanity.

Have you ever seen a thousand naked men with party hats on? It was insane.

Since the show began at midnight, it was pandemonium the whole night. All during the show, people kept passing drinks and joints up to me and to Joey. During the comic's part of the show, I drank some more. When it was over, Liz invited me to a party with some friends of hers, but I passed on it. I had had enough and was ready to go home to Bagel, who probably was crossing her paws needing to pee.

On my way out the door, Joey stopped me and convinced me to have one more drink. Since the traffic was going to be insane anyway, I agreed. As it was New Year's Eve, Steven had thrown caution to the wind and allowed co-ed swimming. There were girls sprinkled all around the pool, all of them naked. *Everyone* was naked. We sat around the pool and I looked at myself with my nice black suit still on.

I was feeling very loose from all the booze and the joints.

"Okay, everybody into the pool!" Joey yelled.

Off came Joey's clothes, and in he and the others went.

Not me, of course. I was thinking I'd love to lose my inhibitions and jump in with the rest of them, but it goes against everything in me.

"Come on, Barry! It's great in here!" some girl yelled.

"I can't," I said, getting up, wobbly.

"Sure you can! Come on!"

I stood there and looked at myself with my nice black suit on.

Gramma would kill me, I thought. I don't know why I thought that.

The pool had steam coming from it and looked warm and inviting, and I was feeling pretty loose.

"No, I really can't. I'm going home."

Here I was in the most outrageous situation I'd ever been in: drunk in a bath house on New Year's Eve. My background just wouldn't release me.

"Come *on*! It's New Year's Eve, Barry! Loosen up!" either someone said or Gramma said.

I stood there and smiled stupidly.

Everyone started to cheer as I took off my black suit and my white shirt—

Are you *really* doing this? my upbringing yelled at me.

and my white T-shirt and my black socks,

Yes, I am *really* doing this!

and finally my white jockey shorts, and jumped into the pool at the Continental Baths on New Year's Eve, 1970.

"Welcome to the seventies!" I yelled as I hit the water.

Adventures with Bette

Ladies and Gentlemen, The Divine Miss M!

I was working at my piano one day early in January 1971 with the television on and the sound off (the way I like to watch TV) when I looked up to see a very strange girl on the screen. She was singing and she was so interesting-looking that I turned up the sound.

She was in the middle of some sort of blues number, singing slightly off key, but putting her entire being into the song, flailing her arms and legs, grimacing, shaking, and practically jumping off the screen. Such a performer was unusual for daytime television. I stayed tuned to find out who it was. The show was Virginia Graham's, one of the all time great yentas, and the performer was Bette Midler. Watching the two of them chat after the song was hysterical. When it was done, I went back to the piano chuckling.

Early the next week, the phone rang. "Hello, Barry Manilow please."

"Speaking."

"Hi. This is Bette Midler. I'm working the baths on Saturday night and Steven told me you were playing piano."

"That's right."

"I want an extra rehearsal."

"Oh, really?"

"Steven will pay for it. When can I come over?"

"Tomorrow at two. Okay?"

I told her where I lived.

"Fine. Good-bye."

"Good-bye.

My first meeting with Bette was uncomfortable. She came in with her dukes up and I reacted by putting mine up. She had just come from knocking 'em dead in Chicago opening for Jackie Vernon at Mr. Kelly's, the supper club, and she was feeling cocky. I was becoming successful writing jingles and conducting for singers and I too was feeling cocky. The truth was we were both nobodies.

She was a half hour late for our appointment. She rang the doorbell and Bagel went crazy barking, as usual. When I opened the door to let her into my apartment, she sneered and said, "Oh, a dog," and breezed past me, leaving me holding the door open. She threw her coat on the couch. I followed her in and we both stood in the middle of the room talking politely while we sized each other up.

"Traffic must have been murder, huh?" I asked her. (She's not wearing a bra, I thought. If there's anyone in this world who should be wearing a bra, it's this girl.)

"No. I overslept. I'm sorry," she said. (He's wearing a tie in the afternoon in his own apartment, she must have thought. What a jerk.)

"It's pretty cold out today," I said, gaping at her hair. (It's the strangest shade of red, and it looks like she just stuck her finger in an electric socket.)

"Yep. I'm freezin' my tits off," she said, looking at my hair. (What's with the bangs? He looks like an old Veronica Lake publicity photo.)

"Would you like something to drink?" I asked her. (She's so short. She didn't look that short on television last week.)

"Yeah, what've you got?" she smiled. (He's so tall. And skinny as a rail. Doesn't he ever eat?)

"I think I've got some tea," I offered. (She's got a strange face, but what a great smile.)

"Oh, I was thinking of something harder. Like coffee, maybe?" (Jeez, what a nose on this guy.)

"Lemme see what I have." And I went into the kitchen as she lit up a cigarette. (This is gonna be one tough cookie.)

"Thanks," she sang. (God, this apartment is so neat you could eat off the floors. This is gonna be one tough cookie.)

For the next two hours, although we made music, we seemed to circle one another like two animals in the jungle. We were very suspicious of one another. When we were done, we shared a taxi uptown, and by the time I dropped her off at her apartment, I felt relieved to be away from the pressure of defending myself.

I had never experienced anything like her. She was demanding, her voice was grating, she didn't try to be polite or social. She was downright rude at times.

She was my mother, my grandmother, and all of my female relatives rolled into one, with my high school biology teacher, Mrs. Wurzel, thrown in for good measure. She was every Jewish boy's nightmare come to life.

She was impatient with my piano playing and critical of everything in my apartment. ("What d'ya have people writing on your kitchen wall for?") And she wanted yet *another* rehearsal before the regular Thursday one.

We met on Wednesday at my apartment, and then again on Thursday with Joey Mitchell at the baths. Neither of those meetings went any better than the first one. Her singing during our rehearsals left much to be desired. She'd do one song over and over and over again, singing out of tune, roaming as she sang. I couldn't figure out what the hell she was doing. I'd offer comments and we'd argue. She'd eventually use my musical suggestions, but she'd use them in her own time and in her own way.

It was a frustrating week, and by the time Saturday night rolled around, I was counting the minutes until I could say good-bye to this person.

*   *   *

There are some moments that stay with you all of your life, and when you think of them, they're so vivid you remember exactly where you were when they happened. I call them Thunderbolts. I've had quite a few of them and some of them were so influential they actually changed the course of my life. Hearing about Kennedy's assassination, reading *The Temple of Gold* by William Goldman, listening to Miles Davis's *Sketches of Spain* for the first time, man's landing on the moon, and, yes, seeing Bette work for the first time.

I had already played three Saturday nights at the baths and I looked forward to the crowd that made up the audience. They were great. First of all, except for towels around their waists, they were naked, so they had no inhibitions. Secondly, they were bright, hip, and compassionate. If a performer was sincere and had the slightest bit of talent, these were the most encouraging audiences I'd ever seen.

Bette had already performed at the baths a few months before, so these boys were ready for her. I was not. I could feel a buzz of excitement in the air as Steven Ostrow introduced her. I began to play the introduction to "Friends" the way we had rehearsed, and I hardly looked up from the music in front of me.

Suddenly, out of the barber shop/dressing room on the side of the stage came a whirling red-haired dynamo! She tore her way to the small stage in front of me and began singing "Friends" in a way I hadn't heard her do in rehearsal. She shouted, she screamed, she kicked, she flailed her arms and legs. It was the same song and the same musical arrangement we had rehearsed, but she was finally *performing* it and she was filling it with such energy and personality I could hardly recognize it. The audience, who had never heard this song before, went crazy at the end of it. And I was in shock.

I'd never experienced anything like it. I sat ten inches away from this explosive energy source and I felt as if I had stuck my hand into an electric socket. As the show went on, I found myself laughing hysterically at her outrageous jokes; during "Am I Blue," I welled up with emotion as she poured out her breaking heart, and I played as delicately as I'd ever played before. I played with as much crazy energy as she performed with during "Chattanooga Choo Choo," and at the end, when she sang "I Shall Be Released," I broke three piano strings pounding out the accompaniment to her fury.

The audience wouldn't let her go. They stood, they hollered, they waved their towels in the air until she came back. When she came back onto the stage, I was standing and cheering too. We closed with an encore of "Friends," and when it was done I just sat there stunned.

I think it had the kind of impact on me that it did, not only because Bette was so dynamic, but because I didn't expect it. I didn't expect her to be funny or filthy or dramatic and most of all I didn't expect her to be so musical. I mean, she had given me no indication during our rehearsals that she had all that inside her.

I went backstage and tried to convey to her how knocked out I was with her performance. I must have sounded like a babbling fool, but I made my point and told her to call me any time she needed a pianist. Inside I was feeling uncertain about wanting to work with her again: she was the most exciting performer I'd ever seen, but I wasn't sure whether I wanted to put up with a steady diet of the craziness I had experienced during the week. But the choice really wasn't mine, because Bette had already made up her mind about me. I was going to be her music director whether I liked it or not.

She wanted me to play for her the next weekend. I said I couldn't because I was working at the baths.

She smiled that great smile. "How convenient!" she shouted. "So am I!"

We played the baths together for three weeks and worked up eight new arrangements. And they were good. Even though it was still only Joey and me, Bette made my charts sound great, and because she was so unconventional, I could do *anything* and she would make it work. Her choices were eclectic—from the old "Empty Bed Blues" to "Chapel of Love." I was crazy about her as an artist and envious of her impulsiveness.

The audiences at the baths loved her and let her do everything. She was such a hit that Steven roped off a little area for people wearing clothes. I would bring Linda and other friends down each weekend and they never quite got over it.

One night, a huge black man got so carried away he jumped up on stage and danced with Bette. Suddenly, his towel fell off. Everyone screamed and laughed and Bette just kept looking from his organ, flapping in the breeze, to the audience and back in shock.

"Put that thing away, honey," Miss M finally said in mock horror. "You could hurt somebody with it!"

"Hurt *me!*" someone in the audience yelled. "Hurt *me!*"

After the third week, I was again ready to say good-bye, but Bette wasn't. She'd gotten a booking at the Downstairs at the Upstairs, the same place I had worked for two seasons with Jeanne.

"Just stay with me until I finish the Downstairs," she pleaded.

I've never been able to say no to Bette. Certainly not then. I stayed. Frankly, I enjoyed her so much, that even though it was a step backward for me to work the Downstairs, I agreed to stay because I wanted to.

Bette and I put a little combo together comprised of Kevin Ellman on drums and her then-boyfriend, singer-guitarist Michael Federal. The owner of the club, Irving Haber, offered me and the band $50 more a week if we would play music for twenty minutes before Bette came on, and we accepted. I had loads of my songs available and Michael and I worked up twenty minutes of original material in which we both sang.

Bette was a huge success at the Downstairs, and we stayed there for three months. The word began spreading about her throughout New York's gay crowd, and the audiences loved her. Our twenty-minute opener went over well, too, especially my song "Sweet Life."

Bette and I stayed together for three years. Every time I'd try to leave, she'd plead,

"Just stay with me until I finish Bermuda"

or "until I finish Vegas"

or "until I do *The Tonight Show*"

or "until I do Carnegie Hall."

I tried, but I couldn't say no. She was just too good.

Even though we worked and rehearsed together for years, I was never quite prepared, each time, for her performances on stage. As illogical and sometimes exasperating as she might be during the day, when it came time to perform at night, she was inspired, always creating something new: a new joke, a new musical twist, a new piece of choreography. She would drive me and the band nuts trying to keep up with her, but it kept us sharp and she was never, ever wrong in her choices.

Slowly, I began to see what Bette needed from me and what she didn't need from me. She needed to be organized. She needed dynamic and innovative arrangements. She needed a solid band. She needed an environment in which she could be free to create. She didn't need me to select songs, or write jokes, or come up with theatrical gimmicks.

One time she said, "Let's do 'Lullaby of Broadway' like it was right out of the forties!"

That's all I needed. I ran to the record store to find "You're Out of The Woods" from *The Wizard of Oz* to be used as the intro. I suggested that she sing the beginning an octave lower so that she'd sound like Alice Faye. And then I'd spend hours and hours at the piano inventing just the right layout for the song.

I would supply the setting and she'd supply the genius.

She was and is the consummate pro. She challenged me, and stimulated me.

She also sent me straight to a shrink.

I may have had long hair, but I was still an uptight square. Smashing headlong into this unbridled crazy woman was too much for me. I didn't realize what a turning point it would be for me professionally, but I knew that personally, something was happening that I needed. My jumping into the pool at the baths was just an indication that I wanted to break free from my uptight bonds. I knew that there were many things I wanted to change about myself and Bette was offering me a way to begin.

I envied Bette for her ability to be in touch with her feelings, and although I dreaded our continual confrontations, I knew that I was gaining strength from them. Her attitude and approach to life represented everything that terrified and attracted me. She was strong, crude, sexual, opinionated, and very bright. She saw through crap before I even knew it *was* crap.

I loved her honesty. I felt the same things that she felt, but she would *say* them—out loud! Who would have the guts to say those things? Her audiences reacted the same way I did. Everybody would think outrageous thoughts now and then, but who would have the nerve to say them out loud?

I would lose every argument not because I was wrong, but because I didn't know how to fight with her. Ironically, Bette saw me as an authority figure. I was, after all, the *music director.* And there was no doubt that I knew more about that field than she did, and she hated that. She would try every which way to bully me into seeing musical things her way. But in that area, I was confident and strong.

I really didn't know how to handle her, and I knew that I was in trouble. I wanted to work with her badly, and yet I *was* working with her and she was driving me crazy. Yes, she had her own problems, but I knew that this problem was with me, not her.

She must have thought I was such a putz. I was the living definition of *uptight.* I never let myself go, I was inhibited, I didn't like losing control. God only knew what would happen if I lost control! I couldn't risk making a fool of myself, so I never did anything dangerous. I still dressed neatly, spoke softly, and kept my feelings bottled up. The white suit Gramma had dressed me in to go to school had changed to a black suit, but it was having the same effect. Trying to work with Bette showed me that there were emotions available in me that I wanted to experience, but I couldn't seem to get to.

Anger—when had I ever really shown anger? Why hadn't I screamed bloody murder at Edna when she had moved into the apartment above me? *Sadness*—when had I ever really sat and sobbed and let out my sorrows? The sadness I felt over my divorce was overwhelming, yet I had hardly shed a tear. *Joy*—had I ever laughed hysterically without wondering if I was being too loud? Had I ever really *felt anything*?

So I went out looking for someone to help me deal with her and myself.

*   *   *

I began seeking out therapists, and wound up changing every few weeks. Some would talk too much, and some wouldn't talk at all. During an especially emotional moment for me, I caught one looking at his watch, and I never went back.

One weekend, I was invited out to the Hamptons on Long Island by an old CBS friend. I took Bagel on the long bus ride and began reading *The Primal Scream* by Arthur Janov. I finished it that weekend and by the time I got home I was hooked. Primal scream therapy dealt with getting in touch with your emotions physically rather than through conversation. You'd actually let your feelings out by screaming at the top of your lungs and eventually you'd get back to that "primal scream" you experienced when you were born.

It sounded scary, but also like the right thing for me. After all, back in my old neighborhood they were primal screaming every night! Larry Rosenfeld's mother was the best little primal screamer you ever heard. If she could do it, so could I!

The primal scream clinic was located in California (although I thought that Brooklyn would've been a natural place for it). They weren't planning on opening a New York center, so they recommended me to a similar-type therapy being done in New York called bio-energetics.

I began a series of appointments with a doctor on Park Avenue, and for the next six months, twice a week, I would lie on a bed stark naked and scream. Or sometimes, I would be bent backward across a bar stool till I thought my back would break. Or sometimes I would kneel on the floor in front of a bed and pound on it while I yelled profanities as loud as I could. I know it sounds very bizarre, but it worked for me. It was a way of getting my feelings out in the open immediately.

What with Bette punching me from one side ("Would you dump that skinny tie already?") and therapy punching me on the other ("Yell *no* at the top of your lungs for the next fifteen minutes."), I was slowly taking off the uptight little black suit.

Superstar

I think Bette and I were our most inspired and most creative during those early days. The ideas were flowing nonstop from all of us. Bette and her collaborator Bill Hennessey would sit in her tiny dressing room at the Downstairs, laughing hysterically at new material or screaming at one another. Bette and I would work in the afternoons at my apartment on song after song. Each one was better than the last. "Leader of the Pack," "Hello in There," "Delta Dawn," blues songs, forties songs, rock 'n' roll. We'd fight, we'd laugh, we'd gossip.

Record companies began to appear at the club to check her out. Ahmet Ertegun, president of Atlantic records, saw an especially enthusiastic show. At the end of the show, the entire audience stood not on their chairs but on the *tables,* screaming for more. They finally actually carried Bette around the room on their shoulders. Ahmet signed her then and there.

A few weeks later, Bette rushed into the club and excitedly told me that Joel Dorn had agreed to produce her first album. I didn't know his work, but she told me he had produced Roberta Flack's records. I was confused. Roberta Flack's records were *sooo* tasteful, they really were. Delicate as crystal, cool as a cucumber, controlled, serious—everything Bette wasn't. It made no sense to me that she'd picked him.

She was running late and putting on her makeup at lightning

speed. Because I hadn't reacted, she was giving me grief, telling me how right he was for her, and that I should be as thrilled as she was.

"All right, all right, I'm thrilled," I said.

I wasn't really, but it was the only way I could get out of the dressing room.

Joel was due at the club for that show, and I figured I'd say hello afterward. Bette's show was great, as usual, but I kept my eye on Joel in the audience. I was very protective when it came to Bette. She needed my protection like she needed another leg, but I was always watching out for her.

He was enraptured, like the entire audience. He was also charming after the show. He told Bette he was going to produce a great album for her.

He asked me if my arrangements were written out. I told him they were.

I could feel right then that Joel was not going to be asking for my input in the creation of Bette's album. Really, why should he? I was only her piano player anyway. But presenting Bette correctly on her first record had become very important to me. I had invested time, energy, and a lot of my heart in her music. I felt that I really knew what the final record should be, but I could see that I was going to have very little say in this project. I went home that night hoping for the best.

About a month later, Bette was scheduled to begin recording. She was very insecure. So was I. I hadn't heard anything from anyone and I assumed Joel wasn't going to need me. I felt bad, but I swallowed it.

The day before Bette was to begin the session, Joel called and told me he wanted me to bring in the arrangements to three songs: "Superstar," "Do You Wanna Dance," and "Friends."

"But what about 'Boogie Woogie Bugle Boy'?" I said.

"Taken care of," said Joel.

"What about 'Hello in There'?"

"Taken care of."

" 'Chapel of Love'? 'Leader of the Pack'?"

"Taken care of."

"What do you mean, taken care of?" I asked.

"I've had them rearranged."

"Oh."

"Can you bring the other songs in?"

"When do you need them?"

"Tomorrow."

"Okay."

I was very disappointed. I had worked on perfecting those charts for Bette for months. They were important to me and right for her but nothing said he was obligated to use them. I bit the bullet and showed up with the charts.

We did the session and it was okay, but Joel considered me a lightweight and he made sure I knew it. No conferring with me, no chatting, just get the arrangements on tape, and let him continue producing the album.

During the playback of "Do You Wanna Dance" the chart sounded so good I was bursting with pride. The original song was a nice, simple rock 'n' roll song, but I had changed the chords, slowed it down, and made it sultry and sexy so Bette could interpret it sensually.

When we were done with the session, I hung back as the musicians said good night to Joel, Bette, and the engineers.

Joel finally noticed me and said, "Oh thanks, Barry, bye-bye."

"Bye, Barry," said Bette.

I took a deep breath and stammered that I would really like to finish the arrangements, because I had the rest of the instrumental parts written out and they really sounded good. Joel said that he had already hired an arranger to finish them.

I said, "But they're my arrangements, Joel."

"Oh, yeah. Well, I'll see if I can give you credit for arranging the basic rhythm tracks."

I couldn't hold back any longer. "But Joel, you've got to let me finish them. Bette and I have been working on these charts for two years. I know how they're supposed to sound, and everything is all ready! Hey, listen, Bette's even *paid* for them already. So what do you say? Let me have a shot at them, huh?"

He didn't even hear me. He was talking to the engineer. I looked at Bette for some help. She hadn't heard me either. She was frozen. She was just staring at the glass booth where she would have to go in a minute and sing. So I left, pissed, hurt, helpless.

I didn't hear from Bette or from anyone about the album for a few weeks. I felt frustrated, but I threw myself into getting the music ready for Bette's Carnegie Hall concert.

This was a monumental occasion for both Bette and me. It had only been a year ago that she was singing at the Continental Baths. Carnegie Hall had sold out in days, and she didn't even have an album out.

For me, it was the realization of a dream. Conducting at Carnegie Hall! It was exhilarating, and yet frightening. I'm sure she felt the same way. Success was happening so fast. Weren't you supposed to suffer more? I was only in my twenties and the dream of my lifetime was already here. What was I supposed to dream about now?

Bette had agreed, after much arguing, to hire an orchestra for Carnegie Hall. We were always at odds about the kind of approach she should take to her music. She always veered toward the rock 'n' roll approach of having the band jam and be loose behind her; I, being the prepared, uptight worrier, always took the safer approach of rehearsals and arrangements written out legibly. The shows came out somewhere in the middle. But when her agency booked Carnegie Hall, I fought to have an orchestra on that stage playing all those charts we had worked so hard on.

When Bette and I started to rehearse for the Carnegie Hall concert, I asked her how the album was going. She said it was no fun. She was having a terrible time, but Joel thought it was coming along great. I told her I thought that she should have insisted that he use my arrangements that day in the studio. She apologized, but she was so into her own thing I didn't bother to make an issue of it.

About a week before the Carnegie Hall concert, it was rumored that Ahmet Ertegun wasn't happy with the Bette Midler album. I hadn't heard it yet.

One day during the last rehearsals, Bette asked me to come to the studio to hear the final mix. I brought Marty and we listened to a delicate, tasteful, controlled, cool, serious, wonderful-sounding record. Just like Roberta Flack. Only it was Bette Midler singing. And there wasn't any Bette Midler in it.

I should have opened up my mouth and given them my opinion. It would have helped Bette, but I was gun-shy of Joel and anyway, they all seemed very pleased with it. What did I know about records?

I was very upset when I left the studio. I had devoted so much time and concern to Bette's career that hearing this nice-sounding album was distressing. As I saw it, the Bette Midler album should be a milestone in records, not unlike Streisand's debut on records. This album wasn't. It was ordinary. Bette wasn't. Bette was an original. But there was nothing I could do.

The day of the Carnegie Hall concert arrived and during the afternoon orchestra rehearsal, I had a little cassette machine sitting on the piano taping everything as we ran down the show. I had planned to give my cassette machine to Linda during the show so she could tape it from her seat, as usual. I mean, I just *had* to have a copy of this. I just knew that this night was going to be an event.

During the rehearsal, I noticed a very serious-looking guy watching me from the wings. When we had a break, he came over to me and told me, in a solemn tone, to get rid of the cassette machine. He said it was against union rules to tape-record any part of the show. I told him that it was only a home machine, and that it was just for my own personal use. He didn't care. He said that the whole orchestra would walk if I continued to tape. And he said that cassettes of the performance were absolutely forbidden. This guy meant business. I reluctantly took the machine to my dressing room and put it in my briefcase. I wasn't going to take any chances. But I was deeply disappointed. I had just about resigned myself to never hearing my arrangements on a record, but not being able to tape this evening's show was a crime. There was nothing I could do.

I had decided I would wear a marching band leader's outfit while conducting. It was off white, with tails and epaulets on the shoulders, and it looked real spiffy. As I was putting on my jacket, there was a knock on my door. It was a little old man who introduced himself as "Doc." He asked if he could talk to me privately. I said yes. He kept looking around to see if anyone was in the room or if anyone was listening. I was intrigued. Then he quietly asked me if I would like a tape of tonight's performance.

"Yes!" I yelled.

He nearly jumped out of his skin when I yelled. I apologized. He told me he was the house sound man at Carnegie Hall. He'd been there for twenty years, and although he knew that it was illegal to tape shows there, he also knew how much it meant to artists and conductors to have a tape of their performances.

Hanging over the stage in Carnegie Hall is a microphone which is used when an orchestra or soloist needs amplification. When the performer brings in a sound system, as we did, the house system isn't used. But that little beauty still can pick up the entire show. And it is connected to a reel-to-reel tape recorder in the house sound booth controlled by none other than Doc.

"How much?" I said.

"Two hundred and seventy-five dollars," said Doc.

I quickly calculated what I had left in my checking account. I could not afford $275. I didn't care. I made out a check right there and gave it to him. I had no idea what I was buying, but it was better than nothing.

The Carnegie Hall concert was a killer. For the people who were there, it will go down in show-business history. Magic like that usually happens once in a career. For Bette it happens every night—but even for Bette this was special.

As I stood in the wings, I saw the lights go down in the audience and heard, for the first time, the roar of the crowd. I'll never forget that moment. We'd never played a concert hall before and I'd only heard that sound in the movies or on television.

It didn't sound real. It didn't sound like individual people applauding or yelling. It was like an animal called "the crowd" and the animal was roaring. I walked out onto the stage of Carnegie Hall and was hit in the eyes with the brightest light I'd ever felt.

After I gave the downbeat to the orchestra, I was fine. I can just imagine how Bette must have felt. This was her first "legitimate" concert. She was at Carnegie Hall and it was sold out. When she came out to the musical vamp of "Friends," she stopped and looked out into the crowd. Before she sang, she said, breathing hard, "Oh my dears, your mother is freaking out."

The show was spectacular. Bette was in her finest form. I think that concert is my favorite of all Bette's performances. She was saucy and haughty as usual, but the enormity of playing the hallowed Carnegie Hall was clearly having an effect. From within that confident, wise-cracking character she showed a genuine vulnerability I had never seen.

For me, conducting for Bette at Carnegie Hall is an experience that's hard to top.

Backstage, with the applause still going, the band, the Harlettes, and even Bette jumped and laughed and carried on. We all knew we had been involved in something very special.

Within minutes there were hundreds of people backstage to see Bette. In my tiny dressing room, Linda, Marty, Bruce, Gramma, Grampa, and Edna crowded in. Even Fred Katz and his wife were there. Mom had spotted them heading toward their seats in the balcony and insisted they sit next to her in my available house seats.

I was in the middle of meeting and greeting when I spotted Doc. I hadn't forgotten about him. I excused myself from the crowd and took him over to a corner. "So? So? Did you get it?"

He said that he had, but that the first song was a little distorted. After that, it seemed fine. He handed me two tapes. They couldn't have been more valuable to me if they had been diamonds.

I couldn't think of anything else but hearing them. I couldn't think of a celebration party, I couldn't think of backstage guests, I had to hear them. Now. So I told Bette I would meet her at the party, and Marty, Bruce, Linda, and I ran. We hailed a cab to my apartment and raced to the tape recorder.

I held my breath as it started. There was the overture! It sounded fine! Then the first song started, and, as Doc said, it got very distorted. But somewhere near the end of the song, it cleared up and sounded not fine, but great! It was like a live album. The enthusiasm of the audience was as clear as it could be, which made the tape exciting. The orchestra sounded as if it had been individually miked. And Bette sounded as if she was in the living room. I had it! On tape! Forever!

Bette called me the next week and sounded very down. It was true Ahmet didn't like the album, and, frankly, neither did she. Of course, she was blaming herself.

I said, "Hey, Bette, you wanna hear something great?"

So she came over to my apartment. I sat her in my recliner, gave her a glass of wine and a joint, and put my headphones on her ears. I turned out most of the lights in the room, and let her listen to her Carnegie Hall performance. She laughed, she cried, she was as moved as she should have been.

I said, "Bette, why don't I show this to Ahmet?"

She said, "Go ahead, it can't hurt."

So I called Ahmet Ertegun. He didn't know me, I didn't know him, but he took my phone call. I told him I had a tape of Bette's concert that I wanted him to hear. He told me to come on over.

He had a big office overlooking Columbus Circle. A real Record Company President. The walls were lined with gold records for people I had only read about. Aretha Franklin, the Rolling Stones, Dusty Springfield, Ray Charles. Talk about intimidation. I didn't know how I had the guts to go through with this. What did I want, anyway?

I knew that this tape had all the ingredients needed to present Bette to the world. It was fun, exciting, musical, explosive. But what did I want Ahmet to say? I didn't know. I just wanted him to hear what Bette should sound like coming through speakers in your own living room.

He sat and listened through most of the tape, and after every song he'd nod his head. Finally, he slammed his hand on his desk and said, "That's what Bette Midler should sound like! That's the performer I signed."

I was really glad that he liked the tape. I sat there quietly, with a thought being born in my head.

The thought was, Never in a million years could I possibly produce the album we were describing.

But what I said was, "I can produce an album for her."

Ahmet said, "You can?"

Of course I couldn't.

"Yes, I can."

"Have you ever produced a record before?"

Never. I had only *been* in a recording studio twice.

"Yes, I have."

"You think you could give me that kind of excitement on a record?"

If you give me about ten years.

"No problem."

"Okay, you do three cuts. I'll come into the studio and give you a hand. Next week. Wednesday."

I knew Ahmet knew I'd never done anything like that, but I really think he believed I could do it. My knees were shaking as I walked down Broadway. I lit a cigarette, and my emotions went from overwhelming joy to absolute terror. What had I gotten myself into? I'd been in this position a few times before, and every time it had felt the same.

I'd bullshitted my way into playing with the Jazz Partners, into music-directing *The Pajama Game,* into writing the score to *The Drunkard,* into my first commercial. When they would ask me if I had done it before or if I thought I could do it, I always said, "Sure," not knowing if I could do it at all. So here I was again.

Bette reluctantly approved of the experiment. She was right to be reluctant. It was her life! It was her reputation! It was her money! It was my ass.

I decided to approach the project like this. Ahmet wanted

excitement. I wanted spontaneity. Joel had produced a beautiful-sounding record (delicate as china, cool as a cucumber, boring as shit, etc.). But there was no life in it. Typically, when you record an album, the lead vocal is put on last. That is, after the band is done and after the background vocals are completed and after the orchestra has been recorded.

It's a lonely process. You go into a small booth. They put a pair of headphones on you and ask you if you want the lights turned down any more. The microphone is the only thing you have to sing to. Usually, you wind up singing to the brand name printed on the mike or a little kidney-shaped button on the mike. (I have sung everything I've ever recorded to a little kidney-shaped button.)

They adjust the sound of the background tracks in your earphones, and when it seems in balance, the producer says, "Okay, should we try one?" It's scary and lonely. Unless you've been doing it for years and feel very comfortable in that recording booth, being spontaneous and exciting is really rough. All you think about is whether or not you're flat or sharp. If your phrasing is great, that will come through, but honestly, you don't even think about that. You just want to sing in tune with the band and get out of that booth!

It must have been agony for Bette. Knowing what she wanted to sound like, and then coming into the control room and hearing an ordinary vocal sound. Bette eventually learned to make brilliant records, but this first one must have been very painful.

I decided I wouldn't let her go through that again. I would create an atmosphere as close to a live performance as I possibly could. I hired Bette's band instead of the veteran studio musicians Joel had hired. Bette's band was fresh, enthusiastic, and excited to be there. Then I rented some theatrical lighting and had it hung in the recording studio. I invited an audience of about twenty close friends of Bette's and the band's. I set up the Harlettes and the band as if we were doing a live performance. I had some drinks and food brought in for the audience and kept Bette busy outside in the hallway while Ahmet and the engineer got the levels set on the band.

When they were ready in the control booth, I lowered the

lights, brought Bette into the studio, and handed her a mike. We did "Chapel of Love," with that funny ending, "Leader of the Pack," "Friends," "Delta Dawn," "Daytime Hustler," and "Superstar."

From the outset, we knew it was going to work. As soon as Bette could feel and react and play to a live audience, the previously missing energy was there. Ahmet, who was in the control booth, kept giving me the thumbs-up sign. Even Bette was having a good time.

A few days later, I had my first violin recording session. I had no idea what the violins were going to sound like because I had never made a record before.

The first song up was "Superstar." I ran it down with the strings. It seemed okay, but you really can't tell until the playback. I was sweating and smoking nervously, while Bette sat quietly and listened to the strings and the vocal she had already recorded.

Lew, the engineer, had the strings up very loud in the headphones, so I didn't know what the whole arrangement really sounded like until he told me to come in to the control room and listen.

He pushed playback, and the song started. There is no thrill equal to the first time an arranger hears his music being played back in a recording studio. All those sounds that were in my head were coming out of those enormous speakers, just the way I had heard them. I knew then and there that I wanted to feel that kind of thrill again and again, and that I would do everything I could to make a career for myself in records.

When the song ended, I looked up and into the studio through the glass booth. I was deeply moved to see the violin players tapping their bows, their way of applauding. It probably was that moment—when the violins filled the room with the sweetest sounds—that got me into the record business for real.

Oh, by the way, Bette hated those strings. Said it made her sound like Eydie Gorme. So there you go.

Who Woulda Thunk It?

Bette's album was released and it was a smash. The single was the ballad version of "Do You Wanna Dance" and it was doing great. The next single was going to be Joel's authentic 1940s-sounding version of "Boogie Woogie Bugle Boy."

When Bette and I went to London to tape the Burt Bacharach show, I had to reproduce Bette's recording of "Boogie Woogie Bugle Boy," because of the British Musicians Union rulings. I chose not to use Joel's hollow forties sound, but rather I produced it like a pop record. There was a difficult three-part harmony for Bette to master, but after hours of rehearsals in a banquet room of the hotel, she got it down. The next day, she recorded all three vocals in one take each. When Ahmet heard it he insisted on that version being released as Bette's next single instead of Joel's album version. Ahmet was a strong supporter of mine even back then, and I'll always be grateful to him for his encouragement during those insecure times.

With all its problems, Bette's first album, *The Divine Miss M,* went on to win her a Grammy for Best New Artist. When she won, I was very proud of her and glad that I had fought for an album that would show her off to be the gifted performer that she was.

*   *   *

I greeted the beginning of 1973 from the piano as I conducted for Bette at Philharmonic Hall on New Year's Eve. At midnight, she rose on an elevator in the giant stage, dressed as the New Year baby in a diaper, while the audience lit sparklers and yelled louder than the orchestra could play.

We had rehearsed all day long at the hall, and all of us spent the last hour secretly taping marijuana joints to the bottom of each seat in the auditorium. They were to be the climax of the evening. An usher snitched at the last minute and they were never used, but the evening was a blast anyway. At the end of the evening we all said our good-byes to each other. Aaron Russo, Bette's new manager and boyfriend, whisked her away on an open-ended vacation, and I went home to relax.

I was very happy with my career and my life. I had conducted at Carnegie Hall, at Philharmonic Hall, and had co-produced an album for my favorite performer. My phone was ringing with offers for conducting jobs and commercials. Since I had left CBS and Susan, I had created a fulfilling professional life. I was ready to start that climb to the next plateau, which I was sure would be as a conductor, producer, songwriter.

My number-one songwriting collaborator at the time was my friend Marty Panzer. He is still one of the finest lyricists I've ever worked with, and we wrote together as much as we could. He was still at CBS, now as an executive, but we wrote together constantly even though I was on the road with Bette.

His job at CBS kept him on alert for eight to ten hours a day, sometimes way into the evening. Like me, years before, Marty spent hours each day on the subway traveling from Brooklyn to Manhattan. He'd get most of his lyric writing done on those subway rides. He'd have me hysterical describing how people would look at him with concern as he wept silently while jotting down an especially poignant line. Or how they'd clear away from him as he shouted to no one, "That's it!" and wrote down a great line.

Sometimes he'd call me during the madness that constantly surrounded him in the On Air Control division at CBS.

"Hi, it's me," he'd whisper excitedly. "Listen to this. 'When I think of your eyes—'*Go to camera one, goddammit!*" he'd shout at someone. " 'Scuse me. 'When I think of your eyes—' *You putz! I said one!*" And on and on he'd go.

Marty and I wrote our first movie theme song for a powerful film about Viet Nam called *Parades*. The film wasn't successful, but on the day of the screening, it was a thrill for us to see our names flash by during the credits. The song we wrote for the film was called "I Am Your Child."

Like a squirrel, I'd been saving my pennies and finally was able to afford my first grand piano. It was a six-foot Steinway, and it fit right into the apartment. Only trouble was it was the *only* thing that fit into the apartment. All my other furniture was smashed up against the walls, and when the convertible sofa became a bed at night, it would have to slide under the piano—and that's the way I slept.

The top of the piano became my dining table and my desk and even Linda's creative arranging couldn't make it look right, but I didn't care. I was nuts about my new piano and it didn't matter that in order to get out to the garden, you had to suck in your gut to get to the door.

A few months later, I heard about a one-bedroom apartment available directly across the street for not much more than what I was paying. I was feeling a little cramped and getting tired of sleeping under the piano, so I moved into the new apartment.

One day in October 1972 I was asked to write the melody for a Shasta Cola commercial. After recording the background music tracks, I waited to be part of the singing group. We had a great time that afternoon. The group consisted of my friend Melissa Manchester, who had worked with Bette as a Harlette for a few months, Valerie Simpson of Ashford and Simpson, who had written some of the most popular songs of our time, and Ron Dante, lead singer of the Archies, the group that recorded "Sugar, Sugar." Ron became a close friend and was later to become very important in my career.

After the session, Melissa and Ron and I went to lunch. I didn't know Ron, but we got along great during lunch. I told him that I was excited about some songs I had been writing and he asked me if he could hear them. After lunch we went back to my new apartment. He was enthusiastic about the songs and during the next few weeks, whenever we'd meet at jingle dates, we'd talk about my original material.

Linda and I became very close with Ron and his wife Penny, and after the New Year's Eve concert we all went to Jamaica for a few weeks in the sun. Ron would continue to talk about my songwriting. He was still excited about it and suggested that both of us go into a studio and record demos of the three songs I had played for him so that singers could hear them properly. I agreed, and when we returned to New York Ron and I booked a recording studio and co-produced demonstration records on three of my songs.

When it came time to put the lead vocals on, I asked him to do it. He said that it would be quicker if I did them since I knew the words. The songs we recorded were "I Am Your Child," "Sweet Life (Mamma Can You Hear Me)," and "One of These Days."

It was my second time singing in a professional surrounding and it felt just as weird as it did when I was singing "Amy" for Tony Orlando and Adrienne. When the engineer played back my vocals, I remember really hating the sound of my voice. To me, although it sounded sincere, it sounded too clean—so clean, you could eat off my voice. When we got to "Sweet Life," I rebelled. Here was a song I had always imagined should be sung by a soulful, gruff-voiced singer.

Just that weekend I had read an article about a singer who also wanted to rough up his voice and had discovered that the way to do it was to holler at the top of his lungs for fifteen minutes. I decided to try that approach. I went into the soundproof vocal booth, shut the door, and lit a cigarette. Then I started to holler at the top of my lungs. Ron and the engineer in the control room watched as I turned blue and red, my eyes bulging out as I screamed and screamed.

Fifteen minutes later, I emerged from the booth, sure that when I sang this time, I would sound like the soulful singer I wanted to be. But when I opened my mouth to sing, not only did I have hardly any voice, the voice I did have sounded more like Donald Duck than Ray Charles. We had to cancel the entire session until a few days later when my voice repaired itself.

When we were done with the demos, I called Miles Lourie, the attorney I had used to handle my Featherbed records, and asked him to show the songs to record companies for their artists. He said he would, and I went back to writing commercials and conducting for singers.

Then the most surprising thing happened.

I was walking in the door from taking Bagel for her morning walk, when the phone rang. It was Miles. "Hi. I just got off the phone with Irv Biegel, president of Bell Records," he told me.

"Yeah, and . . . ," I prompted.

"Well, he's heard your demonstration tape and told me what he thinks," he said.

"Yeah, and . . . ," I said again.

"Well, it's very interesting. I think you should come to my office and let me tell you in person," he said.

I couldn't imagine what he had to tell me, but I agreed and hopped in a taxi up to his office.

Miles Lourie had taste. In art, music, furniture, women. His office on Fifty-seventh Street reflected it. His secretary was very pretty and his offices were simple and stylish. He loved pre-Columbian art, and as I sat in front of his desk I was surrounded with these little ugly statues of men with gigantic penises and women with their breasts hanging to the ground.

This was Miles's turquoise period, too (remember that Indian turquoise stuff that was so popular in the seventies?). He himself was Turquoise City. His belt and his ring were made of turquoise. The stuff was around his neck and hanging from his wrists. There were big paperweights of it on his desk. The paintings hanging on the walls were abstract. You know, the kind of painting that you're sure your four-year-old nephew could paint, but you also know probably cost a fortune. I know I'm not describing anything tasteful, but take my word for it, it really was.

He was a tall man, kind of handsome. Although he tried his best to be lighthearted, he was possibly the most serious man I've ever met. And very smart.

Miles got right to the point, as usual. "Bell Records likes your tape," he said, lighting his pipe with that sweet-smelling cherry blend that I'll never forget.

"You mean they like the songs," I corrected him.

"No. They like the tape. They like your voice, they like you as a singer," he told me dead seriously.

I knew Miles wasn't joking.

"So what are you saying?" I asked him.

"They're offering you a record contract as a singer," he told me, puffing on his pipe.

I sat there stunned. Then I started to laugh.

"Well . . . I don't know what to say . . . I never really considered—" I stammered.

"Here's what I suggest," he told me. "They want to meet with you. Let's go hear what they have to say."

That sounded good. So the next afternoon, I met with Irv Biegel at Bell Records on West Fifty-seventh Street and Broadway.

Bell was a very happy record company. When you walked off the elevator there were framed colorful posters of their famous artists such as Tony Orlando and Dawn and Vicki Lawrence hanging on the walls staring at you. I felt very out of place, but the company bustled with excitement and enthusiasm and there was music coming out of offices up and down hallways. It was a sharp contrast to the quiet and serious feeling at Atlantic Records, four blocks away. Irv Biegel's door was open and he was on the phone. He motioned for us to come in and sit down.

He greeted us and told us that he wanted us to meet with his superior, Larry Utahl. So off we went to another office. This one was in the corner of the floor.

The corner office, I thought. Must be the Big Cheese.

He was.

The conversation was very flattering. They both liked the tape Ron and I had made. They especially liked "Sweet Life." They thought the songs had commercial potential and liked the sound of my voice.

At one point, Larry leaned over and looked at me intensely.

"Barry," he said, "I want you here at Bell Records. I love your songwriting. You are the next Burt Bacharach, *and* you can sing."

"I am? I can?"

"Yes. We believe in your talent and are offering you a singles deal," Irv said.

I floated out of his office on those words and in the elevator I joked to Miles, "Sign me up!"

Miles said, "Down, boy, haven't you ever had a compliment before? Why don't you go home and sleep on it. I'll call you in the morning," and we parted on the corner. I walked down Broadway with an idiotic grin on my face.

Miles was right in advising me to sleep on it. I did. I thought about it all night long. I phoned friends and talked to them about it. Ron, of course, was very excited. Everyone was. Everyone except me. By the next morning I had misgivings. I finally gave Miles the go-ahead to begin negotiations for my very own recording contract, but not because I wanted to begin a serious career as a singer. I was content with my developing career as a songwriter/arranger/conductor. The opportunities I had been given to perform had been pleasant, but they hadn't made me want to drop everything else. The prospect of becoming a recording artist and performer frightened me. I played a great piano when I was backing someone or leading the band, but when I was up front, I felt I was making millions of mistakes. I didn't sing badly in the studio or as part of the group, but solo, I thought I was awful. My voice cracked, I went out of tune, I'd forget the words. I didn't like the sound of my voice and never took singing seriously.

And as for performing, well, I had seen how difficult it was for all those clients of mine to get anywhere and how humiliating it was for them, to say nothing of Jeanne's struggles and Bette's frustrations. I mean, if Bette Midler, the greatest entertainer I had ever seen, was having trouble becoming recognized, what chance could I possibly have? And anyway, who needed it? Not me. I was happy in the background being supportive to the talents that needed me.

The reason I gave Miles permission to negotiate a recording deal for me was that I loved writing songs and I had loved my few experiences in the recording studio. I loved working with the musicians, the singers, the engineers. I loved hearing my music come to life, and a record contract would mean that I could do all the things I loved doing, even if it also meant that I had to be the lead singer.

Bell Records was offering me a singles deal, meaning they would only invest in a few single records, not an entire album. But during those first few days of conversations, they said they would be interested in an entire album. Since they had never seen me perform, they could not justify the investment of a big budget in someone whose claim to fame was as Bette Midler's pianist and the guy who wrote the Stridex pimple cream commercial.

Making my very own album was becoming more and more tempting to me. It was so close I could nearly touch it, and since Bette was on a vacation with no end in sight, I decided that I would attempt to put together some sort of presentation to prove to Bell Records that I could put on an entertaining show of my own. There was only one minor problem. I had never done it before.

But that didn't stop me.

Since I had made friends with many studio musicians, I put together a band of the finest talent in New York. I paid for a great sound system, hired Bette's Harlettes as background singers, and rehearsed for two weeks. I reasoned that the music would be so strong and solid that the executives at Bell would never even know that I had no idea what I was doing as a performer.

Finally, I was able to arrange "Could It Be Magic" the way I had always heard it in my head. I prepared "I Am Your Child" and "Sweet Life," "One of These Days" and "Sweetwater Jones." I did a rockier version of "Friends" as a tribute to Bette, Ron did an updated version of his "Sugar, Sugar," and for the "novelty" spot I learned the old Lambert-Hendricks-Ross jazz piece "Cloudburst." I also threw together a medley of commercials that all of us had done. I booked this showcase at the Continental Baths.

We put a small ad in the paper so there would be more than just our friends and family. I expected a few hundred people. Nearly seven hundred showed up. I was shocked. So was Bell Records!

The night of the show I remember waiting in the wings trembling and thinking, This is like going to my own execution or something!

My heart flopped around inside my chest and I had trouble breathing. When the Harlettes introduced me, I ran from the wings to the piano bench as quickly as I could. I had no idea what to do with my legs, but there was safety sitting at the piano!

I really don't remember too much of that night. It's all a blur. I only know that as a performer, I was very uncomfortable. Standing on the stage, I felt as if I had two left feet. I stammered when I spoke, the spotlights blinded me, and I got hoarse after the third song.

But the reaction of the crowd was enthusiastic. Even my harshest critic, Marty, came back and told me that I had moved him with "Could It Be Magic." And the commercials medley brought the house down.

The next day, I woke up with a hangover from the celebration of the night before. I was sure glad *that* was over with. I poured myself a cup of coffee and went out on the terrace. The phone rang. It was Miles.

Bell Records had loved what they had seen and had offered me the album deal I wanted. I couldn't believe what I was hearing.

I hung up the phone and sat on the couch with my empty coffee cup. Bagel sat at my feet. I was being offered a new career. A new life. Did I really want it? Did I really want all the pressure and responsibility that would come along with it?

The times I had sung with Jeanne or before Bette began her show had been amusing. I had never wanted to become a performer or a singer. I wanted to make music, I wanted to be in music, but being a performer had never crossed my mind. Now here I was being offered the opportunity to make my own album—something that other people would kill for.

I decided to turn the offer down. I felt I was too old to begin another career. I was doing just fine as a musician, and this was just too big a responsibility to undertake.

I went to one last meeting with Irv and Larry. During the meeting they told me how ecstatic they were over the show I had put together. They knew I was shaky on stage, but they believed in me as a songwriter, singer, and performer. They predicted such huge success for me that even I began to become a little excited about performing and singing. I mean, the reaction of the crowd at the baths had been so positive. How could I turn this opportunity down?

So I agreed to make an album for them and undertake a small tour of clubs across the country to promote it. My friends were amazed and delighted, and my clients were stunned.

Then the phone rang.

"Hello Manilla? It's me, Bette. I'm back. Whatcha been up to?"

"Not much, Bette, but we have to talk."

"We sure do. We're going on tour again. Get out the music and the luggage."

The Red Rocks

Bette said, "But you have to do it, Barry. I insist that you use the second half of my show to promote your first album. You know how I love to hear you sing, and how much I adore your songs. I think that you're ready to do this as a performer, and, just think, since you'll still be conducting for me, you can use my band and still receive the generous salary I pay you. And by the way, I think that your idea of wearing all white is great! You're gonna knock 'em dead, Bar!"

And then I woke up.

In reality, when I told Bette I was going to make an album, she said, "Why?"

"Well—" I began.

She said, "Oh, you're going to make an album of piano music!"

"No, I'm going to sing."

"But you *can't* sing."

"Well, the record company thinks different."

"Barry, you're not going to record the one about the stallions meeting the sun, are you?" She was talking about "Could It Be Magic." "They'll laugh at you, Barry. Take my advice, just play the piano."

Words from The Divine One.

*   *   *

When Bette called and told me to get ready to go on tour with her, I found myself in a dilemma. Should I undertake the small club tour to promote the album I had agreed to do? After all, I had promised Bell Records I would support my album and they were expecting me to honor my word. But I had invested three years of hard work in Bette's career and I wasn't ready to leave her. She also asked me to co-produce her second album with Arif Mardin, a top producer at Atlantic Records.

The tour she was about to embark upon was going to be her first major national tour. It would last for four months, ending in New York at the Palace Theater on Broadway. She was the hottest star in the country and would be playing in front of thousands of people each night. It was important to me that she be presented perfectly. I wanted the music, the arrangements, the band, the background singers, the whole show to reflect all the effort I had put in for three years. Protecting Bette's music was more important to me than my own project.

I finally came up with a compromise. I would ask Bette and Aaron if I could open the second half of her show, thereby promoting my album and remaining on her tour to oversee the music. Neither Miles nor Bell Records was thrilled with my decision, but they saw how important it was to me to finish what I had begun with Bette.

It wasn't easy convincing Bette and Aaron to let me open the second half of her show and still conduct and music-direct her concerts. But they finally came around and agreed to take a chance on me.

I spent the months of June and July balancing the recording of my first album with producing Bette's second album and rehearsing and helping to create her show. It was an exciting time. Ron Dante and I had signed a partnership agreement as co-producers of my albums. I had hired Miles Lourie, my attorney, to be my manager. Dick Fox, an agent from William Morris who had signed Jeanne and me, was now my agent. The solo career that I had hesitated about was actually beginning to happen. Now

I had a manager, an agent, and a record co-producer, and I was even interviewing press agents!

I loved going to the recording studio each morning. I'd meet Ron in the coffee shop and we'd work on my songs with the musicians all afternoon. Then I'd run to Bette's recording studio and work with Arif and Bette way into the night. At the end of July Bette's concert rehearsals began, and I'd spend hours creating the charts and rehearsing everyone.

We began the tour one very humid weekend in August. I left Bagel with Sheilah and hoped Bagel wouldn't forget me or get too lonely. On the plane, I kept thinking that I absolutely did not believe that I was doing this. I asked the representatives from Bell Records not to come to the first performance because I knew I would be nervous enough without knowing they were in the audience.

We started the tour at the Merriwether Post Pavilion outside Washington, D.C. It seated five thousand people under a shell and there was room for ten thousand people on an enormous expanse of lawn if it was a sellout. We were sold out. Fifteen thousand people and my first time out.

Sound checks are always rushed, and because this was the first performance, it was even more chaotic. So much so that there was no time for a sound check for my three songs. The piano was far back into the band, and I knew that half the audience wouldn't be able to see me when it came time for my spot. Aaron and I had an argument in front of everyone, but finally he agreed to have the stagehands move the piano out during the intermission.

It was the beginning of what was to be a constant battle between my twenty-minute spot and Bette's entire show. It wasn't that anyone was against me, it was merely that I was the only one looking out for me. The band, the Harlettes, and even Bette, for that matter, were all encouraging, but I was really on my own.

Although our first act was shaky, the crowd loved it, and by the time we got to "Do You Wanna Dance," the last song of the first act, they were all on their feet, screaming.

During the intermission, I changed from the casual outfit I wore as Bette's conductor to the all-white outfit I would wear to sing in. I must have finished an entire pack of cigarettes during those twenty minutes, I was so terrified. My stomach landed in my throat and I actually felt faint.

Linda had flown in during the afternoon and was frightened at how pale I looked. When I held her hand, I squeezed so hard I hurt her.

I went into Bette's dressing room to check in and she wished me good luck.

During the first act, the sun was still out and I could actually see the massive audience. There were so many people you couldn't see where they ended. Thank God the sun had gone down by the time I did my spot, because with four huge spotlights on me, all I could see was the first few rows.

When the house lights went down and I was supposed to make my entrance, I stood there in the wings, frozen. Wuzzy, our stage manager, had to physically push me out onto the stage. I went through my three songs as though I were sleepwalking. I think I had about as much charisma as a fire plug. The response was decent, though.

There was an orchestra pit right in front of the stage, and no one was allowed in it, but of course Linda sweet-talked a guard into letting her stay in it for my set. So there she was taking pictures like crazy, smiling at me and giving me a shot of confidence.

Back at the hotel, Linda and I talked way into the night about what I was doing. I was so unsure. What could this terrifying experience possibly do for me? I loved conducting for Bette, but my ten minutes were not enjoyable.

Linda left the next day and the tour continued. I actually began to loosen up during the next few days, and my spot became bearable for me, but I felt very much alone during that entire tour. And I was. I just kept doing my spot every night. Some nights the piano was so far back into the band I would have to get up and physically push it out a bit so that some of the audience could see me. Aaron would always forget to give me a sound check and I'd have to remind him continually that I was singing too. Bette's co-writer, Bill Hennessey, and all the band and singers were always sympathetic, but they couldn't really help.

Bette's audiences were never rude to me—except for one never-to-be-forgotten raspberry given by an asshole in the front row. Otherwise they were always polite. But as the tour chugged along, I began seriously to question the sense of what I was doing. Why was I putting myself through this? Singing three songs each night to an audience that really wanted to see Bette began to seem foolish. No one involved in the show really gave a shit about my music except me, and the business boys and my friends were back in New York working on their own things. Moreover, the act of performing was nerve-racking for me. I had almost made up my mind to stop doing my spot in the show—but one night in Denver, something happened.

We were staying at a very nice hotel that overlooked the city and the surrounding mountains. The sky was clear and the air and weather were beautiful.

When I got to the gig, I discovered we were playing in a place called the Red Rocks Amphitheater. It's carved into a mountain and it was the most beautiful place I'd ever seen.

We couldn't use any backdrops because of the wind. We had just the natural backdrop of the most enormous mountain I'd ever seen. And the sky. Very blue, high up in Denver.

They had let the audience in all day long, because it was a public park. The audience sat and watched the sound check and applauded, and they were so friendly with their Kentucky Fried Chicken and picnic baskets and wine. I sat in the audience for a while chatting with a few people and feeling not so alone.

That night, during the first act, Bette had a horrible time. The sound of the applause would go straight into the air, and she couldn't hear it at all. It's really hard to work to a crowd when you can't hear their reaction, especially if you're counting on laughs for your timing.

During the intermission she was a wreck. I went to her dressing room and asked if I could help. She just shook her head. I felt so bad for her, but there was nothing I could possibly do. I suggested she relax on stage and not push so hard. I felt they liked it, but they were just laid-back. After all, that setting was so peaceful.

As I stood in the wings, waiting to go on to do my spot, I remember I just couldn't get over the enormous beauty of the place. I kept thinking about Brooklyn and where I had come from, and then I'd look up at the sky and the gorgeous Red Rock Mountains and I felt good. And I felt so small. And suddenly I felt so lucky.

Bette had recommended that I not sing "Could It Be Magic." She felt it took too long to build as a performance piece and that the audience wouldn't sit still through it. She suggested I not take the chance of losing them, and I had agreed with her. I hadn't been singing it on the tour, but I had been rehearsing it with the band and the singers (they loved it), and it sounded great.

I love "Could It Be Magic." It's probably the song I'm proudest of to this day. And right there, in the middle of all that majesty, I decided I was going to do it—for me. Not for the audience. Not for the record company. For me. I told Wuzzy to inform the staff and the band that I would be changing my last song. I checked with Bette and it was fine with her, but she was in such a state that she probably would have agreed to anything.

The reaction to my first two songs was enthusiastic. I could feel that this laid-back audience was with me. But as I sang "Could It Be Magic" I forgot about them. I sang it to the sky and to the mountains and to Brooklyn, and I was lost. Lost in the song. And for a brief moment I felt a glimmer of the euphoria a performer can feel when he becomes one with the work. For a brief moment I understood why Jeanne and Bette and all those singers I played for put up with all the bullshit. It felt so good I was shocked.

When I was done, I took my little bow and tried to start Bette's entrance music, but they wouldn't stop applauding. So I got up from the piano again, and they started yelling. And then, through the spotlights, I saw people moving in the audience. I figured that they were coming back from the rest rooms—but they were giving me a standing ovation. My first.

What a Ride!

My job on Bette's 1973 national tour was music director. I tried not to place too much importance on my own twenty-minute spot. I tried to do my job just as I always had. I'd worry about Bette and her show, I'd be there for the problems of the band and the Harlettes. All the gossip and talk revolved around Bette and Aaron and the show.

It was the hottest tour on the road and there wasn't a seat to be had. Bette was on the cover of every magazine and newspaper. But beginning with my performance of "Could It Be Magic" at the Red Rocks, something happened to my twenty-minute set and even I couldn't ignore it.

The reaction to my little spot began to get stronger. When people would describe what it felt like in the audience, I'd minimize the importance. "Oh, they were just being polite," I'd say. "They were so stoned, they probably thought Bette had learned to play piano." I'd laugh it off.

But then the reviewers began to be very enthusiastic. One said, "Could It Be Magic" was "immortal." I was shocked and thrilled. I'd never really considered being reviewed at all, but when they began to be so positive, I'd look forward to reading the morning paper.

Linda met me in Hawaii for Bette's "hometown" concert. It was the first time I tried to mix business with pleasure. It didn't work. I learned during that week that being on the road is just like being at an office. On the road, even though you only "work" for three hours a night, your mind is on the show all day long. The talk is of the show, the people around you work in the show. It's impossible for someone who is not part of the show to feel comfortable.

By the time we arrived in Los Angeles, Linda and I weren't speaking. She left days earlier than planned, and I was very sad when she did. Once again, as had happened with Susan, it didn't seem as if I could blend the music with my personal life.

After she left, I felt very blue. I went to the lobby and bought *Billboard* magazine, and staring at me was me. There was a full-page ad for my album. I was so shocked I began to shake.

My album came out and there was hardly any negative feedback. I'd phone Miles, Ron, Linda, Marty, and my mother and they raved about the album and would always have someone's positive reaction to tell me about. I was beginning tentatively to pick up on all of the excitement about my set. The audience's reaction was encouraging, the band and the Harlettes loved it, and even the small mentions I had gotten in the papers were positive.

But that changed in San Francisco. After a triumphant show there, Bette and Aaron took the whole troupe out to dinner. At two A.M. the *Chronicle* came out and Bill Hennessey stood up and read aloud what we all thought was going to be a rave review by John Wasserman. It was. But only for Bette:

> And lastly, Barry Manilow has got to go. Somewhere along the line, someone made the mistake of telling him he could sing. Towards this end, he has a new album out on Bell and treated us to four solo numbers to open the second half.
>
> Manilow, who has his hair done at the "Clip and Snip Poodle Salon," apparently thinks he's a potential star. To underscore this hallucination, he has a piano stand-in, like a

movie star has a lighting and blocking stand-in. This fellow comes out first and hits several notes on the piano to make sure it's working.

He swept out onstage in an all white Nehru jumpsuit. His opening number guaranteed instant obscurity and he went downhill from there. . . . Then this second rate singer dared to sing "Cloudburst," the Pointer Sisters hit. The third tune, "Could It Be Magic," was pathetic. The fourth was titled, apparently, "Mama Can You Hear Me?" which needs no comment save Mama's which is, "Yes, son, and you should wash your mouth out with Black Flag."

Well, that sure brought down the party a peg. It was so horrible, no one could even make a joke about it. I tried to pretend it didn't matter, but I couldn't. We all sipped our drinks in silence. Robin Grean, one of the Harlettes, held my hand, and Charlotte Crosley, another Harlette, joked feebly about how Wasserman was probably having trouble with his spike heels last night. Bette and Aaron didn't say anything.

My first negative review had come at a time in my career when I was the most vulnerable. Besides being humiliating, the review just reaffirmed all of my own deep, dark insecurities. Who was I kidding? I wasn't a singer or a performer. I had known that all along and this reviewer had found me out.

I didn't sleep at all that night. The next day I got phone calls from each member of the band and the Harlettes, trying to cheer me up. They were so sweet.

This experience with discouraging reviews was only the beginning. For all my coming career, it would be an up-and-down relationship with the press. My reviews would go from being glowing to mortifying. Never in between.

I never got used to it. I hated it when they'd crucify me. I always felt reviewers should feel a sense of regret when they pan something. But my pans were usually done with a sense of relish, as if, when the reviewers left my shows, they were thinking: "Aha! *Now* I can use that real nasty sentence I've been saving in my top drawer for five years!" When the reviews were raves, I didn't believe I was that good, and when they were lousy, I didn't believe I was that lousy, although I usually tended to side with the negative ones.

I seriously considered throwing in the towel in San Francisco. But my responsibility to Bell Records, to my album, to Ron, to Miles (who was giving up his legal practice to manage me), and to my collaborators was too strong. I took a deep breath and went back into the ring. I would see this tour through and when it was over, my singing career would be too. Then I'd be able to get back to my life as a musician.

Despite the bad review, the reaction to my spot in the show kept getting stronger and stronger. Soon, representatives from Bell Records were showing up and wining and dining me. The press agent I had hired was getting me interviews, and I began to feel important, which is dangerous.

The people who were telling me how great I was were only doing their jobs, but I needed to hear their encouraging words and I began to believe them. I think that the fact I was still the music director stopped me from losing my grip on reality. My career up until that point had been filled with responsibilities and still was. Also, the continuing responsibility for the band, the arrangements, and the entire evening's music helped to balance the dizzying reaction to my own segment.

But with the first hint of success, I found myself surrounded with temptations and they were very enticing. I was offered drugs, booze, and as much sex as I could imagine. While on the road I saw people who were into drugs and I always felt sad watching them get wasted. I would think, I hope to God it doesn't happen to me. The promoters could get anything you wanted. It was very dangerous out there.

My first album began to show encouraging signs, especially in the cities the tour came to. In Jacksonville, Florida, Irv Biegel, vice president of Bell, flew in to see my set. Bette was brilliant, as usual, and the audience received my set enthusiastically. Miles and I went out to dinner with him, and once again he offered support of my own tour.

I was grateful, but I was still hesitant. My own tour? I wanted it and I didn't want it. By agreeing to do it, I'd be committing to a performing career. What if I was successful? What if I wasn't successful?

The album hadn't even made the Top 100. I wasn't really enjoying the performances. Why would I want to continue a solo performing career? It seemed that everyone was excited about me—except me.

We opened in New York at the Palace Theater in December of 1973. Bette had broken all existing attendance records and scalpers were getting hundreds of dollars apiece for tickets.

Bette had worked harder than I'd ever seen her work during the Palace engagement, and she was exhausted. She had decided that this engagement was to be her last for a long time. The audiences went crazy for her. They liked me too. Bell Records sent everyone to see me.

The reviews for me were hot and cold. *Billboard, Cashbox, Variety,* and even the *New York Times* all predicted great things for me. One magazine called me the "next Burt Bacharach," *Rolling Stone* called me a "hack that had grabbed on to the right skirt." Up and down, up and down.

I had my own dressing room at the Palace and it was exciting. I invited Larry and Fred and their wives. All the people I had played piano for came to see the show, as well as my friends from CBS and *The Drunkard.*

Ron and I were already discussing the next album and Miles and Dick Fox were making plans for my tour. I was getting a lot of attention and feeling like a star.

"Hey Fred, remember how I couldn't get dates in high school?" I whispered to him on the way out of the theater one night. "Watch this."

And we walked out the stage door to screams from dozens of girls waiting for me.

All this joy was counterbalanced, because Grampa went into the hospital that week. He was dying. When Gramma and Mom came to see me perform on opening night, it was sad for all of us.

He died on December 15, in the middle of the engagement. When I sang "I Am Your Child" that night, I sang it for Grampa. He would have been so proud to have seen me singing on the stage of the Palace, just four blocks from the "Record-Your-Own-Voice" booth.

The funeral the next day was terrible. It was gray and it rained. Everyone cried and our tears blended in with the raindrops. We stood while the Rabbi moaned and wailed for twenty minutes and made things worse. I had to support Edna, who was on the verge of fainting. When the Rabbi instructed me to throw dirt on Grampa's coffin because I was the youngest male, I wouldn't do it. He insisted and I walked away, letting my cousin Dennis do it.

It was my first experience with death. Grampa's dying was hard enough to take, but the ritual at the gravesite was barbaric. I know Grampa would have hated it. I vowed then that I would never make people go through that for me.

I try to block out that last gloomy association with Grampa. He was alive, the most alive man I ever knew. He was funny and witty and kind. That's my Gramps. That's who I'll always sing to. That's who I'll always remember.

The tour had finally ended and I invited everyone back to my apartment for a final good-bye. During the party, Bette and I sat and had a quiet glass of wine in my bedroom. We both knew this was probably the end of our collaboration together. We toasted, but she looked tired and sad.

I said, "I'm only a phone call away if you ever need me, you know that."

"Thanks, Manilla," she said. She looked at me and smiled a sad smile. "It was a great ride, wasn't it?"

It had been a great ride. I consider those explosive days while I was with Bette some of the most profound times of my life.

I think that what I learned most from her was commitment. Before I met Bette, I thought I was the only one in the world who considered music important enough to give up a normal life for. My passion for music had obliterated everything in its path, and there was no one in my life who had come close to doing what I had done.

But Bette had that same sense of commitment about everything she did. She charged into professional and personal projects with a determination that was frightening. Honesty and commitment were sacred to her, and I excused her every eccentricity. Instead of rebelling or quitting I could only sit back in awe and watch her go after her goals.

I miss her now. I don't miss the craziness, but I miss watching and learning from her. I'm grateful to her for the chance she gave me. Besides opening doors for me, Bette taught me one thing I feel has made a giant difference in my life:

Commitment justifies living.

The Performing Adventures

A Star Is (Reluctantly) Born

Preparing to go on my first solo tour was not an enjoyable prospect for me. I really wasn't thrilled about going back on the road—back to the same little clubs I had just come from with Bette and, before that, with Jeanne. I wasn't thrilled about having to be the opening act for some comedian, and most of all I wasn't thrilled about having to perform. But the possibility of writing songs and making more albums was very tempting, and besides, I had a responsibility to Bell Records, Miles, and Ron. Now I also had co-writers and a small staff of people depending on me.

I began creating a show that was musically solid. I reasoned that I would create such an entertaining set that even if I fell apart on stage, which I was certain I would do, nobody would notice.

I bought flashy costumes for myself and the group. I came up with lines and jokes for the time between songs that fell somewhere between Bette's sarcasm and my optimism and insecurity. Having been with Bette for years, I naturally picked up on her energy trip, which was augmented by my own nervousness and manic New Yorkese.

During our open dress rehearsal a few days before we opened in Boston, I mumbled my way through the introductions. I spoke

151

too fast and stumbled over words. When I watched the videotape playback Marty had made, I cringed at my performance, but the music was admittedly powerful and solid.

The show cost a lot of money to mount and keep on the road. The small clubs were only paying me the bare minimum, and I began to go through Bell's generous advance very quickly. I wanted a first-class show and I decided to pay for it myself. I began to go through my own savings even quicker.

My first night as a soloist was March 4, 1974. We opened at a club called Paul's Mall in Boston, and it was pretty bad. The club was a real dump. The ceiling was extremely low and there were holes in it. It rained on our opening night and water kept dripping on all of us.

I was the opening act for Freddie Hubbard, a black jazz trumpet player. Smart booking, huh? I tried to keep a positive attitude and told myself that it would be good experience for me, if only because it would be the worst booking for a while. It couldn't *get* any worse.

There were no dressing rooms in the club. The band and singers and I found an empty, dusty room with old crates and planks of wood next to the rest rooms, and we all dressed in there. Before we went onstage, I stood in a circle with them. We held hands and gave each other good energy, then we tore out onto the stage with big grins on our faces.

The small audience just sat there. I sped through everything. It was awful. I went to bed that night feeling terrible. I prayed that the next night would be better.

The act didn't seem funky enough to me, especially my part. I wanted to sound soulful, but I opened my mouth and it came out like Pat Boone. I found performing very difficult. I didn't like it. I hoped the audiences and critics would see through to the music. I knew the music was good.

I also realized that anyone in the audience who had come to see me expected a campy Bette Midler–type act. I would begin to try to give it to them and then I'd hate myself for it. I was very confused.

"Well," I told myself, "I'll just keep on truckin' and if it doesn't work, I don't think I'll die. I can always go back to writing commercials. State Farm is always there."

The second night at Paul's Mall got worse. All the reviewers were there and the show was awful. The sound system was all screwed up, the audience talked through the songs, and my voice gave out halfway through.

We found out that Freddie Hubbard refused to go on with me as his opening act. He said he wouldn't follow someone who plays commercials. Beginning on the next night, we did the first show and he did the second show.

"This really stinks," I told Miles on the phone. "I want to go home."

It was humiliating. I couldn't look at the band any more. It was my fault the audience wasn't reacting. The more the audience sat there, the more I retreated into the piano keyboard. It was all wrong. I told Miles to cancel the rest of the tour, but he begged me to wait until the end of the week. I didn't think I would survive.

The third night was even worse. We tried to do an hour and a half because Hubbard wouldn't go on, and it was disaster. I told Miles I wanted out. I didn't want to do this. I began packing, but he convinced me to do the weekend and then we'd talk about it. I hated it.

I was so sure I was going home the next week that I began calling commercial agents and booking dates. But when I hung the phone up, I felt like such a quitter. I didn't have the nerve to phone Marty or Adrienne or Linda to tell them I was quitting.

When we did the show that night, I decided I'd had enough of feeling sorry for myself and blaming the audience. This was a job I had committed to, and even if it wasn't my favorite thing to do, I was going to do it well, goddammit. Instead of hunkering over the keyboard and concentrating only on the music, like my favorite jazz musicians, I looked out at the crowd. The spotlight was too bright and I couldn't really see anyone. But I imagined one person sitting there. And I sang to that person. Sometimes it was Linda. Sometimes it was Grampa. Sometimes it was just a good friend. Instead of laughing with the Harlettes and the band,

I walked to the edge of the stage and spoke to the audience. Instead of singing everything from the piano stool, I dragged the stool to the edge of the stage and sat and sang "One of These Days" to them.

The reaction was noticeably different. The audience seemed to react to the songs more than they had before, and we even did an encore. But on the whole the experience at Paul's Mall was very depressing. I'll never forget trying to hold the small audience's attention during "I Am Your Child," while fighting the noise of the bartender's blender.

We opened at the Bijou Café in Philadelphia the next week. After a few shows with many empty seats, the reviews came out and, surprisingly, they were glowing. By the weekend, business was booming.

I brought in an expensive sound system and hired a sound mixer. I also brought in sophisticated stage lighting.

Shockingly, it was a total turnaround from Boston. We were sold out on the weekend and the crowds became very enthusiastic. The band and the girls and the music were great, but the biggest surprise was that the audiences seemed to like *me*, not just the show. I was sure they liked me because they could see that I didn't have any idea what I was doing.

"There must be *something* that they're relating to," I told Marty on the phone.

"It's probably the lights," he told me.

"Yeah, that's it," I agreed.

I'd sit in my hotel room dreading having to go to the club. Even though the crowds were now on my side, I still felt terrified.

I did my first radio interview in Philly with Ed Sciaky on WMMR and he told everyone to watch out for me—that I was going to be very big. I thanked him and I was very happy, but inside I thought, "Me? Big?" He played cuts from the album and went on and on about "Could It Be Magic."

*   *   *

The tour continued to draw audiences. We played Chicago, Atlanta, Memphis, and New York. I was still determined to put on a first-class show, even though we were playing less-than-first-class places. The owners of the clubs would stand, gaping, as my road crew dragged in the expensive sound system and lighting equipment to set up shows.

The act got stronger and the reaction was terrific. I was trying really hard to get this performing thing down. I called rehearsals all the time. Since I was my own music director, I'd invent new medleys and arrangements. I changed the show constantly. I worked at it all day long in my hotel room. I'd talk to myself in the mirror, making believe I was talking to that night's audience. One time the maid walked in while I was introducing my make-believe band to the bathtub and I'm sure she thought I was nuts.

One night, as one of the girls was singing, I looked at her skirt and I decided that we needed more sparkle. The next day, I went out and bought six Ronko rhinestone studders and we all sat and studded our costumes with rhinestones.

By the time we got to New York, I was tired. The Bottom Line was sold out, but I was hoarse and tired. The newspapers were encouraging (that would be the last time *that* happened!) and, of all things, groupies began to appear. When I looked out into the audience, I saw lots of teeny-boppers that looked as if they had made a wrong turn at a Donny Osmond concert! They came clutching roses and stuffed dolls.

"Tom Jones gets underpants and hotel-room keys thrown at him," I moaned to the band. "I get Snoopy dolls."

They'd line up during the day and fill the club at night. They'd scream the way the girls did for Sinatra and Elvis. None of us knew why, least of all me. There were lots of things I'd hoped to become, but a teenage idol?

The Bottom Line in New York was the end of that first tour. What a dramatic ending! On Thursday night, before a sold-out audience, I opened my mouth and nothing came out. Nothing. I looked at the audience and smiled and mouthed, "Nothing seems to want to come out."

Some girl yelled, "That's okay, just stand there!"

I played an instrumental version of "Could It Be Magic" and gave the rest of the show to the girls and the band and cut the last few songs.

I went to the doctor the next day. He looked down my throat and told me a vocal cord had hemorrhaged. He shot me up with medicine and we canceled the next night's show. But I was back for the weekend and finished the tour.

I was excited, thrilled, confused, tired, and windblown. This experiment as a performer seemed to want to work, but I didn't know what to make of it.

Closing night, when the girls announced my name to start the show, the whole audience gave me a standing ovation as I came onstage. My mother was in the audience and told me she thought there was a fire and started to run for the exit. She couldn't figure out why everyone was standing up.

Neither could I, Mom, neither could I.

Mandy

Larry Utahl, president of Bell Records, was out, and Clive Davis, ex-president of Columbia Records, was in. He'd been out of the business for a few years and there had been rumors he was going to be coming back, but no one knew where. Now we knew where.

Clive was coming back into the record business with a vengeance. He was determined to show the world not only that he had been wronged by Columbia Records, but that he could run a record company without having a huge parent company like CBS get in his way.

He dropped just about every artist on the Bell roster. He would have gladly dropped me too, because he didn't like my first album. But two things stopped him: I was in the middle of making my second album and had already spent money on it; and everyone in the company believed in me.

The name of the company was changed from Bell to Arista, and I was sad to see Larry and Irv go because they had become friends. But most of all their leaving made me nervous about my future as a record artist. Clive had not yet made up his mind about me, so I continued making my second album. I knew exactly what I wanted the album to sound like. I wanted it to be smart, I wanted it to be musical and inventive, I wanted to say things that affected people. Marty and I wrote "The Two of Us," about an unhappy married couple, and Enoch Anderson and I wrote "Sandra," about a housewife. I tackled "Avenue C," the Count Basie monster. "It's a Miracle," written about my time on Bette's tour, sounded very danceable. I knew I didn't want an album of little jingle-y tunes.

I agreed to perform one more show with my old group in New York at the Schaefer Concert in Central Park. Clive came down to check me out, and after the show he came backstage and told me he was happy to have me on the label.

I was surprised at what he looked like. He had a very hip reputation. He had been the one who had signed Janis Joplin, Blood, Sweat and Tears, Dylan, and Sly and the Family Stone, so I naturally thought I was going to meet some hippy-dippy jive-talking guy. But he was the total opposite. Serious, balding, and soft spoken, he looked more like a banker than a music man.

I was relieved he hadn't dropped me from the label. I loved the album I was making. "Home Again," written by Marty and me, was wonderful to record, and "I Want to Be Somebody's Baby," written by Enoch Anderson and me, was exciting to play and sing. Plus my responsibilities had multiplied once again. I had already hired a band, girl singers, and a crew. The tour was being booked and I already owed people money.

When we were nearly done recording, I decided to show Clive our product.

Ron and Miles and I stepped out of the elevator to the offices that had been Bell Records. There were still the framed posters of the company's big stars staring at us opposite the elevators, but somehow the feeling had become more subdued. It had become much more of a serious record company practically overnight.

We were guided into his office, the same office where Irv Biegel and Larry Utahl had flattered and convinced me into signing a deal with them less than a year before. The office was filled with photos of Clive and some of the legends in the business. Janis, hugging him, stared down at me as I sat in front of his desk; Paul Simon shook hands with him to my right; and Sly and Clive laughed behind the desk. It was a little intimidating, but I didn't care. I could see a skinny place on the wall where a photo of Clive and me would fit perfectly. I believed in my new album.

He was polite about it, and very honest. He thought the album was nice, but he was looking for hits. He told me I was a very strong performer, but that I'd need hits to sell records. Ron and Miles said that they thought "It's a Miracle" could be a smash. Clive wasn't sure.

While he listened to "Home Again," I told him I thought that ballads were my strong point. "Clive," I said as the record played, "if I'm ever going to have a hit, it's going to be with a ballad."

When we left his office, I was a little confused.

Clive had talked about "hit songs" and "hit singles." He was looking for those monster hit singles that are played on the radio all day long. An album can be filled with fine songs and productions, but they'll never be heard unless the record company can release one of those songs, a single, put it on a 45-rpm record, and make sure the record is played and sold all day long. Usually kids in their teens buy singles.

A single is successful when it is "commercial."

I found out that a commercial record means a record that appeals to the broadest market, the largest number of people—not necessarily that which is best. With a commercial record, the ingredients push the right buttons.

So I went back to the drawing board and tried to write hit songs. I'd hardly ever listened to the Top 40 radio. So I turned on my radio and listened to what the kids were buying. I found out that the number-one record in the country was a thing called "The Streak," a song about naked people running around.

I didn't have a prayer.

It was a big shock to me and to my friends to digest what Clive was saying. For years, I had been convinced that we were writing quality songs and potential hit songs. The heads of Bell Records had invested a lot of money in my first album and tour and were still committed to supporting my next tour. Bette's audiences had stood and cheered for "Could It Be Magic." People wept over "I Am Your Child." Even the reviews had suggested that I had a promising future as a songwriter.

Now my future seemed to be hanging on teenagers reacting to my "hit songs." I went to work and wrote and wrote. One day Clive called to tell me he had heard a song that he thought had all the ingredients of a hit song. It was called "Brandy."

It was a strange phone call and I didn't know exactly how to respond because I was supposed to be the songwriter. Yet here was the president of my record company, whose support I needed, saying I should sing another songwriter's song. I told him to send it over and I'd listen to it.

I sat down on my sofa and Bagel came over and sat at my feet. I knew this was an important decision. Although I didn't know it at the time, this decision would affect my entire life.

"Well, now . . . what would Laura Nyro do?" I asked myself. I knew what she'd do. She'd tell him no thanks.

What would Paul Simon do? I knew what he'd do too. He'd tell Clive he wasn't interested.

What would Elton John do? Same thing.

What should I do? I should tell him thanks, but I'm really not interested in that kind of success. I'd rather do it with my own material, even if it doesn't go all the way to the top.

But did I? No.

And that was the beginning of a frustrating and infuriating problem, and, I found out years later, one that wasn't unique to me.

When I heard the demonstration record, the arranger/producer part of me could see how to make it interesting and powerful. And that excited me. If I were doing that job for another singer, there would have been no problem. But since it was going to represent me out there in the world, I hesitated for days before I came to a decision.

"Well," I told myself, "I'll book a band and some studio time and see what I can do with it. I don't *have* to put it out, but how will I ever know if I don't try?" You can convince yourself to do anything if you really want to, you know.

The truth was I needed Clive Davis's support and I reasoned that if I recorded something he was excited about, I'd get it. I ran into the same problem with each record album: my own music versus Clive's discoveries. Sometimes it was funny, sometimes it was sad, most times it was damn frustrating.

The demonstration record of "Brandy" was a cute, up-tempo rock song. Clive was nuts about it and told me that with the right treatment, it could be a hit record. I really didn't get it, but his enthusiasm was so infectious I decided to try to record the song just like the demonstration record. I reasoned that beauty is in the ear of the beholder.

When I sang it at home, I felt awkward. I hadn't written or even found it, and when I tried to sing it the bright tempo bothered me. I played it slowly and it felt better, but what did I know?

We spent a frustrating evening in the recording studio that night. Ronnie and I knew how to make good-sounding records, but neither of us felt very much at all for this song. We worked for hours trying to copy the demo and eventually added different elements. By nine P.M. we were beginning to get used to it. Then Clive showed up.

When we played it for him, he hated it. He couldn't tell me what he didn't like about it. Ronnie kept turning knobs on the control board and Michael Delugg, our new engineer, did everything he could. I finally asked Clive to come into the studio with me. I sat down at the piano and Clive and Ron sat around the piano.

I said, "Clive, I've been playing this all day long. Let me show you something." I played him the slow, ballad version of "Brandy." He had his eyes closed and he was swaying; I could swear I heard him moaning. When I finished he said, "That's it. Do it like that."

I called the band back in and we did it slow. We changed the title to "Mandy."

Working with Clive was frustrating but exciting. I felt as if he knew what he wanted but just couldn't express himself technically or musically. Most of all, I liked him. He was very intense. He wouldn't settle. He didn't "yes" me, as people were beginning to do. He fought. I wished he heard hits in my own songs, but I liked him.

Ron and I finished recording my second album and I began rehearsing for the upcoming tour. I was crazy about every song on the album except "Mandy." I mean, it was nice, but it was just another pretty ballad.

Clive, on the other hand, was nuts about it. He called me and told me it was "a career-making record." I didn't believe him, and I didn't know what he meant, but it sure sounded good to me!

We went on the road with the new show and band and it was very successful. This time we headlined in all the clubs. We did the Bijou in Philly again, and Memphis and Nashville and Boston. The shows went over really well. The audiences got a big kick out of the commercials medley, but they loved "Mandy." *Loved* it. I began to love it too.

Andy Kaufman opened for us in Philly and turned the audience so off that it took me the first two songs to get them back. One night he just sat there and *read Moby Dick* to the audience. Another night he tried to play the congas and sing in some African language for the whole thirty minutes. The audience started throwing things at him. I thought it was kind of funny, actually.

"Mandy" began getting a great reaction on the radio. I really couldn't believe that this pleasant little ballad could be a hit record. I turned on the radio in my hotel room in Memphis and heard "Kung Fu Fighting" followed by "Bungle in the Jungle." What chance did I have?

During the visit to Philadelphia, I met up with Ed Sciaky, the disk jockey that had interviewed me during the Bijou shows. He didn't like "Mandy"; he said it was too commercial. He said he thought I had sold out. He still loved "Could It Be Magic" and "I Am Your Child."

That night we went to see Billy Joel's show at the Academy of Music. Billy was very popular in Philly, but hadn't hit it big anywhere else yet. Ed invited me out to a late supper after the show. I met him and his wife, Judy, across the street at the Eagle Diner. He walked in with Billy and a very scruffy-looking guy. Ed introduced us. The scruffy-looking guy was Bruce Springsteen.

Bruce was very somber and drank water. He had taken a bus to Philadelphia and was sleeping on the couch in Ed's living room because he couldn't afford anything better. A guy from Columbia Records who sat at another table was appalled when he heard that. He offered Bruce a wad of cash, but Bruce wouldn't accept it.

"Just push the fuckin' record," Bruce said disgustedly.

Bruce was skinny and looked sickly. He sat and brooded.

It surprised me that after two sold-out shows, Billy was alone. He didn't say very much either, and what he did say was negative and cynical. He just kept downing Black Russians.

I felt out of place. I kept talking and drinking coffee. I felt on a par with them, musically, but it began to dawn on me that I might be the one making the most blatantly commercial music at the table. I was the one who had wanted to be Edgar Winter or Bill Evans, but sitting next to these two brooding young men, I felt more like Bobby Sherman and it was a strange feeling.

During that last year, Bruce Sussman and I had begun a friendship. Bruce was a budding Broadway lyricist—sharp, witty, cynical, and very bright. I always felt smarter after spending time with him. He was a real New Yorker. Like Adrienne and Marty, Bruce was another friend who challenged me and represented quality to me. He was crazy about well-written songs and had no time for most of the drivel on the radio, no matter how much fun the music was.

As December of 1974 began, "Mandy" blazed up the charts and I began to feel nervous. I had never had a hit record before and it looked as if this was going all the way. Because of the upcoming Christmas holidays, everything in the record business began to shut down. There was nothing to do but bite my nails and smoke until the holidays were over. I decided to get away from New York for a week. I tried to convince Linda to come to Florida with me, but she couldn't get away from her job at CBS. So Bruce went along with me.

We arrived in Miami late at night and as we drove from the

airport to the hotel, I opened the window and breathed in the warm Florida air. I loved it. I felt my body beginning to relax.

"Maybe I'll be able to sleep down here," I said to Bruce as I turned on the radio. I flipped around for a nice, quiet classical station. I landed on one as a commercial was ending.

Only it wasn't a classical station. Suddenly the announcer shouted, "Well, it's time for the final song in this week's countdown! It's a song that's been getting the most requests since I've been at this station."

Bruce and I looked at each other. Nah, it couldn't possibly be.

"It's sung and produced by a guy who comes from Brooklyn, New York," the announcer said.

I didn't believe it.

"It's his very first hit record, and boy what a giant this one is going to be!" the guy shouted.

We held our breaths.

"And now, the number-one record in all of South Florida— Barry Manilow's 'Mandy'!"

Bruce and I started to holler so loud that even when the cop pulled us over to the side to see what the trouble was, it couldn't dampen our excitement.

I had a number-one record!

What did this all mean?

The Good News and the Bad News Joke

After my week in Florida, I joined my band in Los Angeles, where we were appearing for the first time at a small but important club called the Troubador. The shows were received very well and there was a good buzz about us in the street.

We were staying at the Hollywood Franklin Hotel, which we affectionately dubbed the Hollywood Flotzky. On that sunny Wednesday afternoon, I was a bundle of anticipation, waiting for a very important telephone call. "Mandy" was hitting the Top 10 on nearly all the regional Top 40 radio stations. It had climbed rapidly to the top of the national pop singles charts and was sitting impatiently at number three with a bullet. Today was the day we would find out how much higher it would go. I might find out today that I had a number-two record, or even, please God, a number-one record.

Technically it didn't matter that much, because "Mandy" was already being played and bought so much that it wouldn't really make much difference in the impact it was having. But a number-one record was something very few people ever experience, and I was crossing everything I could cross in the hopes that it would happen.

I had already gone through a half pack of Pall Malls by noon. My room was adjoining Wuzzy's room. Wuzzy was my road

165

manager and I was driving him crazy. Every time his phone would ring, I'd run into his room, hoping it was Clive trying to get through to me with the new numbers.

His phone rang.

"Who is it?" I shouted as I ran into his room for the tenth time.

"Hold on a minute," he said into the phone. "It's room service checking on our lunch order," he said exasperated.

"Sorry," I mumbled, and went back into my room and lit another cigarette.

We had been on the road for three months. I'd finished the second album, which included "Mandy" and "It's a Miracle," and I was on tour to promote it. We were playing a lot of the same clubs that we had played on my first tour last year, but we were headlining. We were doing very good business too.

The shows were grueling. We'd do two shows a night and three on weekends. I had hired a new band and new girl backup singers. The lights, sound system, and costumes had cost a fortune, to say nothing of the plane fares and hotel expenses.

I knew we couldn't be making very much money and that I was probably over budget. Miles, my manager, kept warning me to watch the expenses, but I was much more concerned with the performances every night. Things were moving very quickly and life on the road was frantic.

At the Troubador, after a nerve-racking opening night, I began to relax a little. The reviews were really good and the audiences made me feel very welcome. What a Christmas present it would be, I thought, if "Mandy" actually went to the number-one spot.

My phone rang. I grabbed it on the first ring.

"Hello," I said.

"I have a call for you from a Mr. Clive Davis from New York. Should I put it through?" the operator asked.

"Yes!" I told her.

"Barry?" Clive said.

"Yeah, hi—well, well?" I couldn't wait to hear.

" 'Mandy' will be the number-one record in the country on the first week of 1975. Congratulations," he told me excitedly.

"Holy mackerel!" I yelled.

I could hear Wuzzy's phone ringing.

"Clive, this is unbelievable! I really thought that it would only make it to the number-two spot. I can't believe—"

Wuzzy had come running into my room. He looked agitated.

"Miles *has* to talk to you. Right *now*," he mouthed.

"Clive, could you hold on a minute, let me just see what Miles wants, he's on the other phone. Hang on a minute, okay?" And I ran into Wuzzy's room.

I picked up the phone. "Miles, Miles! I'm on the phone with Clive. 'Mandy' will be number one in two weeks! Isn't it fantastic?" I shouted to him.

"Barry, it's great!" he said, but he didn't sound excited.

"What's wrong? Is something wrong?" I asked him.

"Listen, I hate to throw a wet blanket on this good news, but I'm afraid we've got some trouble," he said.

"What is it?"

"Well, I've just spent the last few days going over your finances with your accountant," he said.

"Oh, money problems again?" I said. "Can't we discuss this later? I've got Clive holding on next door," I said.

"No. Listen to me. I've told you about my fears that you were spending more than you were making. You're in trouble. You're in big trouble," he said.

"How much trouble can I be in?" I asked him. "I've got the number-one record in the country!"

"Yeah, well, by the end of the week at the Troubador, you will have gone through all of your money. You went through Bell's advance a few months ago. You told me that you and your accountant would get you through the next few months, but you were wrong. You've got nothing left. You're broke," he said.

"What?" I was sure I hadn't heard right.

"Broke. You are broke. You can't pay the band this week. *B-R-O-K-E*," he spelled.

Wuzzy came running in. "Clive wants to talk to you," he mouthed.

"Miles, I . . . lemme call you back, okay?" I said.

"Yeah, but make it fast. We have a lot to talk about," he told me.

I hung up and went back into my room.

"I'm sorry to have kept you waiting so long, Clive. Miles had important news for me," I told him.

"Well, it couldn't top this news, huh?" he said happily.

"Weeell . . . ," I said.

It was the good news and the bad news joke. I had the number-one record in the country and I was so broke that I couldn't get my band home!

I had not been prepared for how fast this success would happen. I was not prepared for the stratosphere I found myself in. Less than six months before, I had been balancing my own modest checking account. I had hired a sweet girl to do my taxes and my accounting. Suddenly, I was on tour, supporting eleven people, paying for airplane fares, hotels, and per diems (whatever *that* was). My name and voice were all over the radio and people were beginning to recognize me in the streets. It seemed that without any warning or preparation, I had entered a totally foreign arena, but all of my values and associates had remained the same as before.

I thought that by having a hit record, my financial problems would be solved, but I found out that before I'd see any money, I would have to repay the record company all their advances. I wasn't going to see any profits from "Mandy" for a long time.

So there I was, sitting three thousand miles away from home, asking myself what I should do. I couldn't just leave everyone and take a bus and go home, although the thought did cross my mind. The only thing I could do was to work my way back home.

While in Los Angeles, I performed on *The Midnight Special* and on *The Smothers Brothers Show*. There I was, singing happily away, joking with the hosts, and I'm sure everyone watching must have thought I was sitting pretty. Far from sitting pretty, I was in deep shit.

By the end of our week at the Troubador, Miles and Dick Fox

and I had put together a plan that would enable us to get home. Between advances, loans, and extending the tour, we might manage to make it back to New York. Miles had also hired a new accountant for me.

"So," Miles told me, "I think you'll make it, but it's going to be a lot of work."

"Okay," I sighed. "Anything else?"

"Oh yeah. There is something. I've been hesitating telling you this," he said.

"What is it now?" I braced myself.

"Well, do you know a Deborah Collins from Omaha?" he asked me.

"I don't think so," I said.

"Well, she knows you. She's just hit you with a paternity suit."

"What?"

It was the last straw and we both laughed for fifteen straight minutes.

The tour was grueling and seemed to last forever. I think those months would have been bearable, even with all the pressures, if I hadn't broken my ankle the next week in Denver.

As I ran off the small cluttered stage in a club called Ebbetts Field, I stepped on a bunch of cables and heard my ankle crack. The cast that the doctor put me in went up to my knee, but at least it had a little stub to walk on.

I would gladly have canceled the entire tour, but I couldn't. So we worked our way back east, me hobbling along on my cast. We did three shows a night in dumps and played to half-filled concert halls nearly every night of the week. We lived from week to week and, because of "Mandy," things slowly began to pick up. We'd hear rumors of people beginning to stand in line for tickets for hours. Arista came to the rescue too and I pulled myself out of debt.

Being broke really didn't frighten me. I sort of liked it. I was afraid of what a lot of money might do. I might relax too much.

Poverty, I reasoned, would make me struggle and work harder. I was much more comfortable being poor. Brooklyn doesn't rub off that fast!

I think that deep inside, I was sort of hoping for failure. The kind of huge success I was looking at was very scary. I didn't want to be the one to quit, and really, who would quit on his way up? When I went broke, it felt like maybe all this craziness would just go away by itself. I imagined I'd say to everyone, "Let's all shake hands and walk away friends, okay? We gave it a good try, but now I've got to go back to work being a struggling musician."

Of course, that never happened. Thank God that never happened!

Weeks later, somewhere in the middle of the country, my spot on *The Midnight Special* was aired. There I was looking happy and singing and dancing as if I didn't have a care in the world.

Things are never as they seem, you know.

Father's Day

Nineteen seventy-five came in with a bang for me. I felt I was on a roller-coaster ride, but it hadn't smashed to the bottom as I had expected. Instead, it was just going way up and then way down and then way up again. I sure was getting nauseous.

I moved into a bigger apartment in the same building and Linda and I spent a lot of time together. She was the only calming influence in my life and I couldn't be with her enough. The apartment I moved into had a huge terrace with trees on it and a few more rooms. Linda decorated it beautifully and I was very happy. Our romance was on again, and we were having a great time. She was the only person in my life at the time that had nothing to do with my music career.

She introduced me to Japanese food and Mexican food. I went crazy for both of them. She showed me how to plant strawberries on the terrace. I relied on her to get me out of the show-biz world. She was interested in my work and was always very supportive, but our relationship was based on the fun that we had together, not music.

We'd spend Sundays reading and doing the *New York Times* crossword puzzle while classical music played on the radio. We discovered backgammon and found ourselves playing way into the night. Sometimes we'd take Bagel for a walk in Central Park. Sometimes we were together for hours and hours and never had to talk. She became the best friend I had.

Bagel loved the place and, being the perfect dog, learned how to use the box full of kitty litter on the terrace so I didn't have to walk her all the time. (Of course, the strawberries never tasted the same after that!)

My family was very excited about my mushrooming success. I think it finally sunk into Gramma's head that I was becoming famous when she saw me on her favorite show, *The Mike Douglas Show*.

"Barry, *tateleh,* you were always clever and I knew you'd be a success," she told me. "You were always talented and I knew you'd be famous. But you were so homely! How you got to be sexy and good-looking, I'll never know."

Gramma had died on January fifth. She had been to the doctor and was leaving the grocery store. She had a heart attack in the street. At least she didn't suffer. During the year since Grampa died, she had just lost her desire to go on. Every time I'd spoken to her she'd sounded weaker and weaker. Near the end she'd hinted she felt as if she wouldn't be here much longer.

I really loved my grandmother. Gramma and I were connected to each other by a bond of love and love alone. To this day, my love for her is the purest form of love I've ever experienced because we never judged one another. I could do no wrong in her eyes, and she could do no wrong in mine. When she died I knew I had lost something very profound. I'll never experience it again, because what Gramma and I had only happens once in a lifetime. Even though she's gone, that feeling of true, nonjudgmental love lives within me and I know that Gramma will live with me forever.

In April 1975 I played the Westbury Music Fair in Long Island. I had finished the last show of the night. Linda was in my dressing room with me and I was getting out of my show clothes and into my street clothes. She was sitting at the makeup table and I had my show pants down around my ankles when the door opened and an older man popped his head in. At first I began to get angry, because the security guard was supposed to announce visitors, but he looked familiar.

"Yes?" I said. "Isn't there a guard out there, for Pete's sake?"

"Don't get all heated up. I ain't comin' in. I just wanted to see ya. I'm your father."

That's why he looked familiar.

"Oh. Hi," I stammered. I still had my pants down around my ankles.

"I just wanted to see ya one more time. You did good out there," he said in his thick Brooklyn accent.

"Thanks. You wanna come in?"

"Nope. Don't wanna bother you." We stood and stared at each other like that for a long minute. Then, "Gotta go. Bye."

And he was gone.

I pulled my pants up and zipped up my fly and ran to the door, but he was gone. There was nobody outside except for a guard.

"Hey! How'd that guy get back here?" I asked the guard.

"Oh, I'm sorry, Mr. Manilow. Wasn't I supposed to let your father back? He said he was your father, so naturally I thought. . . ."

I told him it was okay and went back inside the room. Linda was crying. I was stunned.

He looked older, but of course the last time I'd seen him was when I was eleven years old and he had given me my first tape recorder in the street.

Watching Linda cry made me want to get emotional too, but I couldn't. I didn't feel anything for this man.

I don't even know why I ran after him. Maybe I was curious about him. But maybe it was more than that. My life that year was literally exploding. Pieces of me were being flung in all directions. Maybe I thought that he represented some sort of stability. I was giving Clive and Miles amazing amounts of authority and power, something I'd never done. I seemed to be looking for a father figure and suddenly here was my real father.

Maybe I wanted to miss him. I never had missed him and it had always bothered me. I was hoping he would say something or do something that would be emotionally potent for me. Something that would open up all the feeling for him that I thought *must* be buried deep down inside me. But he was gone. Again.

There is no replacement for a father to a growing son. I understand that my mother and he could never live together. I appreciate my mother's and grandparents' raising me with all the love and devotion they had. But there is still an emptiness; it's there all the time. There are still dozens of questions unanswered.

I hear my friends calling their fathers Dad, and I wonder how that word would sound on my tongue. Sometimes I say it to myself and it feels funny.

Hi Dad.

Hey Pop, I'm home.

Happy Father's Day, Daddy.

I wonder sometimes what it would have been like to play ball with him in the park.

I wonder what ails him. Does he have the same kind of sensitive stomach I do? Does he tan well the way I do? Is he moody like me? How musical is he? How much have I inherited from his genes? Will we both live to be one hundred?

Not having been raised with a father has probably not really affected my life. But I'll never know, will I?

I stood looking at the empty hallway and trying to think of what I needed from him. I needed him to have been there when I was growing up. And he couldn't give me that back. So I came back into the dressing room and watched Linda cry and I let her cry for me because I couldn't.

It's Bananas at the Top

There were more and more people around me, smiling, opening doors, getting me drinks. Some had that glazed look of awe. Because of two hit records and a few television appearances, I had become a "celebrity," and many people around me stopped treating me like a regular person.

It's a problem that's unique to stardom. I wasn't prepared for it and it plagued me for years afterward.

"We didn't want to bother you" became the excuse I hated to hear most.

I'd walk into a room filled with laughing, comfortable people and suddenly there was tension in the air. I found it difficult making friends. I'd befriend someone on the crew, or a stranger at a restaurant, and I'd try everything to loosen them up. But they were always on their best behavior when I was around and just couldn't break through my "celebrity" status.

When I think back on that period of my life and career, it seems that it was filled with work and confusion. I barely made it to the next plane on time. I spent most of the days worrying about the show and how the ticket sales were going. I drove everyone around me crazy with the desire for more rehearsals. The reviews were mixed and every time a bad one came out, I'd go under for the day and make everyone around me miserable.

No matter how good the news was, I always felt it would all be over any minute. I still felt uncomfortable as a performer and was waiting for this silly explosion to die down so that I could get back to my normal life.

I wound up staying in my hotel room most days, and I chose two or three of my band members to socialize with. I just wanted to get home to Linda, my dog, my friends and collaborators, who treated me like a human being and not some kind of statue. I just wanted to get back to my apartment and write some more music. At least it was safe at the piano.

I guess I was really very naïve in 1975. I had always heard about those crazy mixed-up superstars who weren't able to handle their success and I had judged them as being weak and temperamental. Drugs, suicide attempts, alcoholism, tantrums—I'd read about them for years. Those poor weak people, I used to think. When fame and stardom hit me it was months before I realized I had turned into a banana.

It's mostly the shock of trying to deal with elements that are completely foreign that makes it so difficult. There's no school to go to to learn how to deal with it. Go take a look at the latest popularity polls. Ten to one says that the newcomers to the list are acting like assholes. It's hard not to. It's very heady when it hits you. Here you are being told that your record (or movie or show) is the greatest (but *you* know it's an accident) and everyone around you is kissing your ass.

For me, success came with a bang, and before I knew it, there was no place to run or hide. Fame and celebrity had invaded each and every part of my old normal life—no aspect remained untouched.

Going bananas began when my self-esteem as a creator was questioned. My strength as a songwriter was continually challenged. Clive and I played the game of *his* hit songs versus *my* hit songs after "Mandy" became number one. I had vowed that "Mandy" was going to be the only outside song I'd ever record, but for the very next album, *Tryin' to Get the Feeling* (1975), Clive found what he considered to be another smash hit. The irony was that its title was "I Write the Songs."

Clive sent three versions of it to my apartment that day in August. I was working at the piano when the messenger arrived. Attached was a note saying what huge potential the song had for me. Three artists had already recorded the song, with no success. I listened as its writer Bruce Johnston sang it, then as David Cassidy sang it, and finally the Captain and Tennille's version.

It was an intriguing song. The melody was simple but the lyric was ambitious. It gave credit to "music" for having written every song. "I am music, and I write the songs" the lyric went. I liked that. Many times I had felt that another force was helping me to create the music I made. Sometimes when I'd listen to my own work, I'd be surprised at what I'd been able to do. Sometimes it had felt that I really had nothing to do with the writing. The problem with the song was that if you didn't listen carefully to the lyric, you would think that the singer was singing about himself. It could be misinterpreted as a monumental ego trip.

Given that, and the fact that I really wanted to write my own songs, I decided to thank Clive, but to turn it down. I made an appointment with him through Rose, his beautiful secretary, and went uptown to see him.

When I emerged from the elevator to the now-familiar halls of Arista Records, I was greeted with the same colorful framed posters on the wall. Only now I was looking at a poster of myself. Times sure had changed.

Clive and I had become very close. Since "Mandy," and with the success of "Could It Be Magic" and "It's a Miracle" and the tours, we had been in constant touch. He'd cheered me on in Los Angeles and in New York, thrown receptions in my honor, and taken out full-page ads celebrating our success. My success was as much his success.

"This 'I Write the Songs' thing, Clive," I said. "I really don't want to do it."

"But it's a smash hit for you, Barry," he said, surprised.

"Maybe, but I want to write my own songs," I explained.

"You're being foolish and childish," he told me. "You're a

terrific arranger and producer. With the right elements, this could be a number-one record for you. They don't come along so easily, Barry. You really shouldn't turn this down."

But I did. I left his office, feeling good that I had stood up for what I believed in. Laura Nyro would have been proud.

But it didn't end there. Clive called and called and became more and more insistent that I go in and give it a try.

"What can you lose? Go in and play with it," he chided. "What could one more outside song hurt?"

Clive probably thought: I have more experience than you. I've been down this road before. I've been right so far. Trust me. I only want the best for you.

But I felt: I know what's right for me too (maybe). I'm a professional, why won't you let me follow my own light? Listen to *me*. Maybe I'll fail, but at least let me try. And then my insecure side would chime in: Do you *really* know what's best for you? You've never been in this Top 40 arena. You don't really want to fail—maybe you should do it his way. After all, he's been right so far and he does want what's best for you.

I knew he meant well, and I was becoming very insecure. I didn't want to risk my own career, plus I wanted him to believe in my records so that he would support them. So I scheduled recording-studio time and began recording "I Write the Songs."

Ron and I used every commercial trick we could think of on it. I changed keys three times, the orchestra was huge, we used tons of background vocals, and I hit the highest note I've ever sung at the end. To this day, whenever I listen to that song, I swell with pride at our work on the record.

The problems were that the public was beginning to identify me with big booming commercial ballads, which I felt was only a small part of me, and also that I didn't want to be identified with songs I hadn't written. But, I reasoned again, I would do it this one time and never again.

Out of the ten songs on the *Tryin' to Get the Feeling* album, "I Write the Songs" was released as the first single from the album and, as Clive had predicted, shot to number one in two months.

Becoming known for singing other people's songs was be-

With the Harlettes

With Lady Flash

First recording session

Postcard to Linda from first tour

With Grampa. (Someone
cut this person's hair!)

With Melissa Manchester in 1975

First solo tour

Thanksgiving Day Parade, New York, 1976

With Bagel and beard in Florida

On Golden Beach, Florida, 1977

With Linda at the Beverly Hills palazzo in front of the Dancing Waters

With Clive Davis

Jay Thompson

A little light reading

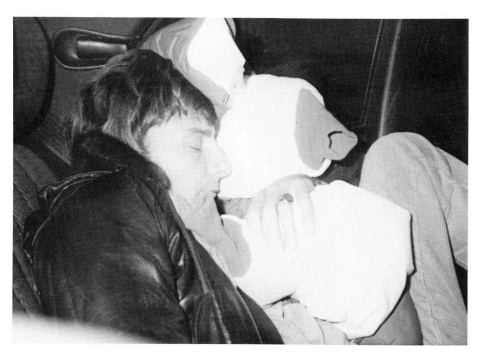

On the road. Ah, the glamorous life!

At Blenheim Palace

Giving a lecture at a high school

With Marty Panzer and Adrienne Anderson

Roberta Kent

With Roberta

With Bagel and Biscuit

Singing the National Anthem at the Super Bowl

With Garry Kief and Roberta in London

In concert

Mark Weiss

In concert

The musicians that played on *2:00 A.M.—Paradise Cafe*: Mundell Lowe, George Duvivier, Shelly Manne, Mel Tormé, Gerry Mulligan, me, and Billy May coming frustrating, but I took it as a challenge and I'm pretty sure I could have dealt with it on its own. The problem was that it was only one element in the package that began to shake me up.

Something had changed about me as a performer, too. During my time on the road, the show had gotten bigger and more produced. I had added an orchestra and had hired more musicians. I had invested in expensive costumes and a flashy set. No Ronko rhinestone studder or bubble machine any more! We were playing for fifteen thousand people a night. The audiences were enormously responsive to the commercial approach of "Mandy" and "I Write the Songs." When I'd try to sing "Sandra" or "I Am Your Child" now, they would seem to sit there impatiently waiting for me to finish so that I could give them more flash and pizazz. They went nuts for the commercials; they loved those big endings. Actually I loved them too, so I gave it to them by the barrelful.

By the middle of that tour I'd watch videotapes of the shows and I could see that I was turning into an "entertainer." An entertainer named BARRY MANILOW. In capital letters. I liked him, yet I wasn't sure about him. I kept searching for that innocent, pure songwriter somewhere in there, and month after month it was harder to find him. I wondered, who was the audience really responding to? Me or *him*?

Backstage, while I'd get ready to perform, I'd sit at my dressing table feeling my old insecurities each night.

"Who am I kidding?" I'd ask myself. "I don't sing well. I don't really know the first thing about performing. If they saw the real me, they'd throw tomatoes." Then I'd get out of my normal workshirt into a sparkling shirt, trying to cover the real me up. For the hour before I went onstage, I'd blow myself up. I'd pump myself into a bigger version of me. I'd have different images in mind. I'd pretend that I could sing terrifically. I'd pretend that I was good-looking and sexy. And you know what? People began to believe it.

The shows got bigger and the crowds got bigger. It was tough trying to keep my head on straight. It was wonderful and terrible.

It was a new world for me. I wasn't prepared for it and didn't know whom to ask about it.

As the tour chugged along, I could feel an undercurrent of explosiveness. Everything around me seemed to rumble as if in anticipation of an earthquake.

Here's a sample of my journals on that tour.

October 17, 1975, Oklahoma City

We played Wichita last night. Hate. Very much hate. Hated the auditorium, hated the dressing rooms. The promoter served us ham and cheese sandwiches for dinner.

I think the audience liked the show, but it was like pulling teeth. David Brenner opened for us and on his way into the wings after his set he said to me, "Lots a luck, kid. There's not one Jew out there." Great.

October 25, 1975, Chicago

Chicago was like a movie. Sold out, screaming people. Can't walk through the streets here. Can't even get to the limo from the stage door. In order to get me to the car, a dozen guards form two lines and make a path for me. It still didn't help last night. As soon as the crowd saw me, they surged. My glasses were broken, I got scratched from someone's long fingernails. I just sat there in the car, breathing hard as we drove away with the crowd screaming and pounding on the car. It's crazy.

Am I having a good time yet?

November 17, 1975, Memphis

In Jackson, Tennessee, the mayor proclaimed it Barry Manilow day! At the end of the show, they wouldn't stop cheering and we had to come back and do another song.

When we got off the plane here in Memphis, I was met with hundreds of people with banners, champagne, TV and radio crews. The mayor made it Barry Manilow day here too. They're calling it Manilow-mania.

They say that I'm the next Frank Sinatra. Isn't that strange? No one can be like Sinatra.

All these years I've been reading about the Beatles and Sinatra and Presley and Elton John and now they're mentioning me in the same breath. It's very scary—I don't know what to think.

I hope I'm not losing touch. I can't relate to the whole thing. It's just me! I'm the same. It really got me crazy over the last few days because of all the strangers following me and pointing at me and waiting outside the hotel room and on and on. Somehow it makes me really angry.

The monitors weren't good during the shows and I flew into a rage during the intermission, yelling at everyone, throwing things around and being generally obnoxious. How can I be angry? I'm a success. I've got to get used to this life.

Am I going crazy?

I had done over eighty-six shows on that tour and had come home and begun recording another album. I was exhausted and confused.

Suddenly my life was out of control. Success had literally exploded over me, wrenching me out of what had been a normal life and thrusting me into something quite different. My roots were pulled out of New York and I felt like a wanderer. Now there were limousines, hotel suites, people taking care of my every whim. I was accepting awards right and left. Of course it was flattering, but it was terrifying too.

The road was crazy. I would go from up to down in seconds. From as high as you can get, with thousands of people screaming my name, to as low as you can get. Low. The lowest was a slam in the newspaper when I got back to the hotel room that called me a putz—an ugly, talentless jerk.

And then there was the phenomenon of the fan. The letters came pouring in and they were glorious. I was getting an acceptance that I'd never dreamed of. They'd thank me for my encouraging words and uplifting music. They gave me credit for all of their triumphs and gratitude for helping them through hard times. It was as if I were a light in the darkness for them.

Why were the fans acting so fanatically? People were acting

like I was the second coming and it was impossible to deal with. They felt as if they really knew me. Hell, I was just a musician trying my best to learn how to sing and perform.

Who was right? The critics who killed "I Write the Songs" or the fans who loved it?

Many of them were screaming girls. That was a big surprise. I thought I would get popular because of the "substance" of my music. But these screaming girls ripping things off my body had absolutely no interest in the music at all.

My personal life took a beating too. My career had taken over my life totally. Linda and I weren't together very much because I was obsessed with the career. She had begun dating again. I hated being out in crowds who were staring at me and I hated feeling isolated in my hotel room.

It's hard to form relationships when you're famous. Even just making a good friend takes time and nurturing, but looking for love when you're well known is really tough. How do you get to know someone when you're in a town just overnight? How can you learn about the little things that are so important in a relationship? Not that I met that many potential partners anyway. I could see people looking at me differently. They weren't looking at me as a person, they were looking at an image. They'd laugh too fast, they wouldn't look in my eyes. I would spot it immediately and just click off.

It was a very exciting time, but at the same time it was hard to deal with. I had never even fantasized about the kind of success that was now happening to me. It was that dangerous moment in a skyrocketing career where pills and drugs begin to look tempting. Had I been the type to want to lose myself in stimulants, now would have been the time to do it. I thank my lucky stars that I never succumbed to the temptation. But I reacted in my own way to the pressures of stardom.

I turned into a brat.

I'd tell my staff to empty rooms of people before I would walk in. That went for TV studios and restaurants. This was not an easy thing to do without seeming demented. But I'd carry on and stay in the car or in my dressing room until places were cleared out.

"Tell 'em who I am," I whispered to Bruce once.

"If you have to tell them who you are, Barry," Bruce told me, "you aren't anybody."

If things were going wrong on stage, I'd come rushing out, yelling and carrying on like a child in front of ushers or technicians. I would constantly complain about people treating me like a star and not a normal person, and yet when I didn't get star treatment, I'd go nuts. I was rude and demanding. I was daring someone to slap me and stop me. The bad reviews I'd get now and again made me very paranoid and I was always on the defensive and looking for a fight.

Alone in my hotel room, I felt as if a huge cloud had descended upon me and that I was walking around in cotton balls all the time. Now and then, I'd emerge and act human and everything would lighten up for a while, but mostly the success and pressure just pushed me further and further into my own confusion.

When I look back on those days, I'm appalled at my behavior. I have to say thanks to those people who stayed with me, because they must have seen what I was going through. Sometimes now I look at the latest "rising stars" and all I can feel is sympathy for what they must be experiencing. Nobody can possibly get through the explosion of success without accumulating a lot of scars.

We'd been on tour for months and we were all very tired, and I think everyone was fed up with me. Even me.

We ended the tour headlining at the MGM Grand in Las Vegas. My nerves were raw. During the last week in Vegas, I found myself crying or yelling at the drop of a hat. I worked my ass off each night but I still couldn't figure out why the audiences were responding so uproariously. Was it my music and the *real* me, or was it this BARRY MANILOW image that Clive and I had created?

I was fed up with smiling and acting nice to radio men and their wives and to the record men and their girlfriends. I was fed up signing autographs. I wanted to be left alone and found it very difficult controlling my frazzled nerves.

At one point in Vegas during the break between shows, one of the VIPs from the hotel barged into my dressing room with his children without knocking. I lost control and started cursing, slamming doors, and throwing my full brandy glass against the wall.

The band had dressing rooms on another floor, the girls had dressing rooms down the hall, and no one was talking to me. I had a guard sitting outside my dressing room and one on the stairway. I was taking much too much Valium and it was time to stop. I headed to Miami where I rented a house on the beach and tried to pull myself together. I was totally "roaded out."

April 14, 1977, Las Vegas
Last night was the final show of the tour and of this group.

My life has been like a movie. I will try to describe what's happened.

I have become a Superstar—it's ridiculous. I've become one of the most popular singers in pop music—in just two years! I can't do anything wrong. We've broken records all over the country, the albums have gone gold, platinum, and double platinum. The TV special was one of the highest-rated shows of the month.

So my life has totally changed. I have to sit and think about where I am and where I'm going because I'm not sure I like what I've become.

When I arrived at the house in Golden Beach, Florida, I felt like a punch-drunk fighter. I sat and stared at the ocean. Not only is it lonely at the top, I thought to myself, it's bananas there too. Now I could understand why all those superstars I had read about lost control of themselves. Success attacks you in places you're just not ready for.

Soon that terrifying roller-coaster ride I'd been on began to fade away and my heart began to beat at a normal rate for a change. I actually thought about bailing out, but it was impossible. I had dozens of people depending on me, and I was in too deep. But most of all, who on earth would pull out of a career that was incredibly successful and showed no signs of slowing down? I sat on Golden Beach and tried to find me.

May 12, 1977, Miami, Florida
 I've been here for a week and I'm feeling better.

I guess I should bring us up to date. On the way to the last tango in Vegas I had become the number-one pop vocalist in the nation. Imagine my surprise. I still feel pretty much the same inside, but it's murder out there.

This house in Florida is a glorious two-story thing, with a circular driveway, big private entrance, three bedrooms, four baths, den, living room, dining room, kitchen, maid's quarters, swimming pool, and a private beach and the Atlantic Ocean. Just a little different from the apartment I grew up in in Brooklyn.

It's in the most private and unique residential area in all of Miami. Very secluded and very expensive. The house has enough furniture in it for three houses. Whoever owns this place must never throw anything away. Three couches in the living room—you actually have to step over one to get to the den. Coffee tables next to coffee tables, dozens of lamps and dozens of little knickknacks. Once you get used to it, though, it's very comfortable and sort of kinky (if you're into couches).

After the first couple of tension-filled days, I began to relax. The phones stopped ringing. I grew a beard, dyed my hair black, cut it short, and nobody recognized me when I went out, which I hardly ever did. The music station I tuned in to played classical music. I spent the days playing with Bagel, lying on a raft in the ocean and the nights reading or watching *Laverne and Shirley*. Linda met me here and she was a godsend. She always makes houses into homes. Bruce came down for a while and so did Marty. Now and again we'd all go out, but I honestly preferred just sitting outside and staring at the ocean. I began to feel calm. Even though I was living in the kind of luxury I'd never dreamed of, I felt more like myself again.

I felt as if I had awakened from a dream. But my surroundings were unfamiliar, and the past six months seemed like a hazy black-

and-white movie. I tried to make sense of all of it by writing out my feelings in my journals.

June 1, 1977

What's happening to me? I always thought I was so to-gether. How can I have become so undone?

Sometimes I think that the whole thing doesn't matter at all. Like last night. I was sitting outside the house at the edge of the patio where the beach begins and I was looking out at this beautifully calm, enormous Atlantic Ocean. There was a little breeze, but it was still real warm and Bagel was sitting on my lap. And all around us was sky and stars and these mammoth gorgeous clouds and to top it all off there was a full moon being reflected in the ocean. I really felt like tossing in my rhinestone shirts and getting a job in a Pizza Hut. It was glorious. It was awesome. I felt like a little dot. Every-thing seemed so unimportant.

Then of course there's the other way of living my life in which every decision (and I mean *every* decision—like one lump or two) is the end of the world and I shall die in agony if the wrong choice is made.

I really feel like that most of the time. I guess that's the insane energetic part of me that has gotten me where I am in my career, but that's just as unhealthy as lying around in a stoned-out stupor. So the solution is to try and keep in bal-ance, and that takes an enormous effort for me because the work is all-consuming—it leaves no room for anything else in my life. If I choose to make my career in music, then I have chosen to give up a normal life. It seems there's no other way. Someone once said, "It's either art or heart."

I saw *Our Town* a few nights ago. I'd never seen it before and I was enraptured. The message at the end is how fast life passes us by and how most of us never slow down enough to treasure it. It really knocked me out because sometimes I think my life is on "Fast Forward."

I've had so many incredible things happen to me over the past decade and I can barely remember any of them. Oh I remember the real big landmarks, but there was so much more—people—God the people I have shared moments with—places, events, tragedies, successes, I swear, I barely remember any of them. I guess I was too busy thinking about how to get to the next one alive. Well, hopefully this journal will be a reminder to me.

During that time in Florida, I'd spent hours just sitting and staring at the ocean and the sky. Its enormity had made my career seem small and less important, reminding me of how far I had come from my old normal life.

Thankfully, those months in Florida calmed me down. I had even begun to enjoy writing music again. Marty and I had written "Even Now" and "I Was a Fool to Let You Go" and Bruce and his partner Jack Feldman and I had begun writing "Copacabana." Linda and I had played house again. I had gotten to know what was on television and Bagel sat next to me all day long.

"Perspective, perspective," I kept repeating to myself. "The answer to this dilemma is all in perspective."

Keeping things in perspective is not only important to success and fame. I think that keeping things in balance is the answer to a lot of problems. Once I stepped far enough back from myself and looked at the problem, putting things back in order became easier. Easier, but never easy.

At the end of my time in Florida I felt in control of myself once again. I was ready to create and face the pressures and excitement that I knew awaited me. I had survived a very dangerous trip. On the climb up the mountain of success, there are lots of minefields. Some, like me, are lucky, and actually reach the top. But in addition to finding joy, fame, and fortune there, I found a big surprise waiting for me.

Bananas.

The California
Adventures

The Amazing Dancing Waters!

I knew my vacation in Miami couldn't last forever, and before I knew it I was packing. This time I was off to Los Angeles. I was off to begin the next phase of this frightening and exciting adventure I was in. Bagel was flying in baggage, and I was flying first class. As I sat on the plane I thought that since Los Angeles is known for being "laid-back," my few months there would be relaxing.

Fat chance!

As the jumbo jet circled LAX for the third time, I stared out the window with my hand under my chin. *Now* what was I getting myself into, I thought. Looking at Los Angeles from the air is not a pretty sight. The layer of brown-red smog hung over the city and cut the sky in two. Above, the blue of the sky was dazzling, and then, as if someone had drawn a straight line, brown gook just hung over all the houses. How could anyone *breathe* down there?

I'm a New Yorker, I said to myself. I don't know anyone here, I won't like the laid-back feeling here, I don't even know how to drive! What am I doing? As we thumped onto the airstrip,

191

the Muzak came on. It was a dirgelike version of "Mandy," heavy on the violins. An omen?

Next to me, Linda happily applied her lipstick and fluffed herself up for our arrival. She had lost the extra pounds she'd gained in Florida and was looking slim and pretty with her strawberry blond hair down to her shoulders. She was very excited. She loved the idea of living in California and couldn't wait to get to the house we were renting.

Linda and I were going to live in California for a year while I recorded my next album, taped my next special, and invented my next road show. All the facilities for the TV special were in LA and I had decided to give the West Coast musicians a try for the next album.

The past year had been very difficult. The hurricane of success had hurled me around and around and by the time I had finished the last tour, I was a wreck. The success was everything anyone could have dreamed of, but it was having a strange effect on me. The records and the ticket sales had gone through the roof. The first special was up for an Emmy. The audiences at the concerts were beside themselves each night. Along with the exhilaration and joy I was feeling came lots of pressure: pressure to top each success and pressure to sustain it.

I had been soul-searching and questioning myself for three months, and now I felt calmer, but unsure. I wasn't sure that I could possibly top my past successes, but I was going to try. Now, landing here in Fantasyland, my New York cynicism began to take over.

Linda and I hadn't yet seen the house we were going to be living in. I had sent my assistant Michael Devereaux to Los Angeles to scout out possible places with the intention of flying from Florida one weekend to see the final choices. He had called and said the selection wasn't great but that he'd found one that seemed to fit the bill. The owners wanted a commitment then and there.

"Is it a modest home, Michael?" I asked. "I really just want to be normal."

"It's the best one, Barry. Take my word," he said.

"But it's pretty expensive," I said.

"They're all expensive in Beverly Hills. Most of them are

expensive and need a lot of work, or they feel like museums. This one you could live in," he said, "but the owners want an answer this afternoon."

"All right, make the deal," I said. "But is it a regular kind of house? We're going to have to live there for nearly a year, so I want it to feel nice and comfortable, you know."

"Well—it's not what you'd call regular, but it's the best of all of them," he said.

My business manager made arrangements to rent it for a year.

Michael greeted us as we emerged from the walkway. He was tall and thin, with dark hair. He was very together. I had hired him a year ago when my life had started to come unglued. He'd become invaluable to me, not only as a business partner who kept my life in some sort of order. We'd become close friends too. He represented security and foundation. I was happy to see him.

"How was the trip?" he asked.

"Long. The longest plane ride I've ever been on. The food stunk, the movie was boring. And I've never seen such filth in the air like there is here," I answered, ready to hate Los Angeles.

"Oh, stop," Linda said. "The trip was fine, Michael. He's just grouchy because the stewardess called him Mr. Sedaka. Let's go. I'm dying to see this house."

The limousine waited for us at the curb. Limousines, I thought to myself. I've been spending a lot of time in these things. They still give me the creeps. Make me feel like I'm going to a funeral. This one was the longest I'd ever seen. Inside it had a television, a stereo, and compartments filled with liquor and mineral water. Red carpeting surrounded us and the Beach Boys harmonized about surfin' girls on the radio. A handsome, silver-haired driver stood holding the door open. "This is Harry Grovier, your driver," Michael said.

"Welcome to Los Angeles, Mr. Manilow," Harry said, holding the door open as I crawled in after Linda.

"Thanks," I said. "Give my sympathies to the widow," I mumbled under my breath.

"Now let me tell you about this house," Michael said as we drove away from the airport crowds. "It's—different."

"Different from what?" I said suspiciously.

"Different from what you're used to," he said.

"I've got a feeling he's trying to prepare us for something," Linda said, smiling.

"Yes I am. Oh, yes indeedy, I am," Michael said, lighting a cigarette and lighting Linda's. I had quit a few months before, but I really wanted one now.

"Come on, tell us about it," Linda said.

"No, I think you'd better just see it for yourself," he said.

As we drove through Beverly Hills, I kept trying to guess which house was ours. Every time the car would stop for a light, I'd select one, and then the car would move along. Beverly Hills is a beautiful place. The houses are all out of a movie. Manicured lawns, beautiful trees and flowers, hardly any people in sight. I opened the window and could smell the sweet air. I began to feel better.

Finally, we pulled up to a long white wall with a solid black iron gate.

"Well, here we are," Michael said.

"Where we are?" I asked, looking at the wall.

"Home sweet home," he said, and clicked a remote control gadget in his hand. The black gate slowly opened and we drove in.

We drove along a circular driveway and stopped by the front door. Linda and I got out of the car and stared at a pretty white house. It had columns in front like Tara in *Gone With the Wind*. It was bigger than I had imagined.

We went inside and stood there with our mouths open. It was Hollywood, circa 1950. The architecture, the furniture, the rugs, the wallpaper—all of it looked as if it were right out of a glamorous fifties movie. A semicircular couch dominated the living room. Shelves of knickknacks lined the walls. A sunken Formica bar with old-fashioned leather stools on one wall. An old white grand piano with an ornate candelabra sitting on it. The walls were filled with sconces of angels holding lights. And smack in the middle of the room was a huge marble fireplace.

The house kept going and going and going. Six bedrooms, a huge dining room, loads of bathrooms, and a large kitchen. The master bedroom was pink. I mean pink. The bed was up a step and sat under a pink canopy with pink headboard in the shape of a crown. The woman's master bathroom was all marble—pink marble. The bath was styled after the Roman baths, with columns and statues of angels. The man's master bathroom was all marble too—also pink marble, but a darker pink.

Nearly every room in the house opened out on the back acres of land. Trees, lawns, flowers, chaise longues, and a big swimming pool.

As Linda and I stood and gaped, I saw a strange man coming toward us. He had on a butler's uniform and carried a tray with glasses of champagne.

"This is Robert," Michael said, handing us our drinks. "He's your houseman and cook."

"How do you do," said Robert, complete with a British accent.

"Hi," I said.

"Well, I told you it was different," Michael said.

It was different all right. I didn't know what to think. My first instinct was to run. Really. It was getting out of hand. Limousines, Muzak playing my songs, now a giant crazy house and a butler! I was having enough trouble coming to grips with the success of the records and the concerts, but now the thought of living in a ridiculous Beverly Hills palazzo for the next year was frightening. I felt that sense of panic returning as I stood looking at the pool with marble statues flanking it.

"Jeez, Michael, I don't know about this. It's so big—it's so expensive . . . a *butler*?" I stammered.

"Oh come on, honey," Linda said. "Enjoy it. We'll make it fun, you'll see."

"Oh wait! You haven't seen the best part!" Michael shouted, and he ran inside. "Are you ready?" he shouted from the living room.

"Yes!" Linda called back.

There was a quiet rumble and suddenly from the center of the swimming pool dancing waters appeared. They sprayed in all directions as different floodlights lit them different colors. It was too much. It was so silly. It was so ridiculous. Dancing waters!

Suddenly, from the guest cottage, way in the distance, I heard the familiar sound of barking. Just like in a *Lassie* episode, Bagel came running down the lawn toward all of us.

I looked around at us—standing with our champagne glasses, the butler, the pink bedroom in the corner, the statues and the waters dancing merrily—and I began to laugh and laugh. What a trip!

"Here's to Hollyweird!" I toasted, and we all drank to a hopeful year in California.

Looking back now at those months and the fragile emotional state I was in, I see it could have been disastrous. I was under a lot of pressure and there was a lot of work to be done. But Michael's instinct was right. It was going to be a work-filled year and he had decided to recommend these outrageous surroundings. The house was so ridiculous that I just couldn't take anything too seriously when I was there. And when the real disasters did happen, the house served to lighten even those incidents.

Within the first week, Linda and I were comfortable. We'd sit around the fireplace in the evening with the doors open and relax. In the mornings, she'd come swooping out of the bedroom in her new white bathing suit while Robert served us breakfast by the pool. You could get used to this kind of life very easily, I thought.

One by one, I flew my New York collaborators in. We had an album to complete, but mostly I wanted to share this experience with them. We got a lot of wonderful work done during those months and had a lot of laughs too.

I remember finishing the writing of "Copacabana" at that silly white grand piano with the ornate candelabra and the angel sconces looking at me. The melody came easily as I sang Bruce and Jack's wonderful lyric. When I played it back on my little cassette machine, Michael and Linda and Bagel sambaed around the fireplace. How could it not be a success?

Putting together the TV special was a great experience too. The respected director George Shaefer had agreed to direct it, and veteran producer Ernie Chambers was co-producing it with me. I loved the experience of working with these professionals. We'd bounce ideas back and forth for hours. They stimulated and challenged me creatively.

But I think it was Kevin Carlisle who really turned my head around!

During all the time I had been performing, I had never worked with a director-choreographer. I had always undertaken the responsibility of teaching myself how to do things. When I began to work with Kevin and realized that he was actually showing me how to move, where to walk, when to stop or go, I felt an enormous burden taken away from me.

He was smart and compassionate. He knew exactly what I needed and I opened up and just let him teach me. Someone once said, "When the student is ready, the teacher appears." I was ready. Letting Kevin and George and Ernie lead and guide me was a major breakthrough for me. I had always been afraid that if I let go of the reins, I would lose myself and turn into a marionette. Look at what had happened by my just letting Clive suggest "Mandy." I didn't want that to happen in other parts of my career, so I kept a pretty tight grip on creative control. Now here was Kevin, just wanting to help. After the Florida experience and the rejuvenation I was feeling from the new album, I let him teach me and it was a revelation. I knew that I had made a friend and had begun working with someone who was going to be very important to my career.

The day before we began taping the second TV special, my first special won the Emmy award for Outstanding Special, Comedy-Variety or Music. That, plus the fact that the live album went to number one on the charts, helped make the time in Beverly Hills one of the most memorable times of my life.

All of the good times, however, were counterbalanced.

I was alone opening my mail when I got the first death threat. It was written so sloppily and by such an obviously young hand that I didn't pay attention to it. Then they began to arrive every other day. Each one a little more vicious than the one before. I wasn't too concerned, because even though the postmark was from Los Angeles, they were addressed to my manager's address in New York. But it became a little unsettling.

I had flown my co-producer Ron Dante and my engineer Michael Delugg out to LA from New York, and we were in the middle of making the *Even Now* album when Michael, my assistant, had his car accident. It was a beaut, too. Seventy-eight stitches in his face alone after they removed all the glass, to say nothing of the broken bones. He remained in intensive care for two weeks. When I rushed into his room on that first day in the hospital, I thought I was looking at the wrong person. His head was twice its normal size. His car had turned over and over as he swerved to avoid hitting a woman. I kept on making the album and creating the special between my trips to the hospital.

I reluctantly agreed to do a cover story for *People* magazine. I've never been comfortable being the subject of gossip, and agreeing to the interview made me queasy. We met at a restaurant and I sat across from the interviewer and tried to answer his questions as professionally as I could. I wanted to talk about music; he wanted to know who I slept with. My mind was on poor Michael, lying all broken in Cedars hospital; the interviewer's mind was in the gutter.

We began taping the special. It had all become very hectic. But it all seemed to come to a head in the week before the *People* article was due to hit the stands. The threats on my life had gotten more and more violent and I had told Miles, my manager in New York, about them. He was very upset and insisted that I hire a bodyguard and detectives to track down the culprits. I still wasn't taking it seriously and dismissed the idea.

But that Wednesday in my stack of mail there was another one. It was my *Live* album cover in a mailing tube. On it, someone had crossed out the *Live* in *Barry Manilow Live* and replaced it with *Dead,* and there was a knife drawn through my heart with blood dripping from it. The letter was the most violent-sounding of all.

The thing that really convinced me to hire the security people was that the *People* magazine article was about to reveal that I was living in Beverly Hills and recording my next album at the A&M studios in Hollywood. Since the letters were postmarked Los Angeles, I knew it would be easy for the craze-os to find me.

So for the next few weeks, I traveled with an Israeli guerrilla named Shlomo. He and his partners were glued to me. They took different shifts—outside my bedroom while we slept, outside the recording studio while I made the record, in the backseat of the cars I rode in.

I really hated it. But the day I decided to let them go, we arrived at A&M studios to find out that two people had been there an hour before, looking for me. They had left me another death threat.

The detectives finally tracked them down. They were just kids and they claimed they were playing a joke on me. Claimed that they were fans too!

Michael got out of the hospital and went back to New York to recuperate. I finished making the *Even Now* album and the second special and began to create the next tour.

The time at the Beverly Hills palazzo brought home the true meaning of the "double-edged sword." I've lived under that sword all my professional life, and although I've never gotten used to it, I feel that it really does represent reality.

I also think that my stay in the Beverly Hills palazzo was a lesson in perspective for me. I appreciated Linda so much more during those months. Robert, the cook, became part of the family. I'd come home from twenty hours in the studio or taping the show and there'd be a fire going, a glass of wine, and a late supper waiting for me. And during the rough times of the threats and Michael's accident, when I thought things were dismal, I'd turn on the dancing waters and things wouldn't seem so terrible. Bagel even had a litter of puppies in the pink bathroom.

At the end of our stay there, I didn't want to leave. I loved that house. Even with the pressures of creativity and the negative incidents, the house had been a safe harbor. When we left in December to go back to New York and begin the next tour, as usual, I felt excited and apprehensive. But while the limousine and Linda waited for me, I turned on the dancing waters one more time and stood all by myself and laughed and laughed and knew that things would be okay.

Driving

In 1978 I made a permanent move to Los Angeles. Even though I'm a New Yorker, I loved the famous LA lifestyle. And the music business had moved from New York to LA. I had to make a lot of adjustments when I became Californicated. For instance, I was an adult, in my thirties, and I had never learned to drive! And no one would let me forget it, because the most repeated phrase I heard was, "You don't drive??"

After making a business appointment I would ask, "By the way, can I get a cab easily from your office?" and I would hear:

"You don't drive??"

I would make dinner plans with a friend and when I'd ask them to pick me up I'd hear:

"You don't drive!!???"

In New York, you see, *most* people don't drive. You hail a cab, you take a bus, you ride the subway, but you don't drive! That's not to say all of us kids couldn't name every name and model number of every car that came out of Detroit. That's also not to say that some of us didn't know how to hot-wire a car. But drive, no. No driver's ed in my school. The only driver's ed I knew of was Ed Ginsberg the truck driver.

A lot of us had relatives who had somehow managed to relocate to Long Island. Ah, Long Island. People who lived in Long Island were to be envied. Now and again you'd hear someone's mother proudly saying, "Oh, *my* brother and his wife live in— Long Island," and everyone was impressed. Only they'd pronounce it "Long *Guy*land."

My Aunt Rose, her husband Leo, and her children, Dennis and Olivia, lived in Long *Guy*land, and now and again I'd get the chance to visit. It was like going to Mars. They spoke an alien language.

They had

LAWNS.

They had streets with names like

PETUNIA LANE and PEACHY ROAD.

They had

DRIVE-INS.

My cousin Dennis was on the

FOOTBALL TEAM.

My cousin Olivia was a

CHEERLEADER

and she twirled a

BATON.

My uncle Leo was a member of the

VOLUNTEER FIRE DEPARTMENT

and Aunt Rose grew

FLOWERS

in her

GARDEN.

And all the kids would talk about was getting their first car.

I was always very polite and quiet when I visited my family in Long *Guy*land. Gramma would dress me all in white and warn me not to impose. For me, going to Long Island was like going to synagogue. Therefore, it was devastating for me when, at six years old, while driving with Uncle Leo and Dennis for an ice-cream cone, I fell out of his car. I was sitting on the passenger side trying to be very good and quiet when he made a turn and I found myself rolling along the street. The car door must have been open. He didn't realize I wasn't there until he was a few blocks away. I wasn't hurt, but I blamed myself and didn't like cars too much from then on.

When I bought a home in Los Angeles, I realized I had to learn to drive. It really was impossible getting around without a car. And if I heard "You don't drive?" one more time, I was gonna hit someone. So I went to a driving school, passed my exam, and bought a car.

One day while I was driving down Sunset Boulevard, I noticed colored lights flashing behind me. I thought, "How nice, a little parade." When they stayed behind me and gave two blasts from their siren the dawn broke and I pulled over. This was my very first encounter with the *law* and my heart was going a mile a minute. The very serious officer walked slowly over to my window and said, "Let me see your license."

As I fumbled for my brand-new driver's license, I asked him what I had done.

"Just let me have your license," he said.

My heart beat faster. Don't think I hadn't heard about police brutality, itchy trigger fingers, and things like that. I finally found the damn thing and gave it to him. He looked at it for a minute and shouted, "I *knew* it was you!"

"What?" I said.

"I told my partner, Hey there goes Barry Manilow, but he said, No way, and I said, Yeah it's him all right, five bucks says so."

I couldn't get my heart to stop pounding, but more than that I couldn't get my blood to stop boiling! But what was I going to do? Police brutality, itchy trigger fingers, ya know what I mean?

"Yep, it's me," I said through clenched teeth.

Those festive lights were still flashing behind my car and people were slowing down to look at who was being questioned by the cops. Some recognized and waved.

"You going to be appearing anywhere around here? I haven't seen any billboards for you in a while," the officer said.

"Nope."

"Ya know, my girlfriend loves you. You think you could give me an autograph for her?"

"Yep."

"Great! Lemme get a blank piece of paper."

When he left to go to his car, passing drivers could get a very clear look at who was in the criminal's car. I tried to indicate that the cops were just asking for my autograph, but the passing drivers just shook their heads in sympathy.

One wise-ass yelled, "What's the matter, Manilow, doesn't he like your music?"

When I got my car, everyone advised me to tint the front-seat windows so people wouldn't hassle me while I was on the road. But no one told me that in California it's illegal to tint the windows on the front seat. One day while driving in Hollywood, I saw those colorful lights again. I pulled over, and the policeman walked slowly over to my car. They always walk slowly, don't they?

"You've got tinted windows," he said.

Sensing that this wasn't going to be another autograph session, I smiled at him and said, "Yes, that's because they stare at me."

He looked at me funny. Slowly he said, "*Who* stares at you?"

"People," I said.

"People," he repeated.

"Yes, they're not used to seeing me out in public alone."

He nodded, humoring me. "Without the bodyguards," he smirked.

"Yeah, because they're always trying to touch me," I said modestly.

"And rip off your clothes," he sneered.

"Well, no, but once," I told him, wide-eyed, "a girl actually stopped her car in front of me and threw herself on my hood! I thought it was pretty funny myself," I went on casually, "because she crawled up and kissed the windshield and there was this big red lipstick mark on my window—"

"Lemme see your license," he said seriously.

He sort of recognized my name on my driver's license, and I

wiggled out of a ticket by offering to sign albums for the Police-man's Fund celebrity auction.

I had been driving for a while when I decided to buy a Rolls Royce. Don't ask me why I did it. I must have had too much Perrier to drink that day and my brains were bubbly. It was a white Corniche convertible with a red interior. I had a very ex-pensive sound system installed, and when the car arrived I was so in love with it that I nearly had my attorney change my will to read that when I died I was to be buried in the Rolls.

The first day out I was so petrified I would scratch it that I swear I drove at ten miles per hour. I found back streets that hadn't seen a car in years. It took me over an hour to get to the recording studio. It should have taken fifteen minutes. At the end of the first week I was a nervous wreck. Just putting gas in the thing was enough to ruin my day.

"Put your gloves on!" I'd scream at the attendant.

"Do you want your windows washed?" he would ask, trem-bling.

"No! *I'll* do it!" I'd shout.

I eventually sat down and had a long talk with myself.

"It's only a material thing," I said to myself.

"But it's the most expensive material thing you've ever owned," myself answered.

"Money is only folding paper," Yogi Manilow answered.

"You're full of shit," I rationalized.

I finally convinced myself that I should enjoy this wonderful machine and not be so crazy. So what if it got scratched. (*Scratched????!!!*)

One sunny California day, after I'd finished eight hours in a dark recording studio, I decided to put the top down and drive home as the sun was setting.

The parade behind me started at around La Brea Avenue. I didn't notice until I was in Beverly Hills, and by that time it was around five cars long. There were station wagons, sedans, and a motorcycle. At first I wasn't sure it was really for me. So I turned into a side street. The parade turned into the side street. I stopped. The parade stopped. I realized that eventually I would *have* to go home and by then all these cars would be going home with me. So I stopped, said hello, signed autographs, put my top up and my sunglasses on, and raced home.

I didn't realize what a commotion driving a white Rolls Royce convertible would cause. Everyone looks to see who's driving a Rolls. Even me! So I decided on my clever disguise. I bought a chauffeur's cap! Brilliant.

The next day, I put the top down, tucked my hair under the chauffeur's cap, and tried it again. The parade was around five cars long again, only this time they'd yell at me, "Hey Barry, what're you wearin' a chauffeur's cap for?"

One guy yelled, "Hey Rod, what's happenin'!" He thought I was Rod Stewart. He still followed me for a few miles. That was the last straw.

I had to get rid of the Rolls. I was just too on edge driving it. Besides, it really wasn't me. It made me feel like an old fart.

I really enjoy driving. It's practically the only time I'm absolutely alone. I've joined the "cassette-in-the-car" group. I know I should listen to the Top 40 stations, but I invariably opt for some cassette that I've loved for the last hundred years. I listen to my favorite radio stations (there's some weird stuff going on around 89 on the FM dial), and I talk to myself. Sometimes I get so involved in a discussion with myself, I find myself banging on the steering wheel to make a point and naturally I turn to find someone in the next car smiling at me.

When my friend Marty Panzer moved here from New York, I invited him to dinner. He called me and asked me to pick him up, and you know what I said? You got it.

"You don't drive?"

The Surprising Adventures

Control Yourself!

Standing there in the wings waiting for Johnny Carson to introduce me for my first appearance on his show, I felt more nervous than I had ever felt in my life. "Pull yourself together," I kept telling myself, but my heart kept flopping around inside my chest.

As he made a flattering introduction, I kept trying to catch my breath while I thought about what the hell had got me to this agitated state.

I had been making the *One Voice* album and had been off the road for about seven months. When it came time to start promoting it, *The Tonight Show* was suggested because of its huge audience and because I had never done it before. Sounded okay to me. In the weeks leading up to it, I didn't really think about it, but during the final week, I began to feel butterflies in my stomach every time I thought of doing it.

I hadn't slept at all the night before the show. I was working myself into a state of nerves that was way beyond the reality of the situation. I had rehearsed the few songs I was to sing and the band sounded fine. I knew what I was going to say to Johnny and I also knew that he was going to be gentle and easy to deal with. There really was no reason for this case of nerves, but it was there nevertheless.

During the afternoon, I had bitten all my nails off and even had a few cigarettes although I'd stopped smoking years before. I was making everyone around me crazy. On the drive to the show, I began to sweat and shake. My new assistant, Paul Brownstein, began to become concerned.

"Maybe we should just take you to a hospital," he said. "I think that might be better publicity than doing the show!"

"No, I'm fine," I told him.

As we drove past the NBC building on our way to the stage entrance, I could see a crowd of people with signs and banners that had my name on it. Ah, my wonderful fans had come to cheer me on. It made me feel better for a minute, and then it made me feel even more nervous.

What was my worst fear? I kept asking myself. What could possibly happen that would merit this insane state I had worked myself into? I wasn't being rational, I knew, but the closer the time came, the crazier I got.

Back in the dressing room, I could hear commotion going on outside in the hallway. My hands were shaking as I brushed my hair. The makeup man asked me if I was all right. When the stage manager escorted me to the wings, I was at a stage where I couldn't see.

But then the strangest thing happened. As I walked out to the greeting of the audience, I began to feel a little better. When I heard the familiar music we'd rehearsed, I felt stronger, and by the time I was halfway into the song, I was fine!

The interview was a breeze: Johnny was a gentleman and seemed glad to see me on his show. The last song was very strong, the band sounded fine, and when I waved good-bye, I felt good.

Afterward, during dinner with a few friends, I kept trying to figure out what had happened to me. My first instinct was to blame everything else. But the truth was that even though I had somehow managed to pull it off for all these years, basically, I still didn't feel that I knew what I was doing when I was onstage.

When I had signed a record contract with Bell Records in 1973 and agreed to go out and perform with a band so that I could promote my first album, it was really just a means to an end. I loved writing songs and being in the recording studio. Frankly, I figured I had pulled a fast one on them. Never in a million years did I think that I could have a successful career as a singer, but by playing the game I was getting an opportunity to make an album of my own songs. So what if I'd have to suffer and go on the road for a few months and get up in front of audiences and sing? The thrill of being able to hear my songs come to life and to work in a recording studio with those giant speakers and talented musicians was worth the discomfort. The album would probably never sell, and after the tour Bell would drop me and I'd go back to being a struggling studio musician/ writer.

I'm convinced that my success as a performer came because of the music. I surrounded myself with the finest musicians and singers I could find. I continually looked for interesting approaches to the arrangements of the material. We all worked each other to death and by the time we hit the stage, the shows were very solid. My backup girls were always delicious to look at and amusing as well as being fine singers. I'd run around checking the lights and the sound system. I'd make sure that one song blended into another and that each set had a solid form. I'd tighten the shows so that there was absolutely no excess. The pacing of the show was always of prime importance to me and I'd rearrange the order of songs constantly. When we were ready to play to an audience there was always only one element that was unsure.

Me.

My own performances never felt certain. The comments I'd get after performing would always compliment me on how "real" I seemed, or how "regular" I was. I enjoyed hearing that, but I knew the audiences were picking up on the fact that I'd never learned the rules of performing. Musically the shows were working fine. When I was at the piano, or even later, when I sat on a stool and sang, I felt great. But most evenings, I was going by instinct. The instinct, fortunately, was working, but inside I always felt at sea.

When each show was over, I'd heave a sigh of relief and begin praying that I could somehow do it again the next night. It had always been a horrible feeling, and the climax of *The Tonight Show* was the last straw for me. I decided right then that somehow I was going to learn how to conquer this problem. Somehow I had turned into a performer that audiences seemed to enjoy. I didn't know how it had happened, but it had, and it wasn't going to go away.

So I decided I would go out and find someone to teach me the rules of performing.

My friend and backup singer Reparata had been taking acting lessons from Nina Foch for a year. She called me one day and told me I would really enjoy Nina and that I should come by and monitor the class. After the experience on *The Tonight Show*, I decided that Nina's class was a good place to start to look for some rules.

She held her classes on Saturdays in a small building off Santa Monica Boulevard. I arrived as the class was about to start and took a seat in the back. It was a dark room half filled with chairs facing the performing area. Nina sat in the front of the class.

She was a great-looking woman in her late fifties. I was hooked on her as soon as she began talking. She was funny and super-intelligent. She seemed to have it all together.

One by one, the actors would get up and do their scenes, sometimes with a partner, sometimes by themselves. I sat and watched for three hours as these talented young people worked. After they'd finish, Nina criticized them and gave them notes. It was an amazing experience.

These people were intense. They were looking for the truth from the bottom of their souls. They'd laugh, they'd cry, they'd holler, they'd shout. They did things I never could imagine myself ever being free enough to be able to do in front of a roomful of people.

After the class, I met Nina and told her how impressed I was with her and her students. "I'd love to join your class, Nina, but

I can't imagine letting myself go like that in front of strangers," I said.

"What are you saying?" she asked, shocked. "You do that and more every night. The only difference is that you have a band behind you!"

She was right. When the songs worked—really worked—I was doing what a good actor does. But I never approached my songs or my shows like an actor. I didn't know how. Now Nina was telling me I had it all inside me and that I *had* been doing it right all along. I just needed the rules, the tools, so that I could do it again every night and not worry about luck or good vibes from the audience.

Taking acting technique classes from Nina Foch was a turning point in my life. Although it was difficult and awkward in the beginning, I soon began to get the hang of it. Soon I was studying with her privately nearly every day.

Just as an actor breaks down a scene, I would break down my song lyrics.

"Can't smile without you," I would sing to my imagined partner as she walked away from me. "Can't laugh and I can't sing, I'm finding it hard to do anything," I'd tell her as she was threatening to leave me.

My songs became more potent, more intense, when I "partnered." My moves became clearer and sharper when I knew where and why I was moving on the stage. And the best part of all was that I never again had to feel unsure! It was possible to plan everything out so that nothing could throw me. As soon as I knew exactly what I had to do in each song and in between, my nerves left me. Now I could involve myself completely with the audience and never think of myself or my nerves again.

It was like going back to the beginning for me. So much so that when it came time to book the next tour, I decided literally to go back to the beginning.

"Let's do it all again, and maybe this time I'll get it right!" I said to myself. Instead of booking a tour in fifteen-thousand-seat arenas, I convinced my agency and manager to book me on a tour of small clubs. The kind of clubs I had played when I began.

I hired a new band and new backup singers and we played five-hundred-seat nightclubs around the country. We charged five dollars apiece and didn't advertise. When I finished our first show in a small club in Denver, for the first time in my performing career I felt that I was in control.

Oh No, Not Again!

At the end of that tour, I headed toward my little house in Palm Springs. The tour of small nightclubs had grown into a tour of fifteen-thousand-seat arenas and had lasted for six months. The weather in Palm Springs is glorious in January. While the rest of the country freezes and catches colds, it's usually eighty degrees there.

Slowly my shoulders began to relax and resume their natural position instead of being up around my ears. I found myself sleeping late. I caught up on books I had wanted to read, and sometimes I'd even go to the piano and try to write. I'd invite friends to stay with me, and I realized that the house I owned in Palm Springs was too small to accommodate more than three people at a time, so I began to look for a bigger place to live in.

I found it one weekend, a big beautiful home surrounded by fruit trees and lawns. Aside from the master bedroom and living rooms, it had two guest rooms. It had a gigantic swimming pool, a tennis court, and a separate building where I could hide away and write. I had asked Garry Kief to begin handling some of my finances on the West Coast, and I told him to look into buying this new house for me.

The next weekend, Garry dropped by my little Palm Springs

215

home, looking very serious. He told me that he had to talk with me immediately. We walked outside and sat in two chairs near the pool.

Garry Kief is bright, together, and handsome. He's a great businessman and came highly recommended.

"How are you feeling?" he said.

"How am I feeling? I'm feeling fine. Why do you ask? Do I look sick?" I asked him, puzzled.

"No, but what I'm about to tell you might make you nauseous," he said.

"What?" I said.

"I've been looking into your finances and trying to buy that house for you," he said.

"Yes . . . and?" I prompted.

"And the first time I looked through all of your holdings, all I could find was eleven thousand dollars," he said. "I knew that had to be impossible, so I had Tucker Cheadle, your new tax attorney, check through everything you own in New York and Los Angeles."

"And?"

"And . . ." He couldn't get the words out.

"And?" I asked, now sitting at the edge of my chair.

"And . . . all he could find was eleven thousand dollars," he told me.

There was silence.

"What are you saying?" I asked.

"I'm saying that unless you've been hiding your money under your mattress, all you've got is eleven thousand dollars to your name. The rest of your money is tied up in huge investments that won't pay off for years, if at all."

"There's got to be some mistake," I said.

"I don't think so, Barry. We both looked everywhere."

"Can't we take some money out of the investments?" I asked.

"Not only can't we take money out, but you owe lots more on each of them."

"How about stocks and bonds?"

"None."

"Real estate?"

"You're living in them," he said. "You've got the co-op in New York, but there's no market for it now."

"What about all those papers I've been signing for the last seven years?"

"They're worthless. In order to see any kind of profit from those businesses, you'd need to keep pouring money into them for years."

I looked at him for a long minute, waiting for him to smile and say he was joking. He was serious. "You're kidding, right?" I said, trying to stop this conversation.

"No. I'm not kidding," he said, dead serious.

I took a deep breath. "Okay, now, lemme get this straight. You're telling me that out of all the money I've made in the past seven years, all I have is eleven thousand dollars?"

He nodded.

I got up from the chair and jumped into the pool. I swam ten laps back and forth as fast as I could. When I finished, Garry was still sitting there. I hung onto the side of the pool, breathing hard.

"Hey, Gar, come on in. I've got an extra bathing suit in the closet," I told him. "Are ya thirsty? Linda! Could you get Garry some apple juice?" I called. "Is everyone still reeling from John Lennon's assassination? I tell you, it was the most horrible thing. You know, I was in New York, staying three blocks from the Dakota when he was shot . . ." I sped on.

"Barry!" he shouted. "You're broke!"

I was broke. I had sold over forty million records and made fortunes with my successful tours, and I was broke.

"Maybe I can melt down the gold records," I suggested.

"This isn't funny, Barry. You're in trouble."

"Good thing I sold the Rolls!" I said and started doing my laps again.

Garry got up and went into the house.

I had tried to stay on top of my finances, but it was Big Business and I was never good at figures. So I'd hired a highly regarded business manager to invest my money. He had looked just like Jimmy Stewart, so I was sure he would look out for me. Now, I found out I had been wrong.

He would come to me while I was hectic on the road, or in the recording studio during a break. He'd show me a stack of legal papers and try to explain what was in them. They were too complicated for me and finally I would just say to him, "Sam, do you recommend that I sign these papers?" and he would look at me with total honesty written all over his Jimmy Stewart face and say, "Yes, I do." And I would sign them.

Sam wasn't dishonest—he just made bad choices, and I didn't know enough to stop him. He hadn't been able to continue to feed the investments with as much money as they needed and had to sell many of them at a loss. Some of them had gone belly up. To top it off, the IRS was getting set to fine me millions of dollars for owning a personal holding company, a tax shelter my financial advisers had set up for me, and that was about to backfire.

In researching my finances, Garry had found that my money had been invested in questionable projects that would probably *never* pay off. And even these projects needed huge amounts of money each year just to protect my share.

I was, for all intents and purposes, busted, for the second time in my career. Who could deal with such news? All I had to show for seven years of hard work was eleven thousand dollars and a few lousy investments?

Garry could see that he wasn't going to be able to have a coherent conversation with me that afternoon, so we made plans to speak the following morning. It was a killer predicament. I was stunned.

I hardly slept that night. And when I slept, I dreamed strange dreams. I dreamed I was back on Twenty-seventh Street. I was in the basement with the washing machines and I was doing my wash, the way I used to. I dreamed that I was riding on a subway, going to meet a client I played piano for. I dreamed that I was strolling down Madison Avenue looking in the shop windows and no one was bothering me. I dreamed that I was hanging around on my old stoop in Brooklyn with Larry and Fred.

And I was happy.

Losing all my money was probably a good thing for me. Really. It forced me to look at my life and see what things were important to me and what things weren't. It was as if God were telling me, once again, not to get used to all the material things I had accumulated. Success, real success, is measured by your heart, not by your bankbook.

As I did when I went broke six years before, I felt panic, but at the same time I felt a sense of relief. Maybe now I could go back to the time when things were simple and fun. Back to when every little thing wasn't a life-or-death decision. It was a great fantasy, but it was just a fantasy. In reality, I had bills to pay, people to support, and lots of responsibilities. I felt low, but strangely enough, not as low as I had felt during the times when my creativity was being stifled by battling the Top 40.

Now I felt pissed off at the people around me who had let this happen. Most of all I was angry at myself. I had always known that one day I would have to pay for abdicating responsibility and letting other people do things for me. Well, the day had arrived.

But I was not going to let a minor problem like money lick me. I never got into the music business for the money. It still didn't mean very much to me. I had been broke when I was growing up and I survived. Jeanne and I couldn't even afford bus fare to her mother's house, and we had survived. Bette and I were making very little money at the Downstairs and I had survived. I had been broke before and I had survived. I would survive again.

Garry and Tucker were capable and honest men. They would get me out of this mess. *I* would get me out of this mess! After all, wasn't I the guy who had "made it through the rain"? I was always telling everyone not to give up. It was time for me to practice what I preached. I still had my friends and family for moral support. My fans were still out there and I still had my music.

Garry and Tucker pulled me out of the fire temporarily, and we put together a plan of attack. It meant touring and making albums nonstop for three years. Nobody knew any of what had happened and I never told anyone. It was a pretty disgusting story, but ultimately, it was my fault. I had to take responsibility for my life and for my finances.

"You want success? Well, success costs," I told myself.

The press picked up a rumor that I had bought an $11 million mansion in Beverly Hills. It gave Garry, Tucker, and me a great laugh when we read it.

Going broke for a second time opened my eyes to more changes I needed to make in my life. You can't always get what you want, but . . . sometimes you might get what you need, to paraphrase the Stones.

A crisis like that was what I needed. Even though it wasn't totally my fault, I tended to blame myself because I had not been on top of my own affairs. I decided that if I wanted my life to run smoothly, I had to take control of it. Unless you are physically forced into something against your will, I don't believe that you are ever a victim, and I had felt like a victim.

I sat down with Garry and he suggested a very intelligent plan. He introduced me to bright young businessmen he had worked with and trusted. I put together a committee of these men to handle my career, of which Garry and I were the head. There would be meetings each week, and this time I would sit in on them. They would bring me up to date on each aspect of my professional and business life. I would never again just hand over my finances and my career to strangers.

It was an enormous responsibility and sometimes it was difficult wearing two hats—that of the artist and that of the manager. But within a few months I began to get a sense of my life I had never had before. I felt more confident than ever. I promised myself, if possible, that I would never let my professional career out of my control.

Our plan of touring nonstop and making records continued for three years and slowly I pulled my life together. My friends and family would keep asking me why I was working so hard and for so long. I'd tell them it was to support albums or singles, and it was the truth, but in reality I was trying to make up for the loss of years of work.

I am truly blessed. I have bounced back from devastating financial situations twice in my life. It's taken an extraordinary amount of determination and hard work. It's taken the love and wisdom of the brilliant people around me to get me through these times professionally and psychologically.

Whenever I hear people use the word *luck* as the explanation for anyone's success, I always see red. I don't believe in luck. I believe in hard work. I believe in commitment. I believe that anyone who has found success has worked for it.

Nina's definition of *luck* is "When preparation meets opportunity."

Open the Door and See All
the People

Although I had been performing and recording since Bette's tour in 1973, I didn't really meet the public until many years later. Because that's when I met Roberta.

I was putting out records, doing interviews, and touring during those years, but other than the live audience response, I never really knew what the public thought. The "fan" mail was always sent either to Arista, my booking agency, or the halls in which we played. My home address wasn't published, so I never received any mail there.

Now and then a few scattered letters would get through, and mostly they'd ask for an autographed photo. Sometimes there'd be a serious letter about the work I was doing, and I was always so moved and grateful for it that I'd invariably begin a correspondence with the letter writer. I'm still in touch with some to this day.

As I began to become more and more recognized, the public became frightening to me. I'd walk down the street and before I knew it there was a mob of people wanting things from me. I'd get on a plane and soon there'd be people kneeling beside me asking for things. They'd stare and point and take my picture as I tried to have a meal in a restaurant. Little by little I began to become very wary of the public. I hired a special service to take care of the fan mail, and pretty much depended on the reaction from my close friends and the live audiences for feedback.

The last straw came when I discovered that a few "fans" had been going through my garbage and publishing their findings in a local newsletter. It turned me off so much that I stopped reading fan mail and had a different view of people who approached me from then on.

After my first television special aired in 1977, I tried going home to New York to visit my mother. My encounters with people in the airport were more uncomfortable than ever before. It seemed that the TV special had given me a very high profile (because of my nose, I already had a pretty high profile!). But this time I was bombarded with people yelling my name, demanding autographs, demanding that I take a picture with them. Same thing *on* the plane. People came to stare at me, thrusting pieces of paper in front of me for my autograph. Rude, impolite, demanding people. Most of them probably didn't even know any of my music. Those people couldn't have been fans—not what I consider fans. They were probably the ones going through my garbage!

At the airport in New York, some guy walked up to me, didn't even greet me, and just handed me a pen and a piece of paper. He said, "Would you give me your autograph?"

I said, "Sure. Now what are you going to give me?"

I was wrong to say it, but I had had it. I apologized to him as I signed my name.

As I was going to the gate, he came running after me. He said, "You know, I've been thinking about what you said. You're right. I wanted something from you and didn't give you anything. So I'd like to invite you to dinner with my wife and daughter when you're in town," and he handed me a business card with his address and phone number. I'm glad I'd made my point, and I know he was sincere, but I still had a very bad taste in my mouth about the public.

I wanted so desperately to talk to the people and find out what they thought. I knew it would really help me as an artist. But it seemed they didn't want to talk; they just wanted a piece of me.

I began to try disguises, but they didn't help. I'd wear false mustaches or floppy caps. I bought sunglasses that practically covered my entire face. But it was as if I was wearing a flashing neon sign. I began to understand why celebrities get a reputation for being creeps. I found myself being rude to strangers all the time and I always wanted to run after them and apologize.

Because of my alienating experiences, I retreated behind closed doors for years. I made my records and did my shows, but never really knew the kind of people who were enjoying my music. It was difficult creating music for people I never met or for people I didn't like, so I did the next best thing. I made them up.

I fantasized about the kind of people that I hoped were listening to my music; I pictured them as warm, friendly, intelligent. I imagined that they loved *all* the songs, not just the hits. I imagined them devouring my albums, the way I used to devour Laura Nyro's or Crosby, Stills and Nash's albums—memorizing every lyric and musical phrase. I'd pretend they understood all the subtleties in the concerts and television shows. Even though I'd never met that kind of fan, I pretended they were out there somewhere and I continued to create things for them.

Paul Brownstein, my assistant, introduced me to his friend Roberta Kent in late 1979. She was a stand-up comedienne and a comedy writer, a tall blond girl with a sweet face. Paul brought her to a small Christmas party I gave and I liked her the minute I met her. Her sense of humor was astounding. I'd never met anyone who made me laugh so much and so soon.

As I said good night to her, I put my arms around her and said, "Listen, I think you're terrific. I really enjoyed meeting you. I hope we see each other again."

She said, "You really mean that?"

"Yes I do."

"Then I guess I won't be needing these ashtrays," she said as she pulled them out of her purse. I doubled over laughing.

Every time I'd meet her after that, she'd do something crazy.

I asked her out to lunch and we agreed to meet in a parking lot. She was standing there waiting for me as I pulled my car in. When I drove up to her, she slammed her hand against my car and fell to the ground yelling, "Somebody call my attorney, quick! Barry Manilow just hit me!" The parking-lot attendants looked on in horror as I cracked up.

I asked Roberta to help me put my next show together, and we began a wonderful relationship. Just as Nina taught me the basics of acting and performing, and as Kevin helped direct me and the entire show, Roberta helped me create a funny, fast-paced, exciting presentation.

We had a great time working together. Because we didn't need any props or musical instruments, we worked in fun places. She'd tread water in my pool in Palm Springs while I paced around it, trying out different comedy lines. "Don't walk when you say that line. You'll get a bigger laugh," she'd tell me from the water. Since she was an experienced comedienne, she taught me about comic timing. My own instincts were pretty good, but listening to Ro's suggestions sharpened every joke, and when I performed for the public the next time, the laughs were bigger than I'd ever gotten.

I convinced her to come along on the next tour with me. I promised her sandy beaches, exotic places, and luxurious conditions. In reality, we were headed for Largo, Maryland, and hockey rinks, but Ro was a good sport and each day with her was a joy. We laughed from morning till night. We created lots of new jokes for the show, and she'd give me ideas each night on how to make things better for the next night.

When we played the casinos in Las Vegas, Lake Tahoe, and Atlantic City, she opened the show for me and the audiences loved her. She was my favorite warm-up act ever.

This was the first time I had been able to bring along someone from my personal life and include her in my professional life and have it work. Since she'd never been on the road before, it was fun showing her the ropes. I'd forgotten how exciting being a star could be, and I wanted to share the star treatment with her. By showing Roberta life on the road, I also showed it to myself, and for the first time I began to really enjoy it. We spent the afternoons sightseeing and getting to know this beautiful country of ours.

During the summer months, we rented private homes, relaxed

around swimming pools, and walked through wooded glades. Instead of taking airplanes, we'd drive from place to place.

She began to break down the barriers that had been growing higher and higher in front of me. During the first part of the tour, I continued to behave as I always had. My security men would run me through back doors and kitchens and directly up to my hotel room or dressing room. They'd sneak me out of limousines into restaurants. As I dressed for the show, my door would be closed and my room filled with only my clothes or work essentials.

Roberta was troubled when she saw the kind of isolated existence I was living. She had been a friend and fan of Elvis Presley. She was concerned that by isolating myself as I was doing, I might begin to head in the destructive direction that he wound up going in.

When she told me her concerns, I tossed it off. "Don't worry, Tootsie," I told her, "that can't happen to me. I'm Jewish." But I was concerned. I did find myself separated all of the time and it was getting worse. I didn't like it.

She began to open the door to the outside world by introducing me to the public. She knew how fantastic it was outside my isolated lifestyle. Because she knew I never had seen it, she wanted me to see the reaction to what I had created. She read each and every letter that was sent to me. She'd go out into the audience and meet the people, and she'd relate stories about them to me.

During the 1980 tour, Ro would read me the fan letters while I dressed for the show at night, and some letters would bring tears to my eyes. She'd come running in showing me gifts or handmade things. Soon my usually empty dressing rooms were filled with flowers and gifts and letters.

"These people drove one hundred miles to see you tonight!" she'd tell me.

I was amazed.

"I just read this letter from a family who have been waiting for three years for you to come here," she told me, sniffling. "They can't afford to come because the husband is in the hospital."

I'd have her call them and give them tickets.

She'd sneak people into the shows if there were empty house

seats. I could never say no to her and I would end up meeting entire families that she'd usher backstage after the shows. She'd make me peek out from the wings into the crowd and she'd point out things; banners, flags, people with love notes written all over their bodies—things I never saw because of the bright spotlights.

I began to get a sense of my career and how it affected people and I was thunderstruck. I had had no idea that people were reacting to my work with such passion.

Roberta has the kindest heart of anyone I've ever met. She is a genuinely good woman, and she reacted to my loving and caring fans with incredible warmth. Having been touched by Elvis, she was able to relate to them and understand them.

Slowly, I emerged from behind the locked doors of my dressing room and hotel suites and met people. I had been so turned off by the "yes" people I thought surrounded me and by the demanding public I had met that I had hidden behind closed doors whenever I toured. Now, because of Roberta and her outgoing personality and love for people, I began to enjoy meeting strangers. For the first time, there was a channel of communication opened between me and the public and it was a revelation. I began to know names, families. I recognized faces in the crowds. I'd sit and read the letters, and I realized that the job I was doing meant much more to these people than just a few pretty songs.

These people had practically adopted me. It had gone way beyond merely liking my latest album. I was important to them as a person. The support I began to realize I had was amazing. They knew how hard I had worked. They appreciated that I had given my life to my music career and they thanked me for it. Until Roberta showed them to me, I didn't think anybody but my closest friends and family even cared about that. The letters would quote lyrics and mention melodic passages that I thought no one caught. They'd mention moments in concerts that affected them, which I thought had gone unnoticed.

And the most wonderful news was that their favorite songs were my favorite songs! They weren't just buying the records and going to the shows for the commercial hits. They loved the singles for what they were, but they actually loved other songs too. It was the most encouraging news I could receive. And it came at a time when I really needed it.

Along with the support came a responsibility. I began to look at my work in an entirely different light. From now on, I had a new duty. As I read the letters and met the people, I realized they were taking me and my music and what I represented very seriously and I had to take them just as seriously.

"Can't Smile Without You" had actually gotten a woman with severe depression to leave her house. "Daybreak" had helped a family through a daughter's horrible sickness. "All the Time," a song Marty and I had written about feeling like a misfit, had practically saved people's lives.

The letters I read began to have a profound effect on me. I asked for them to be forwarded to me personally, and they came by the bagfuls, day in and day out. Hardly any of them merely wanted an autograph. They wrote to thank me for my work. They understood. I was deeply touched.

My new friend and business associate, Garry Kief, began setting up a new fan club that I became personally involved in. Soon there was an enormous network of people communicating with each other. This network of friends and fans began to grow and grow until it reached over sixty thousand members. To me, it was an overwhelming statement of support and there is no way to convey my gratitude.

It began to go way beyond just me and my music. I was just serving as a catalyst to introduce people to one another. It soon turned into a gigantic family who knew each other and corresponded with each other. There would be charity projects and raffles. There would be engagements and marriages and babies! It was a wonderful feeling to know that my music had started this snowball of love.

Not only did Roberta help me become a better performer, but she did a much more important thing for me. She showed me what had been there all along—people who cared.

What Is the Answer?

During my 1983 concert tour of the United States, I decided I would stop at one or two high schools each week, and talk to the music classes. Maybe I could help someone by relating my experiences. I showed up at one or two schools each week and talked to the music classes.

I chose high schools because the students are in their formative years. I enjoyed speaking with music college students too, but their questions are much more technical, and they've already decided what they want—a career in music. I wanted to rap with kids who weren't sure about their future.

Being successful is a tremendous responsibility. Never was it more clear to me than the first time I stood in front of an auditorium filled with high school students. It would have been really easy to turn the hour into a talk show and give witty answers to cute questions.

For the first fifteen minutes, they didn't stop chattering and giggling. Then every other question was "Can I have a kiss?" or "How's Bagel?" But I wasn't there for fun. I was there for that one possible little kid sitting out there, too shy to ask a legitimate question, too afraid of the undertaking, too talented for words.

As I hoped, after the students got over the initial shock of my actually being in front of them, and after the wise-asses in the back of the auditorium calmed down, I usually spent about an hour or so answering serious questions.

I would start off by telling them that I was not there to encourage or discourage anyone about the music business. I was merely there to share my own experiences with them. Once the questions started rolling, they would come at me pretty fast. It was usually so enjoyable, we would stop only when we had to.

I would stare out at the kids and I could spot those few who were taking it very seriously, asking me question after question. I wanted so much to give them the secret, but I didn't have it. They had it inside themselves and all I could do was start their motors going.

"The only truth I know," I would tell them, "is that if you're going to be great, then you're great now. And you know it. You know it right now. Only you can't believe it. You just need some prodding and you need some proof."

I always knew that I was very musical, but I would constantly deny it. In high school, I just wanted to be like everyone else, but all the time I knew I was different. What I needed were teachers to teach me the language of music and encouragement from the ones I loved and respected.

I was one of the lucky ones, because I did receive the love and encouragement I needed. But it was during those teenage years in high school when I *knew* what I had inside me that I needed to talk to someone who wouldn't look at me as if I were crazy. I hoped I could do that for somebody in that auditorium.

"Believe in yourself," I would tell them. "Oh, I know it's easy to do that today when you're surrounded by your friends, but once you get out in the real world and they begin to beat you up, you might need to be reminded. Believe in yourself. Trust yourself. You have all the answers in you—you really do. Take chances. If you're faced with the choice to play it safe or to gamble—gamble!

"To all you budding performers: *Don't do it for the money or for the applause! It will never be enough.*

"Every career has its difficulties. But show business is unique in that it attacks your self-esteem, your dignity, your self-respect. You'll be humiliated and terrified daily. You'll work for peanuts for years and your chances are very slim that you'll ever see your name in lights.

"And when you do make it, it gets harder. The more success, the more pressure that comes along with it. The more money you make, the more money you spend—on agents and managers and personnel—and the more insecure you feel. The more applause you hear, the more you need it.

"Make sure you're doing it because you love it. Make sure you're doing it because you can't stop it. Make sure that something about the work gives you ultimate pleasure. If you fail, you can't lose, because you did it from the heart.

"To all of you budding Bacharachs and struggling Streisands out there: *Learn to read music!* If you dive into the music business, you'll be up against so much competition, your head will spin. If you can sight-read music (or sight-sing) and transpose, you'll be more in demand than the rest. And you'll always be able to make a living just in case, God forbid, David Merrick doesn't make you the star of his new show.

"To all of you songwriters: *Be neat!* It goes without saying that if you're going to send your songs around, you should try to make the best demonstration tapes you can afford. If you can afford to hire an orchestra, do it. If you can only afford to play your guitar or piano and sing, that's okay too. If it's a good song, it will work. But when you're done with the artistic part, don't stop. Type the lyrics neatly. Label the cassette clearly. Include a professional-sounding letter with a little humor in it and pack up the whole thing in a professional cassette envelope.

"If this sounds obvious to some of you, it's not. I can't tell you how many cassettes don't make it to my machine because of amateur presentations. I know I may be tossing away a number-one song. But probably not. When a cassette arrives and looks as if someone took time and care in its presentation, one can't help but take it more seriously than one that arrives looking like someone just threw it in an envelope and sent it out."

*　　*　　*

Here are some of the most frequently asked questions:

Q: How do you write a song?

A: You make it up as you go along. John Lennon said, "Say what you have to say, try and make it rhyme, and give it a backbeat."

Q: I have no money for demos. What do I do?

A: Beg, borrow, work. Find it somehow. We all did.

Q: Are there any rules to follow in order to write a hit song?

A: Yes. There are three very important rules to writing a hit song. But nobody knows what they are.

I'd usually close by having them roll out a piano and I would play and sing a little. The sessions were always very rewarding for me. Who knows, maybe I pushed someone's button. But in the limousine back to the hotel, I always regretted that I didn't have the guts to give them one more piece of advice.

Here it is: If you're *really* serious about a career in music, get out of this small town, move to Manhattan, and go for it!

Adventures on the
Way to Paradise

The Blenheim Experience

When we made plans to play Britain in 1983, David Simone at Arista Records U.K. suggested putting on a concert at Blenheim Palace, the stately home of the Duke of Marlborough situated on eleven thousand acres in Woodstock Park, Oxfordshire. It was given to the first duke by a grateful England for winning wars against the French in 1705. Winston Churchill was born and died there. It has the finest view in England.

After a year of negotiations with the duke, we finally settled on August 28 and picked the exact spot on the property. The promoters estimated that between forty thousand and fifty thousand people would attend. Everybody thought they were crazy, most of all me. But Garry believed in the project and began organizing it.

It sounded as if it could be an amazing event and we began creating a show that would be comfortable and exciting for all those people. Garry hired an enormous team to concentrate on the Blenheim concert. The event was to begin at noon and would include a full day's worth of jugglers, musicians, clowns, bands, and food, climaxing with the show in the evening. It took a lot of people to coordinate the day.

The stage alone took an entire week to construct. There was

to be a sixty-member orchestra, a thirty-member choir for "One Voice," specialized scenery, and sets and two gigantic video screens on each side of the stage so that the action could be seen by everyone. The cost of this one afternoon was close to one million dollars.

I'd been having a love affair with the British people since 1979. They've made me feel incredible. On the other hand, it was hate at first sight with the British press. In America, at least, it took the press a couple of years to rip me to shreds. In Britain, I could do no right. The reviews of my first concerts in 1979 told the public not to take me seriously because I was just a teenage idol who wouldn't be around for long. The very next year the same reviewers told the public not to take me seriously because I was an old fart who was over the hill!

I decided I just can't take reviewers seriously. I think my music is like anchovies: Some people love them—some people get nauseous.

The Blenheim experience began to be a very exciting trip. Everyone worked his tail off. The stage they built on the meadow at Blenheim Palace was indescribable; I'd never ever seen anything like it. It looked like a combination of Woodstock and the U.S. festival. Enormous. It was on the grounds of the palace where there was only a meadow full of sheep. Now, besides a humongous stage, there were enormous lighting towers, a sound tower, fences, dressing rooms, bleachers, concession stands, flags, ambulances, two giant-screen TVs, sixty musicians, and a thirty-member choir. It was amazing. Everyone was absolutely blown away.

We rehearsed for three days—wonderful, tiring days. Each night ended at three A.M. and my days started at eight-thirty A.M. for radio and TV interviews.

I should have been nervous, but I wasn't. I couldn't wait to do the show. We all were praying it wouldn't rain.

The night before the show, the duke and duchess of Marlborough invited me and a small group of my staff and friends to dinner at the palace. It was a thrill for all of us.

I spent some time alone with the duke. He gave me a private tour of the palace. It was awesome. I tried to say very little, because I knew that whatever I said would have sounded idiotic. "Oh wow," just didn't seem right, but that's about all that kept coming out.

We had dinner in their private quarters. Her Grace is a beautiful and charming woman, as elegant as could be, but down to earth too. We had drinks in the parlor before dinner, and I noticed a small oil painting sitting on the mantelpiece. It was a pack of Marlboro cigarettes! A sign that the Marlboroughs had a sense of humor.

While I was chatting with the duke, I overheard Roberta say to the duchess, "Well, you certainly hooked yourself some catch!" I nearly spit up my champagne. But the duchess held her own. "I think that he could say the same!" she said, and they both laughed and walked away chatting and Roberta winked at me.

Dinner was fun, very relaxed. We all were seated away from our dates or spouses, encouraging conversation. Everyone in my party was thrilled to death. The duke and duchess were royalty in the truest sense, in that they made all of us feel as if we were royalty.

Near the end of dinner, Kevin excused himself and said he had to leave to get back to the site to oversee the end of the lighting run-through. I said I had to go too. The duke and duchess asked if *they* could come with us! So we all piled into about eight limousines and drove right onto the concert field.

All the cars faced the stage with their lights on. What a sight we were! All of us in our dinner clothes, gowns, and tuxedos. The crew didn't know what to make of it. We just leaned up against the cars, opened another bottle of champagne, and watched some of the rehearsal. We finally took some pictures, signed some autographs, vowed that we had to do this again some day, and kissed good-bye.

Some of the next day's crowd had begun to camp outside the site. I felt bad that they were going to have to sleep outside all night long so I went over to say hello to them. They were in fine shape and very prepared for the long night ahead. They had sleeping bags and food and drink. They looked like they were having a great time, and I felt better. I could hear them cheering and singing as the car pulled away and it made me feel great.

The day of the show, at five-thirty P.M., I picked up Edna and Willie and we drove to the helicopter pad. They were really nervous about the flight to Blenheim Palace, but once in the air, they loved it. The ride was just beautiful. It was a perfect day: no rain, not too hot, sunny.

When we got near the palace we could see the mass of people. So many. My mother started yelling, "Oh my God!" I was snapping pictures right and left. Willie was up front with the pilot and didn't say a word. He was stunned. I was so glad I could share this once-in-a-lifetime event with them. Who else in my whole life could I pick that would get a bigger thrill out of all this than they would?

We landed in a meadow behind the stage. I could hear Gerrard Kenny finishing up his set. Everyone was excited. There was no tension in the air at all, just positive excitement. When I got to the backstage area, the band, singers, crew, and all of my friends greeted me with grins from ear to ear. They told me all about the day's events and how well it was going. Roberta and Les Joyce, my tour manager and good friend, showed me around, and after a while it was time to get ready for the show.

As the time drew nearer, we began to get very excited. We could hear the crowd beginning to clap and yell. Ro left the trailer early to get to her place in the lighting tower, and we hugged good-bye.

"Thanks for all the help, tootsie," I told her. "You're very important to me. I don't know what I'd do without you." We hugged each other tight.

"Thank *you* for the free plane ride and don't forget to check your fly. Have a good time out there. I love you." And she was gone.

The Concert at Blenheim Palace

For me, the concert at Blenheim Palace was the high point of my performing career. It was as if all the work for all the years had been leading up to this one glorious night. Although I trembled with excitement, I felt confident I could pull it off.

After Roberta left my trailer, Victor Vanacore, my music director, knocked on the door. As the door opened I could hear the crowd beginning to stomp and holler.

"Kid, kid," he said. "How're you feelin'? Nervous?"

"A little," I said.

"It's just another gig, right?" he told me.

"Right, Victor," I smiled at him.

"I hear Boy George is out there," he said.

"Maybe that's why they're stomping and hollering," I said.

"Good luck, it's gonna be fun," he said.

"Thanks, Vic. Have a good time," I said.

The crowd was getting louder and now I could hear my musicians and singers warming up. A minute later Kevin knocked on the door. "Any changes?" he asked.

"Nope. How're ya doin'," I said.

"I'm doin' great. It's very exciting out there. You can even feel it in the TV truck. Remember this one, Barry."

"Thanks for everything, Kev," I said. He had been invaluable.

"It's been a lot of fun. Hey, let's do another one like this next week, okay?" he joked. "Have a good time out there and don't get too close to the edge of the stage. It's a long drop down!"

Gary Speakman, my stage manager, walked me to the wings, and when the house lights dimmed to half, the roar of the crowd was deafening.

"Should I be nervous about this?" I jokingly asked Charlie Mercuri, my dresser.

"No, but I'm glad it's not me goin' out there!" he shouted over the noise.

Standing in the wings, I began to feel nervous. My heart was going a million miles a minute. I breathed in and out deeply.

Speakman flashed the cue to begin. The overture started and the crowd went nuts and then more nuts. Everyone in the wings was yelling and shouting, but I could hardly hear them over the roar of the crowd.

On stage, Victor conducted the overture, grinning from ear to ear. He saw me standing in the wings and gave me the thumbs-up sign.

The music sounded great. It throbbed, it pulsated, it built.

It was very dark standing there in the wings. I couldn't see anything but Speakman's flashlight. I could see the floor and his feet dancing in time to the music. God, the overture was so exciting. I could hear the audience clapping along and recognizing the melodies from the songs.

My eyes adjusted to the dark, and I groped my way over to the box of tissues near the mirror. Why is it that I always have to blow my nose right before I go onstage? I spend so much time blending my makeup so that it won't look phoney, and then just when I can't see my face to fix it, I blow my nose and probably wipe all of the makeup off my nose. *That's* why the press always puts down my nose—it's probably whiter than the rest of my face and looks enormous! (Yes, I'm sure that's why!)

Who am I kidding? It *is* enormous!

"Hatch closed?" Speakman yelled over the music.

I had instructed him always to ask me if my fly was closed right before I go onstage. If he didn't, I spent all the blackouts checking to see if it was open, as it was one night. So embarrassing.

I peeked out at the crowd through a slit in the drape. It was the most enormous crowd I had ever seen. The size threatened to throw me for a minute, but I did my relaxation exercise that Nina had taught me, and I calmed down. The music continued.

All during the show, pieces of my life kept flashing through my mind, making each song and moment more potent than they had ever been before.

As I stared at the crowd through the curtain, a terrible night in Atlanta in 1975 flashed through my mind. I was waiting in the wings of a beautiful theater, all dressed up and surrounded by my backup group and stage personnel. Only five hundred people in a theater that holds six thousand. Putting on a happy face to the people around me and the audience, but dying inside.

I winced at the memory.

The overture was insistent. I could see the light show accompanying it through the slit in the curtain. It was spectacular.

"How's James feeling?" I asked Speakman over the roar of the music. James Jolis, my backup singer for years, had the flu but wouldn't miss this for anything.

"He's still hoarse."

Amarillo, 1976, flashed through my mind. A 103-degree fever, bones aching, stomach so queasy I couldn't even speak without gagging. I was standing in the wings listening to Lady Flash, my former backup girls, introduce me. Somehow I was still alive.

*   *   *

Denver, 1982. The altitude got me in Denver. Finished "One Voice,"
staggered into the wings, and collapsed on a stairway gasping for air.
Speakman gave me oxygen while the choir of kids who had just come
off the stage after backing me up walked by, thinking that I was taking
the song a little too seriously!

The overture continued. Pounding, soaring, building. I clapped
along and stamped with the drums.

Suddenly, the drums stopped. My heart stopped. Someone
came racing through the cubicle I was standing in.

"Excuse me, chief!" and three men were in and out in a flash.
I heard yelling and shouting. The rest of the band and singers
were still going, but the drums, which were electric, had stopped.
What happened?

"Ming-ee-ahh-yee!" I screamed. It's a warm-up exercise, not a
sign of hysteria. Everyone had heard me do this hundreds of times
so no one paid any attention to me.

With a giant thud, the drums came back.

These live performances can give you heart failure.

Forest Hills, New York City, 1978. This was my first big production.
Lady Flash, an enormous orchestra, Brooklyn kid comes home, sold out
for days. Edna, Willie, cousin Stevie, Aunt Rose—the whole family in
the audience. I knew they were going to love our show. But during the
fourth number, "This One's for You"—I'll never forget it—I smelled
smoke in the wings. I heard crackling. As I sang, I watched the spotlights
go out, one by one. When I finished the song I looked around and saw
it was dark on the stage. All the lights had blown out, short-circuited,
except the one on me. And they never came back. Even during act two.
And at the end of the show I got the longest standing ovation I had gotten
yet. It was one of the worst and one of the best nights of my performing
career. Made me realize that they really were coming for the music and
not the production. But going through it was exhausting and terrifying.

*　　　*　　　*

I could see Blenheim Palace lit up in the distance from the wings as the overture built to its climax. I felt nauseous. Why did I feel nauseous? What had I eaten? Nothing. That's probably why.

"Ming-ee-ahh-yee!"

The music slowed down and became very grand as the band played "Could It Be Magic." A long chord . . . and then it slammed into the pulsating beat of the introduction to "You're Lookin' Hot Tonight," my first song. Everyone around me was clapping and yelling. It was the culmination of months of work for these men. It meant as much to them as it did to me.

I heard my entrance music. I looked at Victor. He was beaming.

"Go get 'em, chief," Speakman yelled.

Getting ready to go, I listened to the excited crowd and told myself, "They're my friends, they're my good friends. They're my dear, old, good friends and I can't wait to see them again," and I was off and running.

I ran out of the wings and onto the riser I stand on. I stood with arms open, welcoming them to my party.

Have you ever heard forty thousand people yell at the top of their lungs? It's something to hear. The band members were going nuts, smiling and dancing and raising fists in the air.

I stood there, waiting, waving, smiling.

Carnegie Hall, New York City, 1971. Opening the second act for Bette. Making my way to the piano to polite applause, I could see one man standing in the audience applauding like mad. My Grampa. But he had his hat on and Gramma jumped up and snatched it off his head. How could I do anything but succeed with that audience? Whenever I get the slightest bit nervous on my entrances, I always remember Grampa standing up for me and all my nerves disappear.

"You're Lookin' Hot Tonight" was a very exciting opening song. I loved it. I couldn't get over the size of the audience.

I raced across the stage to the other side to greet the people there. Arms outstretched. Welcome everyone!

As I headed toward the last note, I knew it was going to be a hot crowd that night!

In the blackout I felt for my fly—was it closed?

Amazing.

"You wouldn't believe where I've been," I sang the opening lines from "It's a Miracle." I remembered Bette's first tour.

New York City, 1973. I had just arrived home from Bette's first national tour. Three whole weeks traveling around the country. Breaking records in every city. Selling out every place we played. A thousand seats a night!

I got home in the middle of the night and Bagel went crazy welcoming me, but I didn't want to wake up the whole twelfth floor in the building so I clamped my hand over her mouth and petted her until she was just whining with excitement. I went right to bed and when I got up the next morning she barked and barked for ten straight minutes. She had kept her welcome in for the whole night and let it go when I woke up. What a great dog.

I went to the piano the next day and wrote "You wouldn't believe where I've been," the opening lines to "It's a Miracle." Little did I know that that tour would be the shortest and easiest tour I would ever do.

After the next ballad, the band ripped into "New York City Rhythm," an especially meaningful song to me. As I sang it to my new British friends, I tried to convey to them the excitement of the city I grew up in.

I'll always consider New York my home. I'll always love my roots. I'll never be able to express my gratitude to New York and its people. How could I have ever survived the life I have lived without the strength and the moxie I learned in New York?

Behind me, as I sang, a gigantic New York City skyline was revealed. The crowd went nuts.

As I played the intro of "Memory" on the piano, I looked at the New York City backdrop and remembered how far I had come. I thought of Larry and of Susan and my old life. I thought of CBS and of Jeanne. I thought of my cousins and Division Avenue and Brighton Beach. I thought of little Barry Pincus— that misfit, that innocent, naïve little guy with braces on his teeth just wanting to be like Fred Katz.

And I sang "Let the memory live again" for all of them, because I never want to forget that they helped make me what I am today.

"Bandstand Boogie" came next, with its forties rhythm. Bette used to do a lot of forties songs when we first began together. As I jitterbugged with Muffy and Donna, my background singers, I remembered an incident that happened during my first year with Bette.

June 1971, Paramus, New Jersey. The Paramus Shopping Mall Thea- *ter. Bette was booked there for a week. Needless to say, Miss M was* *not a star yet. No album contract, no Harlettes, just me and three other* *musicians straight from the Continental Baths. She would come out* *wearing a corset and pedal-pushers and sing some very strange songs, to* *say nothing of her chatter. It was a local theater and attracted a very* *square audience. We were required to do eight shows during the week.* *Which meant two matinees.*

The Wednesday matinee was dismal. Ladies with shopping bags who *stopped in to see anything that was playing there. From the opening note,* *they just sat there with their mouths hanging open. Somehow, Bette's* *fans from the city showed up during each show and got her through.*

But on the Saturday matinee, it was asking too much of even die- *hard fans to drag themselves out to New Jersey at two in the afternoon.* *I guess they figured they'd see her evening show.*

The curtain opened and Bette made her grand entrance to the strains *of her theme song, "Friends," and hardly any applause. The theater was* *filled mostly with shoppers from the mall who had stopped in to rest* *their feet. But the clincher was the first ten rows. They were filled with* *girl scouts. Many, many chattering little girl scouts. A perfect audience* *for a Bette Midler show, wouldn't you say?*

After the third song, the order of the show began to change drastically.
Bette was dropping songs, singing them at breakneck speed, anything to
get off the stage! The Divine Miss M was not amused.

Finally, after twenty of the longest minutes in the world, Bette looked
down at the first row and spotted a very nasty-looking little thing sliding
forward in her seat and sticking her tongue out. Miss M had finally had
it. She stopped what she was doing and surveyed the audience with a
world-weary sigh. She looked at the girl scout through the two slits that
had become her eyes.

"Don't slouch, honey," Miss M said. "Your tits'll sag."

Then she turned and strode into the wings while the band and I
doubled up laughing and fumbled with her exit music.

I laughed at the memory. What a character she was. What times
they were for us. We finished "Bandstand Boogie" and soon I
was singing "No Other Love."

I thought of Susan.

Susan and I. Sweethearts. Don't ask me how I ever found her. We were
so in love. I was so happy with her and she thought I was a prince. She
gave me confidence, made me good-looking, made me laugh. I was her
steady and she was my girl.

Susan and I went to the Copacabana to see Lana Cantrell. We didn't
see too much of Lana because we were just looking at each other. And
when the floor show was done, they played music for dancing and they
lowered this wonderful mirror ball and hit it with spotlights and the whole
room twinkled as if we were in heaven. And we were.

When I got to the lyric in "No Other Love" that went, "I was
Mister Dynamite," the whole place screamed. It had become a
kind of tradition over the last year that whenever I got to that
line the audience would scream their approval. I grinned at them
and we all had a good laugh.

I was Mister Dynamite. Ha.

*   *   *

Camp Ma-Ka-Bee, 1960, when Mr. Dynamite was a camper-waiter, flashed through my mind.

Nancy was one of the prettiest girls in the camp and I had a very big crush on her. Sometimes I'd try and talk to her, and I think that she even tried to be civil to me, but I always blew it. The most embarrassing time of all was when they were choosing sides for the Watermelon League, a baseball game in which the winning team won a giant watermelon. The captains were chosen and one by one each captain chose a team member. Of course, I was the last one left, and Schwartz, the captain of the A team, finally said, "Okay, Manilow," and the whole team groaned. Nancy was watching and I wanted to crawl into the ground and pull it over my head.

Two weeks later the camp musical was announced. It was going to be "The King and I." I was chosen as music director and pianist. From then on, camp was bearable, and as the weeks of rehearsal moved along, I made more and more friends. On the night of the musical, when they announced my name as musical director, I got a big round of applause. I started dating Nancy that night and during that summer I became a man. I'll never forget it. Music had saved me again. That night, at least, I was Mr. Dynamite.

"No Other Love" subtly segued into "Mandy." When I played the opening notes, the audience recognized it and reacted. As the years go by, this song means more and more to me.

December 1974, Florida. Bruce and I in Florida. "Mandy" had just come out and was going crazy in Florida.

We had stopped for a hamburger in a diner near the beach. It was empty and there was a waitress behind the counter and a jukebox in the corner. I walked over to the jukebox and sure enough, "Mandy" was on it. I put a quarter in the jukebox and selected it. Bruce and I sat at the counter and the song came on as we gave the waitress our order. I was feeling a little cocky, and before she could walk away, I said, "Do people play that song a lot?"

"What song?" she said.

"The one playing now, 'Mandy.' "

"Oh, yeah," she said. Just as I was about to tell her that it was me singing, she continued, "and I wish they'd stop. I hate that thing."

It was like the air going out of a balloon, and Bruce spit up his Coke all over the counter.

There was lots of applause after "No Other Love"/"Mandy."

The last song in the first act was "I Made It Through the Rain," and as I sang it, I realized how very appropriate it was. Tonight, I felt as if I really had made it through. I felt good on stage. I loved the audience. I was proud of my work. I sang it that night to tell everyone that hard work and perseverance pay off.

As I turned and ran into the wings, my eyes went from the blinding glare of five Super Trooper spotlights to absolute darkness. I could see nothing. Nothing except for Speakman's ever-ready flashlight. A hand reached out to grab me, a towel landed on my shoulders.

"Everything is working like a charm!" Speakman said excitedly.

"Yeah? Great," I panted.

The band followed me offstage, all of them sweating and talking. We only had twenty minutes to dry off, change clothes, and begin act two.

I got back to my trailer and collapsed into a chair. Within minutes Roberta was there.

"It feels great out in the audience," she said.

"I sound like shit, though, huh?" I said, ever the optimist.

"A little raspy now and then, but no one's listening to you anyway," she joked. "The show looks spectacular and everyone's having a great time."

Kevin knocked on the door, all excited. "It looks great in the TV truck. How does it feel to you?"

"Actually, I'm not having too bad a time," I said.

Victor yelled from outside, "Kid, kid! You're killin' 'em!"

"Ten minutes, chief," Speakman shouted.

I started getting dressed for act two.

"I'm going back outside. Keep it up!" Roberta said, and went out.

"I'm going back into the truck," Kevin said.

"Five minutes, chief!" Speakman yelled from the hallway.

"Okay," I yelled back.

"Any changes in the second act?" Victor asked.

"Nope."

Victor left, and Roger Wall, my new assistant, came in. "Your parents will be back here after the show. You've got promoters to see, and record company people and their families, and the duke will be back too. Okay?" he asked.

"Huh?" I said. I was in the middle of putting on my pants.

"I'll tell you later," he said, and out he went.

I put on the rest of my clothes. I'm always sure I've left something off—or open.

Charlie came in. "Need any help?"

"Yes. Look at me. Have I got all my clothes on?"

"I think so," he said, looking me over.

"Is everything closed?" I asked him, hurrying.

"Looks like it, except your fly is open," he said.

"I don't believe it!" I yelled.

"Can I start the film?" Speakman yelled.

We had a funny travelogue made up to start the second act.

"Okay."

I could hear the band beginning act two. The audience sounded somehow friendlier. I don't know why, but they did. I could hear them yelling people's names. "Go Victor!" "All right, Art!"

"Hatch closed?" Speakman asked me.

"I think so." I checked.

The travelogue film ended in the jungle and segued into our opening song of act two, "The Lion Sleeps Tonight," the old sixties song. We had updated it and I learned how to play conga drums especially for the song.

When we finished, the lights went on and lit the audience. It was a huge crowd and I could barely see faces. I welcomed them back from intermission. They were really friendly. Like my friends and family.

The next song was "Even Now," one of my personal favorites, which never fails to move me. It reminded me of the great times I had collaborating with Marty. Marty and I had written "Even Now" in Florida, on Golden Beach. As I sang I remembered the wonderfully creative period in 1977 and all of the fun and satisfaction I had experienced writing songs with my friends.

After "Even Now," I sat on the edge of the stage, trying to get closer to the audience. I spoke with them, and even though I knew there were thousands of them, I felt as if there were only a roomful.

June 1970, New York City. There were only a roomful of people listening to me finish up my last set at the piano. Most of them were my friends, and Linda sat with them and smiled at me.

When I finished, I joined them, but soon a waiter told me the owner wanted to see me. When I met him in the back of the room, he told me he had to let me go. There wasn't enough business to warrant a piano player each night. I didn't tell anyone at the table. I just couldn't.

As the applause died down I could hear Victor counting off the next song. Before the audience knew it, the band was playing the introduction to "Some Kind of Friend," our aggressive rock 'n' roll tune. As I sang it, I shook my fist, pointed my finger at them, prowled the stage, dropped to my knees, shook my behind at them, straddled the mike stand suggestively. I took a keyboard solo and when I did, the camera zoomed in and the audience reacted with screaming and applauding.

John D. Wells Junior High School, Brooklyn. I watched the guys in line in front of me stuffed into their jeans. Why didn't my jeans look like that? I had no ass. Mine always just hung on me like I had a load in my pants. Fred and Larry's jeans looked decent, but mine were pathetic.

I went home from school that day and ripped a paperback book in two and stuffed it in my back pockets. It still didn't make my pants fit any tighter. I ripped up another book and stuffed it in the pockets. I looked in the mirror. Finally, I had an ass! It was, admittedly, a very strange-looking square ass, but I had an ass!

"Can't Smile Without You" was the next song, and had become my favorite part of the show. During the song, I would pick someone at random out of the audience to sing with. It was a little more complicated than usual at Blenheim, because there were so many people.

I picked a pretty woman named Cathy as my partner. As we sang, she held my hand very tight. Singing in front of any audience is usually nerve-racking for these volunteers, but singing in front of forty thousand people had to be terrifying for her. I looked into her eyes and squeezed her hand, trying to make her feel a little more comfortable. She made it through and the crowd gave her a rousing hand.

As the audience was applauding, I silently thanked Roberta for breaking down the invisible barrier that had existed between me and the public. This performing career had become such a joy for me, and it had all begun when Roberta came into my life.

I went to the piano and started the introduction to "I Write the Songs." As soon as they recognized it, they applauded. It seemed as if it was a very long time ago that I had recorded it, but it had only been eight years.

September 1975.
  "Clive, I can't record this song!"
  "It's a major hit record for you."
  "Clive, they'll think I'm bragging!"
  "Barry, it's a major hit record for you. Nobody will think you're

bragging. And even if they do, you do write songs that make the young girls cry."

"But Clive, I can't sing that! It will turn everyone off!"

"Barry, if you sing and arrange and produce this one right, it will be your biggest hit record."

"Clive, you're dead wrong."

As I headed toward the end of "I Write the Songs," I smiled remembering Clive and me. What a ride! I felt very fortunate to have him in my life.

I bowed to the left, to the right, and to the center, and walked into the wings. Everyone in the wings shouted and stamped as I came toward them. I leaned on Speakman as Charlie wiped my face.

"This one was real hot, chief. I think they're gonna want an encore after "One Voice," Speakman said.

"I'll stay all night for them!" I said and meant it.

I ran back out on stage. The crowd was really excited. Standing, cheering. Lots of guys cheering. Fists in the air. I was so glad that men had finally come around to liking what I did.

As I stood and stared at them cheering, I felt myself begin to become emotional. I pushed the feeling away. I couldn't lose it now! But it was overwhelmingly heavy for me.

I sang the first line of "We'll Meet Again" and they *all* lit candles *at once*. It was a shock to see. The spotlights had been lighting up the enormous crowd all night long at various moments, and I had gotten used to seeing them. But when they all lit candles, I realized that the spotlights had been lighting up only *half* of the crowd. There were twice as many people there as I thought there were. I couldn't see the end of the audience or the candles. I hadn't realized that there were *that* many people, and all of them seemed to have candles. I couldn't sing the next line. The experience took my breath away. I swallowed the big gulp in my throat and tried to continue.

The audience sang most of the song, and it was very difficult to join them. Forty thousand people holding lighted candles and swaying and singing to you is very hard to accept. I did everything I could to remain in control of myself, but the orchestra sounded so sweet and the voices in the crowd so beautiful. I made it through "We'll Meet Again" by the skin of my teeth.

As I sang "One Voice," the choir was revealed in silhouette behind me. We had been recruiting local choirs to sing with us for the last few years and it was always a wonderful moment when they appeared out of nowhere. You could feel one big goosebump go through the audience as they'd see and hear the choir. Usually you could hear a mother or father saying, "There's Tammy, third one from the left!"

I always looked forward to rehearsing them during the afternoon sound check. They were always well rehearsed and on their best behavior. I could see how important it was to them, and when I complimented them on a job well done (which it always was), they beamed.

Oklahoma, 1981.

We couldn't have a choir for the show. The law wouldn't allow children to work past nine P.M. I was so disappointed.

I sat during dinner, moping and looking around at all of my crew eating and laughing. We take so many people on the road with us, to say nothing of the caterers that have been feeding us. Why they must total at least twenty people. Twenty people! Twenty people!

Since the doors hadn't opened to let the audience in, I gathered together the crew that wasn't working during "One Voice," the caterers, and the truck drivers, and lined them up on the choir riser. Then Charlie handed out the red choir robes. When they put them on—why, there was a twenty member choir behind me! A little scruffy maybe, but at least they were there.

When the time came to sing "One Voice," I held my breath as the lights began to come up on the choir and, sure enough, I could hear the audience ooohh and feel that one big goosebump go through them. When I turned around to conduct the choir, I really expected to have to stifle a laugh, but I was met with the most touching sight. There was the crew and the truck drivers and caterers, all cleaned up, smiling and singing at the top of their lungs, throwing their hearts into the song and being the best choir of the tour.

When I turned around at Blenheim to conduct the choir, I stood looking at thirty adorable children singing their hearts out accompanied by the most beautiful sixty-piece orchestra you've ever heard. When I turned back to the audience it seemed the candles had multiplied and the glow of lights seemed to go on for miles. I don't know how I made it to the end of the song.

As we finished "One Voice" I ran into the wings and dissolved into a heap of emotions. I looked at my co-workers in the wings and all of them were in tears. It was a killer show.

I ran back out to the beat of "You're Looking Hot Tonight" and waved good-bye to them. I really loved that audience. I hated to leave them. When I looked out at the crowd, I could see that they were all singing and clapping and smiling.

I never know how to thank them enough for giving me all that support and encouragement. When I saw how happy they seemed, I was glad I could be the catalyst that brought them together and made them smile.

The concert at Blenheim Palace was one I'll never forget. So many things went through my mind in the car on the way back to London. I had enjoyed the show. I had worked hard, using Nina's technique, and I hadn't felt the least bit uncomfortable. It was a *good* feeling—finally! Ro and Kevin and I had created a solid show that I was very proud of. I even enjoyed singing the outside material during the Blenheim show. I finally began to love the songs because I could see how much the audience loved them. I had been singing them for so long that by now they actually felt as if they belonged to me—even if I hadn't written them.

But most of all, the concert at Blenheim Palace made me feel closer to the audience than I had ever felt. I had been able to look into the audience and not feel distanced from them. I had grown to love them and appreciate them. Even though there were thousands of them, I still felt as if I was with my family.

I knew that I was about to begin another climb. I knew that these last ten years—learning the art of the singer/entertainer— were just one chapter in my life. I could feel inside that another one was beginning. It was an exciting and scary feeling. I didn't know what the future held, but I couldn't wait to get there.

Read 'Em and Weep

Each time I've ended a tour, I've gone through a period of depression. I've asked other entertainers and musicians about it and I'm told that it's very common.

When I came off the 1983 tour, I went directly to Palm Springs. I practically chained myself to a chaise longue. I greased myself up and lay in the sun trying to relax, but my mind continued to go at a hundred miles an hour.

I had finished recording Jim Steinman's "Read 'Em and Weep," and everyone at Arista was very excited about it. When I listened to it, I felt proud of my interpretation, but once again, there was an emptiness about singing a song that I hadn't written. I felt especially distant from this record because, due to the craziness of the tour, I hadn't even been able to produce or arrange the song.

The end-of-tour blues turned into a full-blown identity crisis. After an afternoon of reading some especially negative press clippings about my music, my empty feelings about "Read 'Em and Weep" made me reevaluate my entire public image.

I had never imagined that I would wind up being thought of as the King of Commercial Music. I mean, *me*—with all of my snobbish musical taste. Me—who wanted to be the next Edgar

Winter or Laura Nyro! Me—who didn't even like Elvis Presley when I was growing up because he was too commercial! How did this happen?

I had set out to make a living at a job I loved—making music by arranging, conducting, and songwriting. When I found myself in the Top 40 arena, I had to learn new rules and compromise in order to survive. But for a while, the balance between the blatantly commercial songs and my own less commercial songs seemed pretty even. For a while there were just as many "Could It Be Magic"s and "All the Time"s as there were "Can't Smile Without You"s. But now I thought that the scale had become lopsided.

Michelangelo had said about his work: "I'll do one for me, and one for the pope." That had been my attitude, too, but I was now beginning to believe I may have done one too many for the pope!

Even my own writing had become geared toward being "commercial." I'd gotten so far away from where I began I wasn't sure if I could write any other way. I felt very sad because I never played the piano for pleasure any more. Whenever I'd write something, I'd think, "Is this a hit? Is it commercial? Can you hum it back? Am I getting too complicated?"

It was frustrating. I found myself listening only to classical music stations. I loved hearing Mozart, Bach, Chopin. But sometimes I suspected I enjoyed listening to them because they were all dead and they weren't competition!

My favorite singers and musicians made the kind of music that I hadn't even hinted at on my albums. Each time I'd tried to stretch, I'd been told not to—that it was too risky.

Art versus commerce. I was in the middle of the classic dilemma. I'd read and heard about it for years, and here I was, smack in the middle of it. Although I was emotionally attached to my values and tastes, I saw wisdom in the commercial approach as well. BARRY MANILOW (in capital letters) had become successful, and I needed to keep supporting him, but now I was searching for Barry Manilow.

We had done one last group of shows, bringing in New Year's Eve at the Universal Amphitheater in Los Angeles. I performed

"Read 'Em and Weep" during those shows, and, surprisingly, I enjoyed it. It was a very well-written, dramatic song and as a performer, I was really able to sink my teeth into it. But it was emotionally draining for me each night, because I was feeling so ambiguous about its success.

It was a beautiful Palm Springs morning. I got up very early and found myself sitting at the piano with my coffee while the sun came up. Johnny Mercer, one of the all-time greatest lyricists, had passed away that year, and his widow had sent me a stack of his lyrics that had never been put to music. Some were in his own handwriting, some were incomplete with scribbles around them, and some were final.

I chose a beautiful lyric of his called "When October Goes," and wrote a melody to it. It took all of thirty minutes. While I was writing, all my depression and conflicts disappeared. I was in another world. I played my melody over and over, making slight changes here and there. It was an old-fashioned ballad, without a "hook," without a "fade," without a "backbeat." I loved writing it. When I looked up, Roberta was standing there.

"That's beautiful," she said.

"I'm sorry, did I wake you up?" I asked.

"It's a nice way to wake up," she said.

"Do you really like it?"

"I love it. It's the kind of music you should be making. Your fans would love it."

"You know, it felt so good to write that melody that I didn't want to stop," I said. "But it's a waste of time. What am I going to do with something like that?"

During the past ten years, that was always the question that had stopped me from continuing to write from my heart. I was in the business of making Top 40 records. Why be self-indulgent and write songs that no one would ever hear?

But writing "When October Goes" gave me a feeling of inner satisfaction that I hadn't felt in a long time. A lot of the struggle over the years had been because I never really felt totally good inside. This experience was fulfilling, satisfying. I felt complete.

The difference between my feelings for "Read 'Em and Weep" and "When October Goes" was obvious to me now. Would I ever be able to blend the two? Could BARRY MANILOW and Barry Manilow ever live in peaceful coexistence?

I decided to stop bitching and do something about it.

Paradise in One Take

I watched from my piano bench as all the musicians filed into the recording studio after their break. Gerry Mulligan talking with Shelly Manne. Guitarist Mundell Lowe with bassist George Duvivier. The great Mel Tormé singing at the piano while the extraordinary Bill Mays played for him.

I had been rehearsing with them for three days and it was the three most satisfying days of my musical career. We were making my next album. An album I had titled *2:00 A.M.—Paradise Cafe*. The music was smoky jazz. The lyrics were torchy.

It was a milestone in my life, not just because it was a great body of music and performances—and it was—but because for me it was a collection of music and lyrics that came from the heart.

For ten years I had found myself in the middle of a life that was so exciting, exhilarating, and successful that I had lost sight of why I had started in the first place. I was just trying to keep up. With *2:00 A.M.—Paradise Cafe*, the experience of writing music for the sheer joy of writing had been so euphoric and natural that it came to me within one glorious week. When I was done, I couldn't believe I had written those songs. It wasn't as if I was writing them. It was as if I was allowing them to flow through me. I worked with my beloved friends/collaborators on the songs and it was a profound experience for all of us.

Each song, each note served to remind and strengthen me.

"Yes!" I would holler each time I finished a passage. "Yes!" And I would pound on the lid of the piano when I was finished with another tune.

"Yes!" I would shout when I played the cassette back.

Now, getting a chance to record with the finest jazz musicians and singers was another emotional catharsis. Except for Bill, I had never met any of them. I had made a list of my "dream jazz band and vocalists." Then I tracked them down and called them all personally. To my shock and delight, they all agreed to work with me on this project. They all knew one another, but had never worked together in this kind of group, so it was exciting for them.

During the rehearsals I had to keep excusing myself to go to the bathroom and pull myself together. Why had I waited so long to allow myself to experience this?

Hearing Mel Tormé and Sara Vaughan sing songs that I wrote redefined the meaning of breathtaking for me. I actually found it hard to breathe while they sang.

Marty and Adrienne were there for most of it and they grinned like children all day long. I kept calling Bruce Sussman and Jack Feldman in New York, holding the phone up to the speakers so they could hear.

I had written and arranged the music so that each song would flow into the next with no fade-outs and no breaks. But I had intended to record the songs individually, then the connecting themes individually; later on I would edit all of it together so that it would sound as if it were one long piece.

"Well, Barry, what do you want to record first?" Michael Braunstein, our engineer, asked me through the talkback system.

"I had an idea as you were all filing in," I told everyone. "Why don't we put the music in the order of the final album, and let's see how far we can get. I'll sing live too."

Everyone agreed and in a few minutes we were rolling.

As we went from one song into the next, I could feel a special energy beginning to happen. We had been rehearsing all morning long, and the songs were sounding great, but this was something else.

Each song had an individuality. Each connective piece of music felt silky and perfect. The tempos to each song were just right. These musicians had somehow learned the entire album in three days and were playing forty-five minutes of original music as if they had known it all their lives.

And as I sang, I found myself totally lost in each song. It brought back the feeling that I had had years before at the Red Rocks in Denver. Once again I closed my eyes and I sang to the sky and to Brooklyn and once again I felt that euphoria that only happens when an artist becomes one with his work.

As we got to the sixth song, I realized we were actually going to record this album in one take. Impossible, but true.

By the time we reached the last song, "Night Song," the most ambitious piece in the album, the whole room was on edge. No one breathed as Gerry began the notes that would start the theme to "Paradise Cafe" and end the album.

When we finished, it had been forty-five minutes of straight playing and singing. Everyone in the control room burst into applause. Adrienne and Marty were standing and cheering, tears streaming down their faces.

I was wiped out. It was as if all the years in the hotels and the planes and the struggling frustrations and the going broke and the headaches were all washed away. And it had only needed one take.

For me, making the album *2:00 A.M.—Paradise Cafe* was much more than just making another album. It represented taking control of a career in which the light of success had been so bright that it had blinded me. It represented so much more than music to me. It represented love.

The concert at Blenheim Palace had given me a feeling of finally accepting and taking control of the part of me that had become an entertainer. The making of this album represented a new beginning. Getting back to the feeling of making music for the sheer joy of it, for the joy of music. This experience had come from the heart. Nothing could compare to it. I would never be the same.

Coda

As painful as they've sometimes been, I wouldn't trade away one minute of the adventures that I've been through. Being thrown into the stormy sea of success has made me stronger and has reinforced my belief in people, loving, and music. The support I've received over the years still makes my head spin.

I'm very proud of the work I've done. I'm grateful to my friends and associates for seeing me through this insane trip. It's taken me years to learn how useless it is to do things for the approval of others. Because when it's all said and done, you're really on your own. The biggest lesson I've learned through all of this is to follow your heart. If you do, you can't go wrong.

I am a musician. My passion for music has obliterated everything in its path for my entire life. Whenever there was a choice between music and anything else, music won hands down every time. No one person or material thing could ever come close to the feeling I get when the music is right. I imagine it's like a drug addict who keeps going back for more. Once you've experienced it you have to have it again. Along the way, I forgot about my heart's desires and ran around trying to please everyone. Now, for the first time in my life, I can see a glimpse of a future in which I can try to tolerate insecurity and believe in myself.

We are all a composite of those events and people that have

been in our lives. I am the sum total of Jeanne's determination, Bette's commitment, Marty's passion, Linda's gentleness, Bruce's integrity, Clive's brilliance, Garry's shrewdness, Adrienne's taste, Nina's wisdom, Roberta's compassion, Gramma's warmth, my mother's love, Grampa's sweetness, the support of strangers, and the music that was born within me.

I believe that *we are who we choose to be.*

Nobody is going to come and save you. You've got to save yourself.

Nobody is going to give you anything. You've got to go out and fight for it.

Nobody knows what you want except you, and nobody will be as sorry as you if you don't get it.

So don't give up your dreams.

Discography

MANILOW I

Bell #: 1129
Arista #: AB4007
RCA #: AL5-8153
Release: July 1973

Side "A": Sing It, Sweetwater Jones, Cloudburst, One Of These Days, Oh My Lady, I Am Your Child

Side "B": Could It Be Magic, Seven More Years, Flashy Lady, Friends, Sweet Life

MANILOW II

Bell #: 1314
Arista #: AB4016
RCA #: AL5-8085
Release: Oct. 1974

Side "A": I Want To Be Somebody's Baby, Early Morning Strangers, Mandy, The Two Of Us, Something's Comin' Up

Side "B": It's A Miracle, Avenue C, My Baby Loves Me, Sandra, Home Again

TRYIN' TO GET THE FEELING

Arista #: AB 4060
RCA #: AL5-8070
Release: Oct. 1975
Additional Cat. # 68336

Side "A": New York City Rhythm, Trying To Get The Feeling, Why Don't We Live Together, Bandstand Boogie, You're Leavin Too Soon, She's A Star

Side "B": I Write The Songs, As Sure As I'm Standing Here, A Nice Boy Like Me, Lay Me Down, Beautiful Music

THIS ONE'S FOR YOU

Arista #: AB 4090
RCA #: AL5-8160
Release: July 1976
Additional Cat. # 68331

Side "A": This One's For You, Daybreak, You Oughta Be Home With Me, Jump Shout Boogie, Weekend In New England

Side "B": Riders To The Stars, Let Me Go, Looks Like We Made It, Say The Words, All The Time, See The Show Again

BARRY "LIVE"

Arista #: AL 8500
RCA #: AL13-8049
Release: May 1977

Side "A": Riders To The Stars, Why Don't We Live Together, Looks Like We Made It, New York City Rhythm

Side "B": A Very Strange Medley: Grab A Bucket Of Chicken, State Farm Insurance, Stridex, Band-Aid, Green Bowlene, Dr. Pepper, Pepsi-Cola, McDonalds; Jump Shout Boogie Medley: Jump Shout Boogie, Avenue C, Jumpin' At The Woodside, Cloudburst, Bandstand Boogie; This One's For You

Side "C": Beautiful Music (Part I), Daybreak, Lay Me Down, Weekend in New England, Studio Musician

Side "D": Beautiful Music (Part II), Could It Be Magic/Mandy, It's A Miracle, It's Just Another New Year's Eve, I Write The Songs, Beautiful Music (Part III)

EVEN NOW

Arista #: AB 4164
RCA #: AL8-8052
Release: Jan. 1978
Additional Cat. # 68322
　　　　　　　　　58230

Side "A": Copacabana, Somewhere In The Night, A Linda Song, Can't Smile Without You, Leavin' In The Morning, Where Do I Go From Here

Side "B": Even Now, I Was A Fool (To Let You Go), Losing Touch, I Just Want To Be The One In Your Life, Starting Again, Sunrise, Can't Smile Without You

GREATEST HITS-VOL. I

Arista #: A2L-8601
RCA #: AL13-8039
Release: Nov. 1978

Side "A": Mandy, New York City Rhythm, Ready To Take A Chance, Looks Like We Made It, Daybreak, Can't Smile Without You

Side "B": It's A Miracle, Even Now, Bandstand Boogie, Tryin' To Get The Feeling, Could It Be Magic, Somewhere In The Night

ONE VOICE

Arista #: AB 9505
RCA #: AL5-8046
Release: Sept. 1979

Side "A": One Voice, (Why Don't We Try) A Slow Dance, Rain, Ships, You Could Show Me, I Don't Want To Walk Without You

Side "B": Who's Been Sleeping In My Bed?, Where Are They Now, Bobbie Lee (What's The Difference I Gotta Live), When I Wanted You, Sunday Father

BARRY

Arista #: AL 9537
RCA #: AL8-8117
Release: Nov. 1980

Side "A": Lonely Together, Bermuda Triangle, I Made It Through The Rain, 24 Hours A Day, Dance Away

Side "B": Life Will Go On, Only In Chicago, The Last Duet, London, We Still Have Time

IF I SHOULD LOVE AGAIN

Arista #: AL 9573
RCA #: AL8-8123
Release: Sept. 1981

Side "A": The Old Songs, Let's Hang On, If I Should Love Again, Don't Fall In Love With Me, Break Down The Door

Side "B": Somewhere Down The Road, No Other Love, Fools Get Lucky, I Haven't Changed The Room, Let's Take All Night

LIVE IN BRITAIN

Arista #: ARTV-4
Release: April 1982

Side "A": It's A Miracle/London; The Old Songs Medley: The Old Songs, I Don't Wanna Walk W/out You, Let's Hang On; Even Now; Stay; Beautiful Music

Side "B": Bermuda Triangle, Break Down The Door/Who's Been Sleeping In My Bed?, Copacabana (At The Copa), Could It Be Magic/Mandy, London/We'll Meet Again, One Voice

OH JULIE

Arista #: AB 2500
Release: Aug. 1982

Some Kind Of Friend, Oh Julie, I'm Gonna Sit Right Down And Write Myself A Letter, Heaven

HERE COMES THE NIGHT

Arista #: AL 9610
RCA #: AL8-8003
Release: Nov. 1982

Side "A": I Wanna Do It With You, Here Comes The Night, Memory, Let's Get On With It, Some Girls

Side "B": Some Kind Of Friend, I'm Gonna Sit Right Down and Write Myself A Letter, Getting Over Losing You, Heart Of Steel, Stay

GREATEST HITS VOL. II

Arista #: AL8-8102
Release: Nov. 1983
Additional Cat. #: 68291

Side "A": Ships, Some Kind Of Friend, I Made It Through The Rain, Read 'Em And Weep, Put A Quarter In The Juke Box, Somewhere Down The Road

Side "B": One Voice, The Old Songs, Let's Hang On, Memory, You're Looking Hot Tonight

2:00 A.M.-PARADISE CAFE

Arista/RCA #: AL-8-8254
Release Date: Nov. 1984

"First Set": Paradise Cafe, Where Have You Gone, Say No More, Blue (duet -w- Sarah Vaughan), When October Goes

"Second Set": What Am I Doin' Here, Goodbye My Love, Big City Blues (duet -w- Mel Torme), When Love Is Gone, I've Never Been So Low On Love, Night Song

THE MANILOW COLLECTION/TWENTY GREATEST HITS

Arista/RCA #: AL-9-8274
Release Date: April 1985

Side "A": Mandy, This One's For You, Weekend In New England, Even Now, I Made It Through The Rain, It's A Miracle, Can't Smile Without You, Ready To Take A Chance Again, Looks Like We Made It, Somewhere In The Night

Side "B": Copacabana (At The Copa), Some Kind Of Friend, Read 'Em And Weep, Memory, Run To Me (Duet With Dionne), When October Goes, Tryin' To Get The Feeling, I Write The Songs, Could It Be Magic, One Voice

MANILOW

RCA #: AFL1-7044
Release Date: Nov. 1985

Side "A": I'm Your Man, It's All Behind Us Now, In Search Of Love, He Doesn't Care (But I Do), Some Sweet Day

Side "B": At The Dance, If You Were Here With Me Tonight, Sweet Heaven (I'm In Love Again), Ain't Nothing Like The Real Thing, It's A Long Way Up

COPACABANA (THE MOVIE)

RCA #: SML1-7178
Release Date: Jan. 1986

Side "A": Overture, Copacabana (At The Copa) (Barry Manilow), Let's Go Steppin' (The Copa Girls), Changing My Tune (Tony), Blue, Lola (Tony), Who Needs To Dream (Tony), Man Wanted (Lola), Aye Caramba! (The Copa Girls), Call Me Mr. Lucky (Tony)

Side "B": Big City Blues (Tony), Sweet Heaven (I'm In Love Again) (Tony), El Bravo (Lola And The Tropicana Girls), Copacabana (At The Copa) 1985 (Tony), Who Needs to Dream (Tony), Aye Caramba! (Barry Manilow)

# B 971 Date: 2/2/71	Amy b/w Morning	# AS 0273 Date: 9/9/77	Daybreak b/w Jump Shout Boogie
# B 45133 Date: 6/4/75	Could It Be Magic b/w Morning	# SP 11-DJ Only Date: 11/18/77	It's Just Another New Year's Eve
# B 45357 Date: 5/9/73	Sweetwater Jones b/w One Of These Days	# AS 0305 Date: 1/20/78	Can't Smile Without You b/w Sunrise
# B 45422 Date: 12/4/73	Cloudburst b/w Could It Be Magic	# SP 18-DJ Only Date: 4/10/78	Copacabana
# B 45443 Date: 2/1/74	Let's Take Some Time To Say Goodbye b/w Seven More Years	# AS 0330 Date: 4/14/78	Even Now b/w I Was A Fool (To Let You Go)
# B 45613 Date: 10/7/74	Mandy b/w Something's Comin' Up	# AS 0339 Date: 5/24/78	Copacabana b/w Copacabana (Long Version)
# AS 0108 Date: 2/12/75	It's A Miracle b/w One Of These Days	# SP-21-DJ Only Date: 5/24/78	Copacabana b/w Copacabana (Spanish Version)
# AS 0126 Date: 6/4/75	Could It Be Magic b/w I Am Your Child	# SP-25-DJ Only Date: 8/2/78	Ready To Take A Chance Again (one side promo)
# AS 0157 Date: 10/24/75	I Write The Songs b/w A Nice Boy Like Me	# AS 0357 Date: 8/25/78	Ready To Take A Chance Again b/w Sweet Life
# AS 0175 Date: 3/3/75	Tryin To Get The Feeling b/w Beautiful Music	# AS 0382 Date: 11/29/78	Somewhere In The Night b/w Leavin In The Morning
# AS 0206 Date: 9/1/76	This One's For You b/w Riders To The Stars	# AS 0464 Date: 9/26/79	Ships b/w They Gave In To The Blues
# AS 0212 Date: 11/3/76	Weekend In New England b/w Say The Words	# AS 0481 Date: 11/27/79	When I Wanted You b/w Bobbie Lee
# AS 0244 Date: 4/20/76	Looks Like We Made It b/w N.Y. City Rhythm (long version)		

AS 0501
Date: 3/26/80

I Don't Want To Walk
Without You
b/w One Voice

AS 0557
Date: 8/8/80

Bermuda Triangle
b/w 24 Hours A Day

AS 0566
Date: 11/7/80

I Made It Through The
Rain
b/w Only In Chicago

AS 0596
Date: 2/25/81

Lonely Together
b/w The Last Duet

AS 0633
Date: 9/23/81

The Old Songs
b/w Don't Fall In Love
With Me

AS 0658
Date: 12/4/81

Somewhere Down The
Road
b/w Let's Take All
Night To Say Goodbye

AS 0675
Date: 3/3/82

Let's Hang On
b/w No Other Love

AS 0698
Date: 7/14/82

Oh Julie
b/w Break Down The
Door

AS 1025
Date: 11/3/82

Memory
b/w Heart Of Steel

AS 1046
Date: 2/2/83

Some Kind Of Friend
b/w Heaven

AS 1-9101
Date: 11/4/83

Read Em And Weep
b/w One Voice

AFS-9122
Date: 12/2/83

Mandy
b/w It's A Miracle

AFS-9123
Date: 12/2/83

I Write The Songs
b/w Could It Be Magic

AFS 9124
Date: 12/2/83

Weekend In New
England
b/w Can't Smile
Without You

AFS 9125
Date: 12/2/83

Copacabana
b/w Even Now

ADP 9168
Date: 1/6/84

You're Lookin Hot
Tonight
(Promo Only)

ADP-9185
Date: 2/17/84

You're Looking Hot
Tonight
b/w Put Quarter In
The Juke Box

ADP-9295
Date: 10/31/84

When October Goes
(Promo Only)

ADP-9301
Date: 11/84

Paradise Cafe
b/w Big City Blues
(Promo only—12″)

ASI-9318
Date: 1/85

Paradise Cafe
(Promo Only)

PB-14223
Date: 10/7/85

In Search Of Love
b/w At The Dance

PB-14302
Date: 2/28/86

He Doesn't Care (But I
Do)
b/w It's All Behind Us
Now

JD-14330
Date: 4/11/86

I'm Your Man (Club
Mix) 6:10
I'm Your Man (Dub
Mix) 6:25
(Promo Only—12″)

PB-14397
Date: 6/20/86

I'm Your Man (Club
Mix) 3:59
I'm Your Man (Dub
Mix) 3:55

Index